Corrections

Corrections

The Essentials

MELISSA W. BUREK
Bowling Green State University

STEVEN P. LAB
Bowling Green State University

MICHAEL E. BUERGER
Bowling Green State University

New York   Oxford

OXFORD UNIVERSITY PRESS

Oxford University Press is a department of the University of Oxford.
It furthers the University's objective of excellence in research, scholarship,
and education by publishing worldwide. Oxford is a registered trade mark of
Oxford University Press in the UK and certain other countries.

Published in the United States of America by Oxford University Press
198 Madison Avenue, New York, NY 10016, United States of America.

© 2021 by Oxford University Press

Library of Congress Cataloging-in-Publication Data

CIP data is on file at the Library of Congress

978-0-19-088250-1

9 8 7 6 5 4 3 2 1
Printed by LSC Communications, Inc., United States of America

CONTENTS

PREFACE

The intent of this book is to offer a succinct introduction to corrections in the United States. While there are many introduction to corrections textbooks available, they tend to be large tomes replete with lots of tables, graphs, and pictures—and command a high cost to students. Our goal is to provide a concise, yet thorough, discussion of the components of corrections along with a discussion of major issues and challenges facing corrections today. Our intent is to offer the same base content found in larger tomes without all the costly frills of the other texts. We have found this approach to be very effective in another "Essentials" texts we have coauthored. The primary audience for this work are those students who have little knowledge of correctional systems or those who need a refresher on correctional topics. The book can be used as the primary text in introductory corrections courses or serve as a good supplement for other criminal justice courses.

We have incorporated several features to assist the reader in gaining a good understanding of corrections. First, the book provides a general overview of the primary components of corrections along with discussions of major issues facing correctional systems. We have attempted to cite the most relevant scholarship on correctional topics and summarize the current state of the evidence, rather than attempt to review every study on each topic. Second, each chapter includes web activities, critical thinking exercises, and/or discussion questions that ask students to question and assess what they are reading. Many of these items ask students to apply what they have read to real-world and contemporary concerns/issues. Finally, in order to keep the length of the book reasonable, we have placed some materials on the book's website. This site will grow over time as we add materials related to recent events and new materials. We hope both students and instructors will find the book a useful resource in their quest to explore and understand the complexity of corrections in the United States.

We wish to thank the editors and staff and Oxford University Press for their guidance and assistance during the development of this book. We also want to thank the anonymous reviewers as well as the following reviewers for their feedback and insight regarding all of the chapters:

Joseph Rizzo, Rowan College at Burlington County
Chernoh Wurie, Virginia Commonwealth University
Todd Krohn, The University of Georgia
Mario Hesse, St. Cloud State University
Nicole Doctor, Ivy Tech Community College
Monica Solinas-Saunders, Indiana University Northwest
Norman Rose, Kent State University
Ryan M. Labrecque, Portland State University
Lloyd Klein, Laguardia Community College, CUNY
Kelly Henderson, Langston University

We have attempted to incorporate reviewer suggestions to the extent it could be done without altering the basic intent of producing a student-friendly, low cost yet information-packed introductory text.

Corrections

CHAPTER 1

The History and Development of Corrections

AFTER READING THIS CHAPTER, YOU SHOULD BE ABLE TO:

- Discuss the earliest responses to dealing with offenders
- Outline the changes in correction practices throughout the Middle Ages
- Identify the factors related to the emergence of correctional institutions after the Middle Ages and prior to 1800
- Identify and discuss the two styles of penitentiaries that emerged after 1800 in the United States
- Discuss the early development of probation and parole
- Describe and discuss the key elements of the eras of reform, industry, rehabilitation, and retribution
- Discuss reentry
- Outline the development of correctional institutions for women

DEFINING CORRECTIONS

Corrections is one of the three cornerstone institutions comprising the United States criminal justice system, along with the police and the courts. While the term "corrections" typically brings to mind prison and jails, that image is too limited and does not reflect the great diversity in what constitutes corrections today. Academic interest in corrections began under the heading **Penology** in the early and mid-1900s and reflected the interest in studying the operations and the residents of "penitentiaries." Penitentiaries and penology focused primarily on punishing offenders for their actions. That continued until interest shifted in the later part of the twentieth century when "corrections" replaced the "penology" in most discussions. Use of the term "**corrections**" reflects broader responses to crime than simple punishment. Corrections includes punishment, treatment, rehabilitation, and virtually any interventions/actions addressing the behavior and needs of offenders in prisons/institutions or in the community.

The dominant type of correctional intervention in vogue has shifted greatly over time. Many responses have experienced renewed interest and attention at different times and in light of different social situations. The varied responses that comprise modern corrections have not, and do not, exist and operate in full harmony. For example, punishment and rehabilitation may compete for resources and for public and political support. That competition can greatly influence the operations of correctional systems and interventions. The shifting of correctional interventions is not a new phenomenon. Indeed, corrections has changed greatly over time, and the history of correctional activities illustrates the range of responses to offending that have been employed.

THE EARLIEST RESPONSES

Since the beginning of history, the general approach for dealing with offenders has fallen on the victim and/or the victim's family. There was no societal recourse for addressing antisocial behaviors. Throughout most of history people lived in small, intimate communities, there was no need for formal laws or the agencies needed to enforce communal living rules and regulations. Indeed, the earliest known laws left responses to offending in the hands of the victim. The Code of Hammurabi (circa 1750 BCE) outlined a variety of laws, most of which dealt with fair trade issues and concerns of the monarch. When it came to the individual, the rule of *lex talionis*—or "an eye for an eye, a tooth for a tooth"—was established. When someone harmed you, the law allowed you or your family to exact vengeance and to respond in kind. This same approach to dealing with transgressions appears in most other early laws, including the Justinian code (450 BCE).

Web Activity

You can see a translation of the Code of Hammurabi at http://avalon.law.yale.edu/ancient/hamframe.asp.

Vengeance, or the yearning to injure someone who has injured you, is a natural human affinity that has persisted, over the ages, in many forms. Throughout most of history, when a family member was killed, there was no formal system of justice for apprehending and exacting punishment against the offending party. Thus, the affected family would hunt down the murderer and viciously attack this individual to even the score for the loss of the loved one.

More formal responses to crime and transgressions were reserved for the king or monarch and were enforced by the army. The only "court" was that of the monarch; there were no juries, attorneys, prisons or jails. The consequences of transgressions tended to be harsh physical punishment and/or death. During these times, the use of torture, the guillotine, stoning, and other actions was common. Forfeiture of all one's belongings (to the monarch) was customary and the individual and his family were forced to live and beg on the street.

Most societies continued to rely on such draconian measures well into the Middle Ages (5th–15th centuries). The term "draconian" comes from the seventh-century Athenian lawmaker, Draco, who prescribed death for nearly every transgression—including idleness and stealing herbs or fruits—as well as for the more serious crimes of robbery and murder. Draco was asked why he meted out death for even the most minor of crimes. He responded that even these lesser offenses deserved capital punishment. Since that was the ultimate sanction, nothing else was left for the more severe violations.

THE EARLY MIDDLE AGES

In the fifth century, after the fall of Rome, nobles and bishops ruled the towns and principalities into which the empire had fragmented. This meant that these officials also were responsible for keeping order and upholding the law. As these new rulers began to formalize their control, they replaced families and individuals as deliverers of justice. What is striking, however, is that strategies of vengeance continued to receive support and were put into practice by these governments. Punishments based on revenge, when delivered by the state (i.e., the government), could be even more brutal than the crime that had been committed. The rulers saw criminals as menaces to the community and would sanction offenders to whatever punishments seemed to them to be most appropriate.

Another factor underlying the primacy of the revenge principle was the violence that characterized the Middle Ages. Life continued to be insecure, there was no "justice" system to which individuals could turn for assistance, and danger was ever present. Thus, for individuals who committed transgressions against the state or others, severe punishment and torture were considered to be deserved and the only available response.

FEUDALISM AND THE LATER MIDDLE AGES

Beginning in the ninth century (and lasting to the fifteenth century), **feudalism** developed as the primary economic system. Feudalism was a further extension of the changes that came after the fall of Rome in the fifth century; it involved the division of rural land into working estates owned by lords and nobles who did not live on these properties. Instead, landlords would be hired to manage the lands and peasants would farm them. Landlords were responsible for protecting the peasants, their families, and their possessions.

The peasants held the lowest class position in the social order and, in general, did not challenge their place in society. This occurred for at least two reasons. First, the isolated and self-sufficient society of the fief (i.e., the land) kept peasants from being "tainted" by the social change and revolutionary ideas that were occurring at the time. Second, peasants accepted their positions and the despair that accompanied it because of their religious beliefs and pressures. In essence, if peasants broke the rules, they were severely punished. Punishments for peasant law breakers were quite harsh as these penalties were used as a mechanism for keeping the peasants in their place. Ironically, punishment was typically not enforced in feudal times unless the person imposing the sanction was superior in class to the person on whom the punishment was to be inflicted. Thus, formal punishment was imposed by the state (i.e., the ruling class) on the poorer classes. Responses for transgressions between members of the poorer classes remained the purview of the victim and/or his family.

Beyond disputes between the peasants, disputes between the feudal lords was not uncommon. Typically referred to as **blood feuds**, these disputes often continued over long periods of time and involved physical confrontations resulting in serious injuries and death. The actions generally mimicked ongoing war between the battling fiefdoms—even as the feudal system began to crumble.

While physical punishments and vengeance maintained their primacy during this period, the earliest glimmers of imprisonment also emerged. Transgressions by members of the Roman Catholic Church were typically handled by the church. Known as **benefit of clergy**, the church would confine offenders under the auspices of reforming the individual through penance. This action was not reserved just for clergy and the church could provide sanctuary for individuals it felt were wrongly accused or being subjected to inappropriate sanctions. Since the state would be barred from entering the church in order to secure the offender or mete out punishment, the accused would, in essence, be imprisoned in the church. These religious accommodations for offenders, typically in an abbey, came to be called **monastic prisons**.

The development of monastic prisons and the use of benefit of clergy should not be viewed as indicating that religious institutions were against the use of harsh punishment. The idea of reforming an offender was not a consideration shared most individuals or institutions—including religious groups. The Crusades of the eleventh through the thirteenth centuries provide a good illustration of use of physical punishment in the name of religion. During the Crusades, thousands of Christians and Muslims were killed because they were avenging their respective gods. In ensuing years, burnings at the stake, hangings, decapitations, and torture exemplified the punishments during the time of the religious conflicts between the Roman Catholics and the Protestants.

Prior to monastic prisons, incarceration of offenders was a rare occurrence. The accused might be held temporarily, but only until a confession was obtained or the imposed punishment (usually the death penalty) was carried out. What "prisons" existed were constructed and operated privately, mostly by wealthy landowners. Powerful and influential persons at this time, rather than the formal government, were able to build their own institutions to imprison anyone who appeared to these landowners as threatening their way of life.

It was during the Middle Ages that more formal, communal responses to crime and transgressions began to be developed. These changes often resulted from citizen opposition to and revolt against the actions of the monarchy. In AD 1166, the **Assize of Clarendon** set constitutional procedures establishing how crimes were to be handled and processed, including creation of a jury system (similar to what exists today). It also resulted in the first public correctional facility, which was built under the rule of England's King Henry II.

Coordinated responses to crime by the community also emerged during this period and were codified. The **Statutes of Winchester** (AD 1285) outlined early community policing/protection activities, including "watch and ward," "hue and cry," and "assize of arms." **Watch and ward** was a process in which community members would take turns patrolling the local area at night to watch for problem behavior and people committing a crime. If the individual saw an offense or a problem, he was to raise the **hue and cry**, which simply meant the populace would be alerted to the activity and would respond to the call for assistance. Members of the community were expected to keep arms in their homes that they would bring when responding to an alert (the **assize of arms**). While seemingly simple, these actions represented the movement from individual victims responding to transgressors (thus, the problem was viewed as a concern only for the victim) to the community responding (thus, the *community* is the victim and needs to take action).

The **Magna Carta** (AD 1215) represented major changes in England (and formed the basis of laws in England and in other countries, including the Constitution of the United States). Signed into law by King John, the Magna Carta outlined the rights of the citizens in relation to the monarchy. Many of the rights addressed taxes and concerns of feudal lords. For the general citizenry, the royal government could no longer imprison or execute offenders unless they were first tried by a jury of their peers. With the development of trials, there was a need to temporarily hold the accused until the case was heard—this place was called the *gaol*, which is now spelled, "jail." Thus, the Magna Carta furthered the movement toward state-run correctional institutions. Box 1.1 discusses the movement to more communal responses in corrections.

BOX 1.1

Explaining the Shift to Communal Corrections

The move away from individual retribution as the primary response to offending and toward communal responses and more-formal correctional approaches can be understood in terms of the changes in society over time. An easy way to view this move is to consider the move from Gemeinschaft to Gesellschaft types of society, proposed by Ferdinand Tönnies. Early society consisted of **Gemeinschaft** communities, which were small, rural, and agrarian in nature. There was little specialization of roles and tasks in this society (what Émile Durkheim referred to as "mechanical solidarity"). Rather, everyone could see to their own needs. Relationships between people were "primary" relationships, meaning that everyone in the community knew each other almost like family members. Little happened in a community that everyone living there did not know about. Transgressions would not go unnoticed, and informal responses such as shunning and other social disapproval, would be effective at controlling behavior. Everyone in the community would know about the offense and support the punishment. If the offender would choose to leave the community to avoid the social condemnation and punishment, it would have little, if any, impact on the rest of the community. Other members could step in and do whatever the absent person did.

A **Gesellschaft** community is larger, more urban, densely populated, diverse, and technocratic. Most relationships were secondary or mere acquaintance relationships. Primary relationships still exist in this type of community, but typically only between family members and close personal friends. This society is more *organic* in nature, meaning that tasks are more specialized, and people must rely on each other for their needs. In this community, transgressions can occur in relative secrecy from most people. The victim cannot impact the offender effectively with informal controls—other members of the community may not know about the sanction and, even if they do, they may simply ignore the sanction. This would negate any impact on the offender. There is a need for a legitimized process for identifying offenders, passing judgement on the offending behavior, and deciding and carrying out sanctions. All this needs to be recognized and supported by the larger community. Thus, in a Gesellschaft community, formalized policing, courts, and corrections are needed. It is also important to do more than drive offenders away or simply allow them to leave. The organic nature of the community means that offenders need to be corrected so they can again contribute to the community.

MIDDLE AGES TO 1800

Corrections in the later Middle Ages until roughly 1800 continued to rely on physical punishment as the primary response to crime and transgressions. The emerging and existing places of confinement were limited and largely addressed the needs of the monarchy to control threats to its power. Indeed, most confinement was physically grueling and often led to some final form of physical punishment or death. The use of mass executions imposed by royalty to address internal dissidence was common. Mass executions were also popular when particular offenses seemed to be widespread. For example, more than 72,000 thieves were hung under King Henry VIII in England during his reign between 1509 and 1547. Under his daughter Elizabeth I (reign 1558–1603), vagrants were killed 300 to 400 at a time.

Public executions were held in order to deter others from committing offenses. In the eighteenth century, nearly 200 crimes were eligible for the death penalty. Anything from murder to shoplifting could result in a death sentence. Hangings were often carried out as if they were a theatrical work with the hangman, the chaplain, and the offender playing a part in a play. For example, the hangman would not speak, but stood rather deftly and made no mistakes. The chaplain would preach a sermon to the condemned and to the crowd so that the wages of sin could be reinforced. The lines for the person about to die were impromptu and could profess anything from apologies to protests of innocence.

The widespread use of death as a response to offending was not restricted to European countries and the Old World. Indeed, the American colonies followed the same laws as Mother England. William Penn, the founder of the state of Pennsylvania, attempted to address the use of the death penalty (as well as general responses to offending) by leading the enactment of the **Great Law**. These statutes reduced the number of crimes punishable by death to one—murder. Instead, hard labor in a house of correction was advocated for other transgressions.

Punishment was also used as a source of labor. Perhaps the best example of this was enforced galley service that was popular around the sixteenth century in England and France. Naval ships, called galleys, were manned by galley slaves who propelled the vessels with oars. The galley slaves were noncapital crime offenders (i.e., any crime except murder, rape, or burglary as these offenses resulted in execution). Galley service was usually a life sentence. Galley slaves were subjected to hard labor and their needs—whether medical, nutritional or otherwise—were largely neglected. If one galley slave died during service, there was always another one waiting in the jail to take his place.

It was during this period that there were growing calls to do more than simply punish and execute offenders. Many of those who committed crimes and were identified for intervention were the poor and those who had little recourse for survival. Consequently, increased attention was paid to the establishment of houses of correction that focused on both the poor and criminal offenders. One of the earliest of these was the **Bridewell House,** so named because it was established in the former Bridewell Palace in 1553. This institution incorporated elements of several responses to offending, including simple incarceration, hard labor/prison industry, and assistance for the poor (von Hirsh 1992). Those sent to Bridewell House were expected to learn trades so they could be released to live productive lives in society. This institution became a model for other houses of correction in England, France, and other countries.

Web Activity

For more information on Bridewell House and other early English institutions, visit https://www.londonlives.org/static/HousesOfCorrection.jsp.

The outward expansion of European powers in the later Middle Ages opened a new option for handling offenders. Rather than try to house offenders or to simply put them to death, shipping offenders to newly established colonial holdings became an alternative. The sentence of **transportation**, or the sending of convicted offenders to colonies of the mother country, became a frequent practice in England. North America, prior to the Revolutionary War was the main destination for prisoners from England. After the United States gained independence, Australia became the recipient of unwanted English criminals. Both men and women were transported. Most served as indentured servants to planters and tradesman for five to ten years. If the indentured servants tried to return to England before their sentences were completed and they were caught, they would be hung. Some exiled convicts worked under military and naval officers. Those who were skilled or semiskilled had the opportunity to gain paid employment. The unskilled males worked in chain gangs. After their sentences expired, a good number of men and women would remain and become shop owners or farmers. Besides the mainland of North America and Australia, four penal settlements were also locations used for banishment of the most serious offenders. The most famous of these settlements was Norfolk Island where brutality and harsh living conditions were the norm. Convicts sent to Norfolk Island were often subjected to horrendous lashings and beatings.

In addition to the practice of transportation of criminals to the United States, British settlers also brought with them England's laws, punishments, and its system of jails. These jails became the first correctional facilities in America. Similar to English gaols, American jails confined persons waiting trial and those individuals already convicted for their crimes who were awaiting the delivery of their sanction. The idea of "serving time" in jail was still not known at this time.

Another concept that Americans adopted from the British was the fee system for the operations of the jails. For example, in the early seventeenth century, offenders could be charged two pounds of tobacco or other commodity as payment for their admission to or release from jail. Given this fee system, the wealthy were often able to avoid jail altogether. The poor, however, were left locked away in what historical documents show us were horrible facilities where hunger, filth, and disease were widespread. It was not uncommon for people to die of starvation in these early jails.

Immediately prior to the American Revolution, **Newgate Prison** in Simsbury, Connecticut, was established as the first institution to house offenders for the purposes of long-term punishment rather than exclusively for pretrial detention. Newgate was actually an abandoned copper mine. The administrative buildings for this prison were built over the mine's shaft; three excavated caverns with one pool of fresh water constituted the living quarters for those incarcerated there. Essentially, Newgate was much like a dungeon—dark, wretchedly gloomy, unsanitary, and reeking of foul air. To make matters worse, adults (both men and women), children, the ill and the well, criminals, and political prisoners were all housed together. The one incentive that pushed these inmates to survive was the belief that they would one day escape from Newgate—and many frequently did because they were desperate to escape the terrible conditions of their confinement.

By the mid-eighteenth century, a number of factors led to major changes in punishment in Europe and the United States. First, it was widely recognized that penalties for offenders had become grossly disproportionate to the seriousness of the offenses committed. Punishments had also become quite violent. Second, Europe was under the influences of the Enlightenment at this time. Thus, more emphasis began to be placed on individual equality and the importance of being more humane to even the worst among us.

One of the leading figures in the development of the new correctional facilities in the late 1700s was **John Howard**. Howard was appointed as sheriff in Bedfordshire, England. One of his responsibilities was to run the county prison. Upon inspection of the facility he found the conditions to be overcrowded and generally unsanitary, with many of the individuals incarcerated mainly for being poor and unable to pay required fees. His concern over the conditions prompted him to visit and study institutions in England and other European countries, which led him to call for changes in the prisons. His work led the English Parliament to pass the Penitentiary Act of 1779. This act required that prisons were to be kept more sanitary and secure, and that they be subjected to inspections on a regular basis. In addition, the fees to inmates for basic services were repealed and a more reformative, rather than punitive, philosophy was adopted. Howard coined the term "penitentiary" and hence became known as the "Father of the Penitentiary." He believed that these institutions should be based on penance and the contrition of the offender's sins. Howard's concept and principles of the penitentiary would become the model for prisons in the Western world.

THE ERA OF THE PENITENTIARY

Many of the changes in corrections after 1800 can be traced to efforts and institutions in the United States. Incapacitation and deterrence were the philosophies that dominated the purposes for confinement in the 1800s to 1860s. This era was known as the **penitentiary era**, so called because of the development of a formal penal system and a heavy reliance on incarceration. Two different styles of penitentiaries became symbols of this era—*separate* and *congregate*. These penitentiaries are more commonly known by their location names—the **Pennsylvania System** and the **Auburn System**.

The Pennsylvania System

The Eastern State Penitentiary in Philadelphia, Pennsylvania, relied heavily on enforced silence and solitary confinement of inmates twenty-four hours a day, every day. Inmates were housed in individual cells. Eating, working, sleeping, and all other activities were to be performed in the confines of the cells. Prisoners were housed in cells roughly 12 feet by 8 feet, with a private exercise "yard" attached to each cell (to keep the prisoners separate at all times). Inmates were denied visits from family members and friends, access to newspapers, and correspondence of any kind (Rothman 1971). The only reading materials to which they had access to was the Bible and the only visitors allowed were the clergy. The system was highly influenced by the Quakers, a Protestant religious group that stressed salvation through adherence to the teachings of Jesus Christ. The purpose behind this silence and solitude was the belief that the only way to repent and reform for one's wrongdoings was to reflect silently on one's deeds and to accept God. Inmates could take on some forms of work, providing it could be done in isolation.

The Pennsylvania System was studied by many people, including Alexis de Tocqueville, who advocated this approach to incarceration. It was widely adopted in Europe. Despite its wide appeal at the time, the Pennsylvania System faced many challenges. First, the requirement for separate prison cells and exercise areas for every inmate meant that space quickly became an issue. This led to a second major obstacle—cost. The requirement for total isolation meant major construction costs. Third, the enforced, prolonged isolation was considered torture by reformers, and they pointed out that the conditions would cause brain damage and mental problems in the inmates (Woodham 2008). Because of these types of shortcomings, some reformers sought other variations for institutions.

The Auburn System

The Auburn Prison in New York developed a competing model for penitentiaries. This system also operated under the rule of silence, but it differed from the Pennsylvania System in that inmates could congregate with one another during the day while eating or working (thus it is also known as the **congregate system**). Auburn prisoners would return to separate cells at night. These cells were even smaller than those in Pennsylvania, measuring less than 4 feet by 8 feet. Enforced silence was the rule at all times, even while in the presence of other inmates. This rule was in effect at night, at work, at meals, and during exercise. Inmates in New York were also secluded from the outside world: no sight, sound, or contact with anyone or anything beyond the prison walls (Rothman 1971). As with the Pennsylvania System, the only visitor a prisoner could see was a member of the clergy. The institution also relied on corporal punishment to control the inmates.

Not unlike the Pennsylvania System, Auburn suffered from major problems. The requirement for separate cells quickly meant that the institution ran out of space. The fact that inmates worked in common areas did not alleviate the space concerns. The enforced silence led to suicide and mental illness among the inmates, and harsh discipline by the guards led to unrest in the institution. Despite these shortcomings, the Auburn System became the dominant form of penitentiary in the United States, largely due the lower costs compared to the Pennsylvania System.

Web Activity

The Pennsylvania and Auburn Systems set the stage for penitentiaries in the United States and Europe. To read more about these early institutions visit, https://www.smithsonianmag.com/history/eastern-state-penitentiary-a-prison-with-a-past-14274660/ and https://www.britannica.com/topic/Auburn-State-Prison.

The Beginnings of Modern Community Corrections

Interestingly, in the midst of the move toward imprisonment and the development of large institutions to house offenders, two important developments in the growth of community-based correctional interventions had their beginnings. These were probation and parole.

Probation, a form of conditional release by the court in lieu of incarceration, received its start in 1841. **John Augustus**, a Boston bootmaker, happened to be in court when an individual was brought before the court for public drunkenness. Augustus offered to take the individual into his custody and guarantee that he not offend in the future. Augustus had to report to the court regularly about the progress of the individual. The court released the prisoner to Augustus's care and, after a brief period, he was released from the court's oversight. Augustus repeated this arrangement with over 2,000 individuals before his death, and he is considered the "Father of Probation" (Lindner 2006). Augustus often put his "probationers" to work learning a trade in his cobbler shop, saw to their housing and daily subsistence, and made reports to the court on all his charges. The success of Augustus' efforts led to the passage of laws in Massachusetts during the late 1800s making probation a state-recognized alternative to incarceration. The statutes outlined the conditions that probationers and probation officers had to follow, and authorized the hiring of "probation officers." One advantage of probation for the growing correctional system was the fact that it helped to alleviate the need to house and care for those individuals in already overcrowded institutions. A primary goal was to help the offenders become contributing members of society.

Parole served similar functions to that of probation, particularly in terms of alleviating overcrowded institutions and helping offenders become functioning members of the community. Where probation was developed in the United States, parole finds its origins in the English system of *transportation*. Norfolk Island, located east of Australia in the Pacific Ocean, was used as a penal colony by England from 1788 (at the end of the US Revolutionary War) until 1855. **Alexander Maconochie** became the governor of the island in 1840 and quickly noted the harsh treatment of the offenders. As a means of altering the conditions of the prisoners, he established a system of graduated release known as the **mark system**. This system gave the prisoners the chance to earn release by earning marks through progressively demonstrating their ability to act appropriately. They would move from total imprisonment, to work on a chain gang, to freedom to work outside the institution without a chain gang, to monitored release, to full release. This measured release was copied in Ireland by **Sir Walter Crofton**, who gradually released prisoners on parole as long as they adhered to set conditions. Among these conditions was holding employment and refraining from reoffending.

THE ERA OF REFORM

The Civil War detracted attention away from the plight of prisoners being housed in the penitentiaries that were built in the 1800s. By 1870, however, a renewed awareness in the harsh environment of these institutions came to be scrutinized. A more humanitarian approach to the practice of incarceration was advocated based more on the philosophy of rehabilitation than on pure incapacitation or deterrence. The National Prison Association, which is known today as the American Correctional Association, was formed in 1870 to address the problems of the penitentiary system. Prison administrators, members of Congress, and prominent citizens from the United States and abroad gathered in Cincinnati, Ohio, and issued a set of declarations by which prisons would be reformed.

These principles emphasized the value of treatment for inmates based on their individual needs, an indeterminate sentencing scheme by which inmates could earn their way out of prison, vocational and educational training (labor that was purposeful instead of as punishment); and noncorporal methods of discipline, which made use of rewards rather than punishment for conformity. In addition, the rule of silence was abolished by these reformers. The introduction of a system whereby released inmates could continue their treatment in the community was also introduced during the Reform Era.

The **Elmira Reformatory** in New York was the prototype institution whose mission was to carry out the aforementioned principles. Inmates were classified based on their conduct and success in the interventions available at the facility, such as training for trade and academics. Similar to Elmira's predecessors, the reformatory was criticized for the means used to control inmates, inhumane working and living conditions, and its rigid order. Thus, the intentions of the reforms appeared to be sound, but in the end, poor implementation and a lack of funding required a new approach to the use of institutions for punishment.

THE ERA OF INDUSTRY

The period from the late 1800s to the 1930s is best known as the "Era of Industry" in the history of corrections. The idea of convict labor was not new to prison society. Both the Pennsylvania and the Auburn systems required inmates to engage in craft-oriented or factory-oriented labor, respectively. The goods produced by inmates were often sold in the open market. Inmates at the Auburn Prison actually built Sing Sing Prison—New York's second state institution for the incarceration of convicted offenders. Chain gangs were developed during this era, with inmates working on road or canal projects and prison construction for the states. Inmates were also tied to the private sector by being employed contractually with private businesses in the making of furniture, clothing, brooms, baskets, and hosiery. In addition, some inmates were contracted out to work in the stone quarries and coal mines.

These latter practices, known as **convict leasing**, was a Southern development and some authors have purported that convict leasing was basically another way to enslave blacks following the Civil War (Johnson 2002). Convict leasing of inmates often led to their illness, suffering, and even death. For example, in Georgia, convicts were beaten if they did not produce the designated amount of coal per day (Mancini 1978).

Despite such horrific consequences associated with convict labor during the Industrial Era, states and their officials continued their labor programs for inmates until the 1930s when state legislatures and Congress passed a number of measures banning the sale of inmate-produced goods to the public. The major impetus for such legislation was a result of complaints advanced by workers in the organized labor force claiming that inmate-made goods negatively affected the price at which free market products could be sold. Once the Great Depression hit in the 1930s, pressure from workers increased considerably to prohibit inmate labor from interfering with their profits. As would be expected, inmate labor was curtailed.

Interestingly, legislation was reintroduced in the late 1970s that permitted products produced by prison industries to be sold in the open market once again. Today, inmates continue to work, while doing their time, in various industries connected to the private and public sectors. Inmates have been involved in such jobs as assembling graduation gowns for Jostens Inc., making embroidered emblems for Lyon Brothers Manufacturing Company, and even sewing garments for Third Generation, Inc., which were later purchased by J. C. Penny and Victoria's Secret for retail sale (Sexton 1995).

THE ERA OF REHABILITATION

By the early 1930s, there was a strong sense of urgency to do something about the harsh punishments faced by inmates in United States penal institutions. Besides the Great Depression, which led to discontentment among the general public, dissatisfaction in the prison was also on the rise. Several major prison riots occurred in Illinois, Colorado, New York, and Missouri that prompted the government to take notice. Even prison officials began to understand the despondency that prisoners experienced. With a report issued by the Wickersham Commission in 1931, inmate grievances were officially recognized: State prisons do not provide anything more than capricious rules and coercive punishments for inmates and certainly, meaningful programs to actually assist inmates in their reformation were duly lacking. In fact, inmates spent most of their time inactively engaged while doing their time.

The **Wickersham Commission** called for a new philosophy to guide the prison system—**rehabilitation**. The philosophy of rehabilitation soon replaced the ideas of deterrence and incapacitation that had dominated since the inception of the penitentiary. The major players in the move toward more rehabilitative efforts were the progressives who were most active during the first couple decades of the twentieth century. The progressives were known for their indeterminist view that social problems, including crime, were often beyond an individual's control, much like having a disease that needs treatment. The medical model dominated the rehabilitation era with a focus on the needs of the individual offender and less reliance on prisons to carry out the criminal sanction. Probation, indeterminate sentences, classification systems, vocational and educational training, and release from prison based on treatment success were some of the significant practices devised and implemented to carry out the goal of rehabilitation, and to treat the "sick" offender. Many of the recommendations from the 1870 National Prison Association finally came to fruition.

Corrections would follow the rehabilitation philosophy for over forty years, with reported success in some jurisdictions and miserable failure in others. It appeared that states were just not equipped to carry out the rehabilitative ideals. This latter statement especially held true for prisons where the correctional officers were mandated to keep order within the institution while simultaneously attempting to create an environment that was amenable to treatment (Rothman 1980). It soon became clear that the premise of rehabilitation, while altruistic and even efficacious, could not climb over the hurdles blocking its proper implementation where those who carry out the criminal sanction and enforce rules could also benevolently change offenders' behaviors.

THE ERA OF RETRIBUTION

In the 1960s and 1970s, social and political unrest were sweeping across the United States. Crime was on an upswing. Coupled with the ideological struggles taking place in corrections, it should come as little surprise that the philosophy of rehabilitation would soon be replaced with a more punitive philosophy, better known as the "Get Tough" movement. Student uprisings against the Vietnam War, the dawn of the hippies, civil rights demonstrations, increases in poverty and crime rates, and the Watergate scandal led people to question vehemently the government, social institutions, law enforcement, courts, and corrections. Few people could swallow the notion that the government and its officials could "do good" (Cullen and Gilbert 1982). A catalyst that provided further justification that the philosophy of rehabilitation should be abandoned was the publication of a report by Robert Martinson, which indicated that "with few and isolated exceptions, the rehabilitative efforts that have been reported so far have had no appreciable effect on recidivism" (Martinson 1974, 25). This observation was interpreted by many people that "nothing works" and led to a generally negative view of society's ability to rehabilitate offenders.

The "nothing works" doctrine associated with Martinson's publication touting rehabilitation's ineffectiveness provided the ammunition to close the book on the chapter of treatment to reduce recidivism. This opened the door for sentencing and correctional policies to shift back to more punitive ideals. In turn, there was an increased reliance on secure confinement for more offenders for longer periods of time, determinate sentencing models, and the abolishment of parole. Offenders would now be sentenced to a finite amount of time and release was not tied to reformation or rehabilitation. Under the auspices of get tough practices, offenders who committed a crime would get their "just desserts."

Since the 1980s, there has been a general trend in the United States and Western European countries to respond to law violators with more-severe penalties and a decreasing support for rehabilitative efforts toward crime and offenders. In the United States, this has resulted in most jurisdictions passing lengthier prison sentences, more-punitive sanctions (such as "three strikes and you're out"), the establishment of sentencing guidelines that attempt to limit the discretion of judges or correctional administrators to reduce sentence lengths, and other efforts that result in the greater use of incarceration. Although these changes apply to a wide variety of behaviors, violent crimes and drug law violations have been particularly affected by these changes. Perhaps most importantly has been the increasing effort toward the "war on drugs" that has been fought (with intermittent strength) since the mid-1980s. As a consequence, drug law violators make up a significant percentage of offenders in criminal courts and under correctional supervision.

Jurisdictions, from the local level to the federal level, have had to increase correctional funding in response to the constant flow of offenders formally processed in the criminal justice system due to the passage of get tough policies.

While the funding for all aspects of the criminal justice system has increased, the increase for correctional spending has been the most dramatic. To reduce prison overcrowding, many states and the federal government have greatly increased the bed space within their prison systems through massive prison construction programs. Some states, such as Ohio, have attempted to shift inmates from state penitentiaries to local facilities. While this may have temporarily reduced overcrowding in the centralized state institutions, the impact has often been short lived. At the same time, local correctional centers have taken on convicted offenders, Ohio's prison population and overcrowding reached record levels in 2016 (Mangino 2016). This situation is a prime example of net widening at work: The number of incarcerated individuals (in any facility) has increased to overfill the capacity of the system.

The need for additional institutional space has prompted some jurisdictions to turn to private industry for assistance. While the involvement of businesses in corrections goes back hundreds of years (for example, the leasing of inmates to farms and industry), modern private, for-profit prisons emerged in the United States in the 1980s when Tennessee contracted with the **Corrections Corporation of America** (CCA) (now named CoreCivic) to assume total control of a correctional facility. Since that time, CCA and other companies have built prisons and contracted with states and the federal government to house offenders. According to Carson (2018), almost 130,000 prisoners in the United States (roughly 10% of the incarcerated population) are held in private prisons on behalf of twenty-eight different states and the Federal Bureau of Prisons (FBP).

The move toward private prisons was promoted with the ideas that private industry could build and run prisons for less costs and the facilities could be built faster when not bound to tax dollars, construction bonds, and/or government regulations. Evaluations of for-profit prisons have not borne out these claims. The claims of costs savings have not been demonstrated (Lundahl et al. 2009), there is no evidence that private prisons do any better than public facilities in terms of recidivism (US General Accounting Office 1996; Cheung 2002; Mattera and Kahn 2001), and one study notes that escapes from private prisons is a problem (Camp and Gaes 2002). Questions over the effectiveness of private prisons prompted the US Department of Justice to announce in 2017 that it was going to cease contracting with for-profit companies.

The move back to a more retributive approach to crime and corrections has resulted in the great growth of offenders in the system. Unfortunately, the correctional system cannot incarcerate all those sent to it. The United States has the highest incarceration rate of any country (Collier 2014). In addition, there are at least twice as many adults under correctional supervision in the community as in prisons/jails (Kaeble and Glaze 2016). These additional individuals are handled in a wide range of community correctional programs, including probation and parole. This means that, during a time when retribution and get tough are in vogue, the system has had to continue building alternative correctional modalities to handle all the offenders sent to it by the police and the courts. In addition to programs for new offenders, corrections has some responsibility to assist those individuals who have been in prison, have reached the end of their sentence, and are being released back into the community.

THE ERA OF REENTRY

The reentry movement has become a necessary response to decades of sanctioning practices based on retributive and incapacitative philosophies whereby more and more persons were put behind bars for lengthier periods of time—which is a costly enterprise. At a minimum, 95 percent of state inmates will be released from incarceration at some point (Hughes and Wilson 2002). In 2015, over 640,000 inmates were released from state prisons; in 2016, the number was nearly 626,000 (Carson 2018). **Reentry** is the transition period of persons who are soon to be released or who have recently been released from prison or jail back into the community. It involves providing services and assistance to these individuals and their families.

In general, there are two mechanisms to reduce prison crowding and its cost. There are front-door options that involve community-based sanctions like probation instead of prison or jail. Back-door options involve early-release mechanisms such as parole, transitional placement in a community-based correctional facility, or simply being released from prison without any assistance or supervision. The focus on reentry programs and services, most notably in the areas of employment, housing, and behavioral health, becomes important when back-door options are implemented. Given that four in ten offenders return to prison within three years after release, concentrated reentry efforts are vital (Pew Center 2011).

Offenders face a multitude of barriers, such as finding employment, obtaining stable housing, adjusting to life outside prison/jail, and repairing broken ties with friends and family members. Of specific concern are individuals with substance abuse and/or mental health disorders, who have an even greater risk of recidivism. It is estimated that over 70 percent of state prisoners have struggled with either one or both conditions (James and Glaze 2006). Numerous local, state, and federal agencies and nonprofit organizations across the country provide reentry programming and assistance. Reentry efforts that make connections even before inmates return to the community and that continue over the first year after release are essential. Fortunately, there are more formalized reentry programs today than there were five years ago, and there is more financial support through grant funding with the passage of the 2008 Second Chance Act.

Critical Thinking Exercise

What do you think will be the next era or approach to corrections? What will it emphasize (treatment, custody, punishment, something else)? What should it be?

HISTORY OF INCARCERATION FOR WOMEN

The discussion of the history of corrections is mainly one covering the handling of male offenders. This is largely due to the position of females in society over the years. Throughout most of history, females were viewed as the property of their husbands or fathers (Edwards 1989; Pleck 1989). As such, women had no legal status and could not be held culpable for any criminal acts. The father or husband was responsible for the actions of a female. In turn, the husband or father was expected to punish the errant woman (Buzawa and Buzawa 1990). Many Western cultures proscribed official punishment for women in their legal codes, which were to be carried out by the male members of the family.

The fact that women held no (or very little) legal status throughout most of history meant that there was no need for institutions for females offenders. It was not until the later Middle Ages that female behavior came to be viewed as a societal concern and could then be subjected to public punishment. Women who committed adultery or murdered their husbands could be burned at the stake (Kurshan 1995). In the seventeenth century, women were controlled by labeling them as "witches" and burning them. Before 1790, the use of criminal confinement for women was a rare occurrence. When they were confined it was in facilities designed for men. Instead of being housed in single cells, women would be placed in large communal rooms.

From an historical standpoint, the history of institutional corrections for women is relatively short. Rafter (1983) dates the history to 1790. She further breaks up that history into two main periods: the Custodial Model (1790–1870) and the Reformatory Model (1870–1935). Post-1935 follows no distinctive model.

The Custodial Model

Prisons in the late seventeenth and early eighteenth centuries were small and often housed as few as fifty inmates. The number of female inmates was small and prisons likely had one to two female inmates housed in their facilities (Pishko 2015). Typically, early prisons, such as Newgate Prison in New York, did not have private cells. Instead, inmates were housed in communal rooms. Females sent to these institutions would often be in the same rooms with the men. Given the low numbers of women in prison, concern over their needs and treatment was lacking. The institutions were designed to serve male offenders. This situation created a number of problems for female inmates. There was a lack of privacy. This led to sexual exploitation by male correctional workers and inmates. Women also tended not to receive much needed support from visitors, medical personnel, and chaplains in these coed facilities. The idea of women supervising women inmates seldom, if ever, was realized.

It was not until the 1820s that segregating the sexes into separate cells or areas of a prison occurred. With the establishment of new, larger penitentiaries during this time, states began to house women separately from men (Kurshan 1995). In the Auburn prison in New York, for example, men were placed in individual cells, while female inmates were kept in a communal, third floor attic above the prison kitchen (Rafter 1983). The institution also employed a **prison matron** (i.e., a female correctional officer who was more of a mother hen type figure) to oversee the women. An agent of the prison delivered food to the women and removed any waste once daily, but other than that, the women were expected to take care of themselves. The conditions in the attic were quite deplorable and overcrowded. The cellblocks where the males were housed were luxurious in comparison.

While it would seem like any type of separate housing for men and women would improve the daily lives of female inmates, new problems surfaced. As women were given their separate units, they were often far away from the prison's center where the programs and other opportunities for betterment were held. Women were seldom able to access the healthcare, religious services, or exercise facilities. They were also not offered the same work opportunities as men. Women were generally given tasks, such as sewing, to accomplish. The goal was to make them more domesticated and ready to become a mother and housewife. Thus, what women received in these institutions was the appearance of equality with inferior conditions. These communal rooms had no provisions for exercise or for privacy.

The housing of women in communal rooms within prisons persisted until the late 1930s. At that time, many institutions moved women to individual cells just like those of men. Unfortunately, this often came with the same harsh treatment, discipline, and isolation experienced by male inmates. The same recognition of the need to address female inmates that brought about moving females to individual cells eventually led to the establishment of separate institutions for women.

New York established the first separate prison for women. The Mount Pleasant Female Prison opened in 1839, near Sing Sing, a men's prison. While physically separate from Sing Sing, the ultimate administration of the institution was the same as that of Sing Sing (Rafter 1983). A matron was the on-site person in charge. Mount Pleasant adhered to the use of cells, rather than communal areas, and included space for exercise and work. Unfortunately, the institution was quickly overcrowded and experienced a good deal of violence and aggressive behavior. The institutional response to the violence and aggression was the use of severe physical punishment.

The Custodial Model can be characterized by several things (Rafter 1983). First, little space was available for female prisoners, largely as a result of the relatively few women in the system. When space was available, women did not have access to work or exercise as did men. What work and programs were available tended to reinforce traditional female roles of being a wife and mother. Second, the administration of women's facilities was primarily left to men, often as an extension of male facilities. Third, discipline mirrored that for men—strict regimens and harsh physical punishment. In general, prisons for women borrowed the organization and policies found in men's prisons. This model dominated until the end of the Civil War.

The Reformatory Model

Under the Reformatory Model concern for female prisoners became evident. Feminists at this time campaigned in earnest to encourage male legislators to fund separate reformatory institutions for female offenders. Their arguments surfaced around three major ideas: (1) males are not to blame for female criminality; females should be responsible for their own actions; (2) rehabilitation would be more effective if women were not subjected to the negative influences of men; and

(3) women have the ability to control and reform their sisters and should be given every opportunity to do so (Freedman 1984). In essence, it was argued that female inmates and male inmates require different responses in punishment and treatment and the best way to achieve this goal is for women to be separated from men and housed in their own facilities operated by women.

The first female reformatory opened in Indiana in 1873. This was followed by the Massachusetts Reformatory for Women in 1877. Other states followed their lead and by 1933 there were twenty such institutions in the United States. The majority of these were in the Northeast and north central areas of the country. Only three were in located in the South and one was in the West (California) (Rafter 1983). The facilities were administered and run by women. The architectural style of these institutions differed a great deal from the typical male prison. Female prisons were constructed in a cottage plan with inmates living in small units (hence, the term "cottage"), which had a homelike atmosphere rather than built using a cell block design. It was believed that this environment would enable the women to understand and accept their expected role in society. Training in sewing, cooking, washing and ironing clothes, gardening, and farming were the main elements of treatment incarcerated women received at this time.

Separate and different style prisons, different programs, and different labor assignments were just some of the aspects where the differential response to female offenders became evident. Of course, in any number of ways this differential treatment was an improvement over the neglect in earlier years when women were housed with men and supervised by male guards. However, in focusing on the special needs of females and creating this differential response, the reformers (mostly middle class women intent on molding female offenders into homemakers despite the reality that most of these women would have to support themselves upon release from prison) "created a new set of problems by assuming that all women inmates, as women, could be treated alike, by methods aimed at reinforcing true womanhood in an era in which a new woman was emerging" (Freedman 1984, 90).

Other problems also emerged. Over time, the reformatories housed greater numbers of women, including more women who had committed serious felony offenses. This resulted in overcrowding, increased costs, and forced a move away from a primarily rehabilitation/treatment orientation. Harsh discipline became more the norm and the female institutions shifted to a greater emphasis on general custody.

Women's Corrections since the 1930s

Not much change occurred in women's corrections from the 1930s to today. Few new institutions were built in the Northeast and north central parts of the United States. More facilities appeared in the South and the West, largely due to the fact that there were so few in existence in those regions and the number of women being incarcerated steadily increased. Women's facilities continued to mirror those for men and were primarily custodial in orientation. There was a notable lack of work beyond "household chores" and a dearth of skills training and job preparation. Females were not provided the same opportunities as their male counterparts.

This situation was partly due to the fact that, although the number of female prisoners had increased, females represented (and still represent) a small segment of the total correctional population. In addition, most institutions and programs were led by males who had little understanding of the needs of female prisoners.

The unequal handling of men and women in prisons again led to calls for change. One mechanism that jump-started change in corrections for females was the use of legal action by and for female inmates in the late 1960s. Such issues as sentencing disparities between men and women, wherein women were serving longer, indeterminate sentences were brought before the courts. In the 1970s, unequal conditions of confinement were brought forth for the courts to rectify.

The decisions handed down held that there must be substantial equivalence between men and women prisoners across a number of practices. For example, men and women must be given similar opportunities to participate in work-furlough programs, the ability to be assigned to minimum-security institutions should be available to both men and women, and the distance between the location of sentencing and the prison should be equivalent for men and women. These last two holdings were driven by the fact that most states only have one prison for all female inmates, and where there is only one institution for females, it must house all security levels. Outcomes from other cases resulted in the development and implementation of quality treatment and vocational programs equal to those delivered in male prisons. Further, courts held that women must have access to adequate law facilities and legal assistance in their prisons as well.

Critical Thinking Exercise

Should women's corrections mirror the correctional practices for men? Should it have a different emphasis? If a different emphasis, what should that be?

Web Activity

To see a broadcast by Diane Sawyer from ABC's *20/20* program about women in prison today, go to https://www.dailymotion.com/video/x4uloac.

SUMMARY

The history of corrections has led to a system that handles a large number of offenders in a wide range of institutions and programs. Society no longer leaves responses to offenders in the hands of the victim and/or the victim's family. As well, offenders are not widely subjected to death and physical punishment. Many offenders now find themselves being held in residential institutions that are largely custodial in orientation and offer minimal rehabilitation and treatment. The alternative is a wide array of community interventions that may or may not provide the assistance needed to become a contributing member of society.

The current state of corrections focuses on an array of offenders, in a myriad of settings and interventions, with numerous challenges. It is to this current state of affairs that the balance of this book is devoted. Chapters 2 and 3 look at the existing correctional systems and the varying goals/rationales underlying different correctional approaches, including incapacitation, retribution, deterrence and rehabilitation, among others. Chapter 4 examines a myriad of issues in institutional corrections, including prison life, correctional officers, and special offender populations. Community correctional approaches and issues appear in the Chapter 5. The issue of offender reentry into the community is a major topic of concern today and is addressed in Chapter 6. Likewise, a separate discussion of juvenile corrections topics appears in Chapter 7. Youths pose unique challenges that require interventions geared to their age and situations. The final chapter tackles a key issue in corrections, namely what works in correctional treatment.

KEY WORDS

Alexander Maconochie
assize of arms
Assize of Clarendon
Auburn System
back-door options
benefit of clergy
blood feuds
Bridewell House
congregate system
convict leasing
corrections
Corrections Corporation of America

Sir Walter Crofton
Elmira Reformatory
Lex talionis
feudalism
front-door options
Gemeinschaft
Great Law
hue and cry
John Augustus
John Howard
Magna Carta
mark system
monastic prisons
Newgate Prison

parole
Penitentiary Era
Pennsylvania System
penology
prison matron
probation
reentry
rehabilitation
Statutes of Winchester
transportation
watch and ward
Wickersham Commission

DISCUSSION QUESTIONS

1. You have been asked to explain why individual responses to crime have been replaced by more communal responses. While explaining the changes in society over time you can see your audience is confused. Provide examples of what society used to look like and how it has changed, and explain how that change necessitated adjustments in addressing offending behavior.
2. Crime and deviance have always existed but a formal correctional system, particularly one with prisons, is relatively new. Why is that the case?

3. Five eras of corrections have been identified. You are asked to give a presentation to a group of citizens about historic changes in corrections. List the five eras and give a brief explanation of each (i.e., what makes each period unique in comparison to the others).
4. The discussion of corrections focuses mainly on male offenders. Describe how correctional approaches for female offenders differ from and/or parallel those for male offenders.
5. You are with a group of friends and family members and they are discussing the problem of corrections—but the discussion seems to only address aspects of imprisonment. Provide a brief, realistic outline of the many factors of corrections that go beyond the aspect of imprisonment.

SUGGESTED READINGS

Camp, S. D., and G. G. Gaes (2002). "Growth and Quality of U.S. Private Prisons: Evidence from a National Survey." *Criminology and Public Policy* 1:427–449.

Cullen, F. T., and K. E. Gilbert (1982). *Reaffirming Rehabilitation.* Cincinnati, OH: Anderson.

Martinson, R (1974). "What Works? Questions and Answers about Prison Reform." *Public Interest*, 42: 22–54.

Rafter, N. H (1983). "Prisons for Women, 1790–1980." In *Crime and Justice: An Annual Review of Research*, vol. 5, edited by M. Tonry and N. Morris, 129–182. Chicago: University of Chicago Press.

Rothman, D (1971). *The Discovery of the Asylum.* Boston: Little, Brown.

REFERENCES

Buzawa, E. S., & Buzawa, C. G. (1990). *Domestic violence: The criminal justice response.* Newbury Park, CA: Sage.

Camp, S. D., and G. G. Gaes. (2002). "Growth and Quality of U.S. Private Prisons: Evidence from a National Survey." *Criminology and Public Policy* 1:427–449.

Carson, E. A. (2018). *Prisoners in 2016.* Washington, DC: Bureau of Justice Statistics. Accessed February 14, 2018. https://www.bjs.gov/content/pub/pdf/p16.pdf.

Cheung, A. (2002). *Prison Privatization and the Use of Incarceration.* Washington, DC: Sentencing Project.

Collier, L. (2014). "Incarceration Nation." *Monitor on Psychology* 45:56–61. Accessed February 14, 2018. http://www.apa.org/monitor/2014/10/incarceration.aspx.

Cullen, F. T., and K. E. Gilbert (1982). *Reaffirming Rehabilitation.* Cincinnati, OH: Anderson.

Edwards, S.M. (1989). *Policing "domestic" violence: Women, the law and the state.* Newbury Park, CA: Sage.

Freedman, E. B. (1984). *Their Sisters' Keepers: Women's Prison Reform in America, 1830–1930.* Ann Arbor: University of Michigan Press.

Hughes, T., and D.J. Wilson. (2004). *Reentry trends in the United States.* Washington, DC: Bureau of Justice Statistics.

James, D. J., & Glaze, E. (2006). Mental health problems of prison and jail inmates. http://bjs.ojp/usdoj.gov/content/pub/pdf/mhppji.pdf

Johnson, R. (2002). *Hard Time: Understanding and Reforming the Prison.* Belmont, CA: Wadsworth.

Kaeble, D., and L. Glaze. (2016). *Correctional Populations in the United States, 2015.* Washington, DC: Bureau of Justice Statistics. Accessed February 14, 2018. https://www.bjs.gov/content/pub/pdf/cpus15.pdf.

Kurshan, N. (1995). *Women and Imprisonment in the U.S.: History and Current Reality.* Accessed February 15, 2018. https://www.freedomarchives.org/Documents/Finder/DOC3_scans/3.kurshan.women.imprisonment.pdf.

Lindner, C. (2006). "John Augustus, Father of Probation, and the Anonymous Letter." *Federal Probation* 70, no. 1. Accessed February 12, 2018. http://www.uscourts.gov/sites/default/files/fed_probation_june_2006.pdf.

Lundahl, B. W., C. Kunz, L. Brownell, and N. Harris. (2009). "Prison Privatization: A Meta-Analysis of Cost and Quality Confinement Indicators." *Research on Social Work Practice* 19:383–394.

Mancini, M. (1978). "Race, Economics, and the Abandonment of Convict Leasing." *Journal of Negro History* 63:339–352.

Mangino, M. T. (2016). "Ohio's Prison Population Rising." *Youngstown Vindicator*, July 2, 2016. Accessed February 14, 2018. https://csgjusticecenter.org/jr/ohio/media-clips/ohios-prison-population-rising/.

Martinson, R. (1974). "What Works? Questions and Answers about Prison Reform." *Public Interest* 42:22–54.

Mattera, P., and M. Kahn. (2001). *Jail Breaks: Economic Development Subsides Given to Private Prisons.* Washington, DC: Institute on Taxation and Economic Policy.

Pew Center on the States (2011). *State of recidivism: The revolving door of America's prisons.* Washington, DC: The Pew Charitable Trusts.

Pishko, J. (2015). *A History of Women's Prisons.* Accessed February 13, 2018. https://daily.jstor.org/history-of-womens-prisons/.

Pleck, E. (1989). Criminal approaches to family violence, 1640–1980. In L. Ohlin & M. Tonry (Eds.), *Family violence.* Chicago: University of Chicago Press.

Rafter, N. H. (1983). "Prisons for Women, 1790–1980." In *Crime and Justice*, vol. 5, edited by M. Tonry and N. Morris, 129–182. Chicago: University of Chicago Press.

Rothman, D. (1971). *The Discovery of the Asylum.* Boston: Little, Brown.

Rothman, D. (1980). *Conscience and Convenience: The Asylum and Its Alternatives in Progressive America.* Boston: Little, Brown.

Sexton, G. (1995). *Work in American Prisons: Joint Ventures with the Private Sector.* Washington, DC: National Institute of Justice.

US General Accounting Office. (1996). *Private and Public Prisons: Studies Comparing Operational Costs and/or Quality of Service.* Washington, DC: General Accounting Office.

von Hirsch, A. (1992). Proportionality in the Philosophy of Punishment. *Crime and Justice*, vol. 16, 55–98.

Woodham, C. (2008). Eastern State Penitentiary: A Prison with a Past. *Smithsonian Magazine*, September 30, 2008. Accessed February 10, 2018. https://www.smithsonianmag.com/history/eastern-state-penitentiary-a-prison-with-a-past-14274660/.

Correctional Systems

AFTER READING THIS CHAPTER, YOU SHOULD BE ABLE TO:

- Discuss the functions of jails
- List and describe different jail designs
- Identify and describe state prison models
- List and define the different state prison security levels
- Tell the important outcomes of the Three Penitentiary Act
- List and define the different types of federal prisons
- Discuss the growth of federal prisons
- Discuss the privatization of prisons

INTRODUCTION

Corrections involves a wide range of activities aimed at carrying out criminal sentences on those who have been convicted of a crime. While the term "corrections" most often brings to mind incarceration in jail or prison, correctional sentences can also entail probation, parole, fines, and a number of alternative interventions aimed at punishment and/or rehabilitation besides incarceration. Beyond the diversity of forms, corrections exists within a web of local, state, federal, and private agencies and organizations. Each is authorized under specific jurisdictional boundaries and legal codes, although the local, state, and county systems all work within their respective state's criminal code. There is no one system of corrections. Instead, there are individual systems related to the different governmental units operating the correctional agency/unit.

An offender's particular situation may be determined by any number of factors. Although sentencing guidelines exist to increase the penalties for repeat offenses, the courts have considerable discretion to depart upward or downward from the recommendations, so long as they articulate the reasons and conditions that justify the departure. Those may include, among others,

- the type and level of seriousness of the instant offense;
- the offender's age;
- the offender's cooperation with law enforcement and the court;
- the offender's standing in the community where the offense occurred;
- the offender's anchors to the community, such as stable employment, the presence of family, and the like;
- the offender's previous criminal offenses, if any;
- the amount of time elapsed between a prior offense and the current one, and evidence of the individual's commitment to self-improvement in the interim;
- the degree of remorse expressed by the offender for their actions, and their offers of recompense;
- the willingness of the victim to participate in a program of alternative reconciliation or mediation.

This chapter investigates corrections from the point of view of different governmental levels, from local to state to federal. We will also consider private corrections as a separate system, although those companies operate under contract with some governmental entity (typically the state or federal level). While correctional systems also address youthful offenders, we will hold that discussion for a later chapter.

The discussion in this chapter focuses heavily on the structure of incarceration (particularly jails and prisons) related to the various jurisdictional levels. The operation and programming of those facilities is taken up in later chapters. Interestingly, the public's focus on jails and prisons reflects only 30 percent of the correctional population in the United States (Kaeble and Cowhig 2018). Seven out of ten adults under correctional supervision are on probation or parole. A further consideration is that few facilities are federal institutions, with 94 percent of correctional facilities being run by state or local governments (Stephan 2008).

LOCAL CORRECTIONS

Local corrections refers to correctional actions taken by communities (towns, cities, and other similar jurisdictions), and counties. Local corrections includes a wide array of interventions and agencies. Probation and community supervision represent the largest component of local efforts. Incarceration also appears at the local level, typically under the umbrella term of "jails."

Local courts hear cases of violation of two different levels of legal code: local ordinances (which are by definition civil rather than criminal) and misdemeanor offenses under the state's criminal code. Juvenile offenses under the criminal code are almost always heard in local courts, but punishment levels can be elevated to a higher level of correction for serious offenses.

Local juvenile dispositions are aimed at correcting the youths' behavior and giving them an opportunity to earn their way back into the community's good graces. Some form of community service work is often required, along with a period of nominal supervision by the court (called probation in some areas, though it can go by other names locally). Attendance at educational facilities or special presentations may be part of the court's requirement, and adult community members, rather than paid correctional personnel, are often their supervisors.

There are local juvenile probation officers in many cities and counties, however, they are assigned for more serious offenses. Depending on the nature of the offense or the youth's background, however, commitment to a residential facility other than the child's home is a possibility. Treatment of substance abuse or severe anger management problems often require knowledgeable staff and restricted conditions to be effective. In the rare case that incarceration is deemed appropriate, a juvenile usually will be remanded to the care of a state facility, or to a private facility under state authorization

For adult offenders of local ordinances, courts are generally limited to imposing fines as punishment, but they have the authority to require corrective measures, such as taking down an unauthorized structure, or ending unlawful
commercial ventures. When adults are convicted of serious misdemeanors in local
court, the sentence may be a locally supervised probation, or possibly a state-
supervised one. Compensatory actions similar to those required of juveniles are
often imposed on adults as well, usually focusing on community clean-up and
other activities. If the misdemeanor offense is serious enough, or if the offender's
history indicates that lesser measures have been ineffective in the past, the court
may sentence the individual to a jail term of up to one year in the county jail; it
may be a longer sentence in some states.

Local corrections typically do not include residential incarceration, at least
not in terms of a jail or prison cell. Local police departments often do have barred-
cell facilities that resemble a small jail, but they are solely for short-term *detention*,
either while a person in custody "sleeps it off" after being arrested for a drunken
bender, or until a person charged with a more serious offense can be brought
before the court for a preliminary hearing. If continued custody is required by the
court, the accused will be housed in the county jail until trial.

COUNTY CORRECTIONS

The sheriff is the chief law enforcement officer of the county, and responsibility for
the county jail falls under his or her responsibility. The sheriff's office is the only
institution that serves all three branches of the criminal justice system:

- Road deputies have law enforcement power throughout the county.
- Jail deputies serve as guards and maintain the jail.
- Law enforcement deputies provide security in the county courts and serve
  civil writs on behalf of the court.

Service as a jail guard has traditionally been the point of entry for people who
want to be road deputies. They would become eligible for the road enforcement
work after spending a certain amount of time working in the jail (during which
time they would get to know many of the county's more serious repeat offenders, knowledge that could potentially pay benefits when the guards became
road officers). However, a modern trend has been to hire for these separate
duties. Jail guards may still apply for open positions as road deputies but would
not receive automatic preference based on their time with the Sheriff's
Department.

Not all of county corrections occurs inside the jail, of course. County probation officers supervise far more individuals in the community, monitoring
their (presumed) law-abiding behavior, but also conducting unannounced
visits to verify that behavior. Most of the people under supervision will be
adults, but as noted above, some juveniles may be watched by county probation
officers as well.

Jails

Jails are typically under the purview of a county sheriff and serve the needs of the county, the local towns and cities, and possibly the state. County jails serve three distinct purposes, and hold three different types of populations in custody:

- Adults serving felony and misdemeanor sentences comprise the largest group.
- Adults unable to make bail or remanded to custody until trial because of perceived flight risks (or danger to their victims), are the second, though their stay in the jail facility is generally short-term.
- Persons who are potential witnesses in criminal cases are an infrequent, but nonetheless important, custodial group.

Witnesses who are held in jail must be considered flight risks by the court, and their detention is a civil order rather than a criminal one. The charges against the accused must be serious enough to justify the state's interference with the liberty of a citizen, which is a rare occurrence. Nevertheless, protection of a witness in a correctional setting is one of the challenges of running a jail.

Work release under court supervision is also one of the tools in the county's purview that operates out of the county jail. While the popular image is of the chain gang cutting brush and cleaning up trash from county roads, other forms of labor occur as well. Prisoners often help clear the damage from large-scale environmental disasters like floods and tornadoes, and other work opportunities, such as conducting computerized surveys while within the jail's confines. One issue is that prisoners may not be used as an unfair substitute for paid labor on the open market; another—perhaps particular to the use of computers—has been offenders' unauthorized use of computers for illicit means. The latter is more likely to be a problem only when supervision of the workroom is poor.

Alternative sentencing also affects jail populations unevenly. A convicted person may be released during the daytime to work at their regular job (when a longer jail term would cause them to forfeit it, thus hurting their family), and then return to the facility as soon as the workday is over. Others may be sentenced to serve their term on weekends, remaining with their family during the regular work week.

The county jail is also the "cell of last resort" when prison overcrowding requires suppressed sentencing (often under court order). Prisoners held under those conditions will be transferred to a state or federal prison when an opening occurs, but they may constitute a more problematic element of the jail's resident population in the meantime.

Most discussions of jails typically assume that their characteristics and purposes are readily understood. While I am sure that we all have a general idea about jails, there are some elements that deserve attention, especially considering that jails have become a type of purgatory, in that convicted offenders are waiting in jails until space opens up in prison, where they will serve out their sentence. Jails were not designed for this capacity, but as long as the United States remains focused on incarceration as a major form of punishment, we should at least have some background knowledge on the world of jails.

Currently, there are roughly 3,200 jails in the United States (Stephan 2008) and this does not include all the temporary holding cells and lockups that appear in many police departments and small towns. Police-department and small-town holding cells are typically used at the very outset of the arrest and processing of the accused. The subjects have not been convicted. Those held in jails are often awaiting trial or some other court proceeding or are awaiting transfer to a larger jail or other institution. Thus, these "jails" are not the same as those typically included in discussions of correctional institutions.

In the truest sense, **jails** and **detention centers** are facilities designed to hold a variety of offenders for a relatively brief period, usually for less than one year. The size of a jail varies depending on the geographic and legal jurisdictions that the facility serves. While jails in rural areas and small communities may hold relatively few prisoners, the facilities found in America's largest population centers can be quite immense. A total of 727,400 adults were held in local jails in 2016 (Kaeble and Cowhig 2018) for an average of roughly 225 inmates per jail. Counties or municipal governments operate most jails, while some jurisdictions such as the federal government have special facilities for their own detainees in certain areas of the country.

According to one report (see Austin 2014), compared to state prisons with over 1.3 million persons incarcerated with serving an average of three and one-half years, jails house 55 percent fewer individuals with an average length of stay around twenty-three days. Most jail inmates are un-convicted, meaning that they have yet to plead or be found guilty of any offense (i.e., they are in the pretrial process). With rare exceptions, offenders only go to prison post-conviction. Demographically, nearly 46 percent of jail inmates are white males. In comparison to prisons where black males are the most represented racial/ethnic group.

Jails perform several important functions. First, jails are where most offenders are housed following arrest. After arrest, a local judge or magistrate reviews the offenders' charges and flight risk and sets a bail amount, orders the offenders held without bail, or releases the offenders on their own recognizance until their next court date. Second, jails house defendants who have been sentenced to less than one year of incarceration. Some jail sentences are served on weekends, or the offenders may be released to the community for work while residing in the jail. Finally, jails may serve as detention centers to temporarily confine a variety of offenders until their cases are resolved or until authorities from the proper jurisdiction assume custody. Therefore, juvenile and adult, misdemeanor and felony, and state and federal offenders may all be housed briefly in the same facility, but sometimes in different units within that facility.

Although there are exceptions, jails tend to be chaotic environments and face a number of problems. First, jails have historically been the dumping grounds for the poor, deviant, and marginalized individuals in a community. They seem to be continually under pressure from overcrowding, a lack of resources and training, and the issue of local politics. Many individuals processed into the jail are intoxicated or under the influence of behavior-altering substances, highly agitated, suicidal, or mentally unstable when they arrive. Jail personnel often do not have adequate information on an arrestee's needs and risks when he or she is first booked into the facility. This lack of knowledge may lead to otherwise preventable problems. Last, the continuous movement of prisoners in and out of a jail facility presents logistical and safety challenges to jail staff and administration. Jail inmates are frequently moved for court hearings, community service work, and other activities. The high volume of visitors into these facilities can also provide opportunities for violence or smuggling of contraband.

Jail Design

Jail administrators are constantly facing facilities management problems. Jails are often impersonal, with little contact between the guards and the inmates. Many jails, particularly older jails that are part of police departments, follow an **intermittent surveillance** setup (see Figure 2.1). Intermittent surveillance means that inmates are not visually monitored at all times. Instead, jail staff check on the inmates on a regular schedule. Larger jails housing more inmates and possibly serving more than one agency or jurisdiction (such as a regional jail for multiple cities and/or counties) may use a similar intermittent surveillance setup like that of the **radial design** in Figure 2.2. The radial design has several corridors radiating off of a central hub and requires staff to periodically walk down each arm of the jail. In these larger jails, staff may have to monitor hundreds of inmates at once, thereby decreasing safety for all involved. Beyond the ramifications of design, jails also lack necessary services such as medical, psychological, and substance abuse treatment for inmates. It should come as no surprise that stress levels are often heightened in the jail setting, with violence and safety issues in constant need of resolution.

To overcome some of the problems in these jail designs, particularly those with intermittent surveillance, there has been a movement to replace existing jails with what are known as **new-generation jails (NGJs)**. Architecturally, these NGJs are built to house fewer inmates in what are known as pods or modules that contain anywhere from sixteen to thirty separate cells with one or two inmates per cell. Inmates do not have access to other pods in the jail, and the staff does not have to be concerned with managing more than sixty inmates at any given time. These

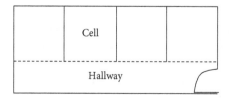

Figure 2.1 Intermittent Surveillance Jail Setup.

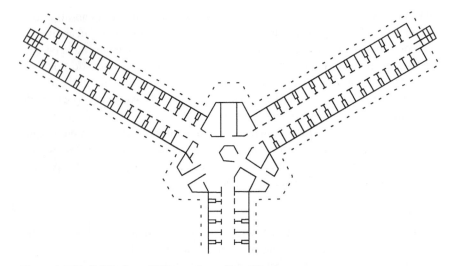

Figure 2.2 Radial Design with Intermittent Surveillance.
SOURCE: Nelson, W.R. (1988). Cost savings in new generation jails: The direct supervision approach. Washington, DC: National Institute of Justice.

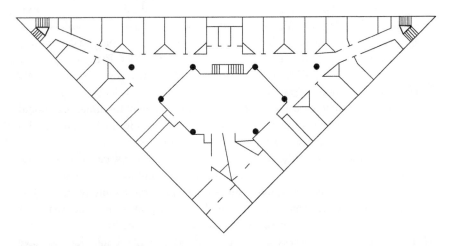

Figure 2.3 NGJ with Direct Supervision.
SOURCE: Nelson, W.R. (1988). Cost savings in new generation jails: The direct supervision approach. Washington, DC: National Institute of Justice.

jails typically also allow for **direct supervision** (see Figure 2.3 for one such layout). In direct-supervision settings, correctional officers are stationed in the pod or central area where they can directly observe the inmates at all times. Officers and inmates are in direct contact with one another.

In the NGJs, inmates eat, sleep, make phone calls, and engage in activities such as game playing or television viewing all in the pod (Zupan 2002). The staff is in closer contact with the inmates and consistently monitors inmate behavior, which not only attenuates problems among the inmates and within the facility but can also provide inmates with more positive social exchanges between inmates and staff. One earlier evaluation of a NGJ found that recidivism of inmates housed in these facilities did not increase and, for some offenders, recidivism decreased when compared with inmates housed in traditional jails (Applegate, Surette, and McCarthy 1999).

A major concern facing our nation's jails is the increasing numbers of individuals with mental illnesses and how jail administrators and staff can effectively deal with this population in the jail setting. Approximately 80 percent of jails conduct mental health exams upon intake (James and Glaze 2006) and it is through this initial screening that persons with mental illnesses are identified. These assessments find that 23 percent of inmates had been treated for a mental illness the year preceding arrest, 17 percent used medication that affects their mental illness, and 7 percent had at least one overnight stay in a psychiatric hospital (James and Glaze 2006). Although some jails provide psychotropic medications, most facilities lack appropriate treatment for affected inmates and the political, physical, and administrative structure of jails are often counterproductive to treatment efforts that might be effective.

Local corrections has experienced increasing diversification in recent years. As noted earlier, regional jails serving several jurisdictions are becoming more commonplace as the costs of jail construction and operations continue to increase. In some locations, states are pushing for the establishment of regional correctional centers that will serve surrounding counties and jurisdictions. These facilities may be governed by the local authorities or the state. The reasons for the state's interest in these more-localized institutions are varied. First, these facilities can handle offenders who otherwise would go to state prison, thereby alleviating overcrowding in the state institutions. Second, the local facilities allow for the inmates to remain closer to their community and families. Third, the facilities can offer specialized programming for specific types of offenders. These programs could address the mental health issues and needs identified above.

STATE CORRECTIONS

State-level correctional systems deal primarily with long-term incarceration of those who have been convicted and sentenced to a prison term. There were over 1,700 state-level correctional facilities (Stephan 2008) housing 1.3 million persons in 2016 (Kaeble and Cowhig 2018). State prison populations are more than double that of local jails. In addition to those held in secure institutions, over 870,000 adults were under parole supervision in 2016 (Kaeble and Cowhig 2018). It is important to note that, while parole supervision typically takes place in the local community by parole officers working out of a local office, the parole authority rests with the state.

Prison Models

While it might seem rudimentary to discuss the basic building models of prisons, they are important to recognize insofar as the designs of a prison affects everything from inmate adaption to inmate discipline to crowding and related issues. Policies attempting to impact these issues have a better chance of success if they, among other items (types of inmates housed therein, sentencing models, programming availability, and so forth), take into consideration prisons' physical structures.

Many of the earliest prisons followed the first model known as the radial design (see Figure 2.2). These resembled a wagon wheel without the outer ring. The center hub, where the axle of a wheel would be, allowed prison staff to look down each corridor. Staff would have to patrol the corridor intermittently to truly monitor activity. Each spoke or corridor could be isolated from the others by closing down the hub. This allowed the institution to deal with disturbances if they arose. There are many examples of these prisons. One example is the New Jersey State Prison. (See http://www.prisonpro.com/content/new-jersey-state-prison for a picture.) New prisons are rarely built based on the radial model. This design has given way to newer layouts.

The second design type resembles a telephone pole, thus the term "**telephone pole design**." A large central corridor (the pole) serves as nexus for crossbeams or cross arms extending from the pole. Cells, medical facilities, classrooms, treatment rooms, kitchens and dining rooms, recreation areas, administration offices, and other areas are housed in the pole and the cross arms. The center pole allows inmates and staff to traverse between locations in the prison. Access to each arm and the various functional areas can be sealed off and controlled by correctional officers. The officers are also able to maintain surveillance from the corridor. The main purpose of this type of design is incapacitation and control. Separation of inmates according to threat levels and needs is a common feature of these institutions. Modern maximum-security prisons (discussed later) typically follow this design. An example of this type is Graterford in Pennsylvania (http://www.prisonpro.com/content/graterford-state-correctional-institution).

The **courtyard design** is another model (see Figure 2.4). A single building or separate buildings are constructed in a perimeter format around a large interior courtyard. Movement from units and areas within buildings is not restricted to tightly controlled corridors like in the radial or telephone designs. Instead, inmates and staff can traverse the center courtyard to access classrooms, work areas, medical offices, libraries, living quarters, and other areas of the institution. The Madison Correctional Institution in London, Ohio, could be considered a courtyard model prison.

Figure 2.4 Courtyard Design.

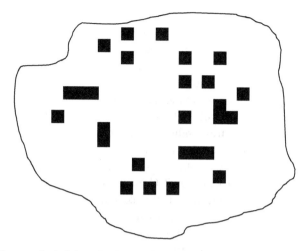

Figure 2.5 Campus Style Prison Design.

The fourth style follows the layout of many colleges and universities and is referred to as the **campus model** (Figure 2.5). Separate buildings are spaced over an open area and house a wide range of functions. The buildings will house cells, dormitories, or other living quarters. Other buildings will house schools, dining facilities, administration, and prison industries, among other activities. This design is commonly used for nonsecure or low-security prisons and institutions housing juveniles and females. Rather than being confined to individual buildings, inmates and staff move from building to building as the need arises. These institutions are still secured by fences or other locked barriers to keep the inmates from escaping. The Wabash Valley Correctional Facility (http://www.prisonpro.com/content/wabash-valley-correctional-facility) is an example of the campus model.

Two prison designs that have emerged since the 1980s are the skyscraper design and the modular prison model. The **skyscraper design** looks like any tall office building with many floors in a major city. The main purpose of these structures is to incapacitate offenders. Many of these designs function as both a long-term prison and a short-term holding facility for offenders awaiting trial or other system processing. The different floors of the institution may contain space for a range of functions, such as classrooms or workspace for prison industries. Exercise space for inmates is often on the roof of the structures. Lower floors are often devoted to administrative offices or related criminal justice agencies, such as a police department, sheriff's office, or courtrooms. Jails and many private prisons (i.e., corporations contracted with the government to operate correctional facilities) are of this design. Many major cities and the federal government also have prisons built using the skyscraper model. The Metropolitan Correctional Center in New York City (https://www.bop.gov/locations/institutions/nym/index.jsp) and the Metropolitan Correctional Center in Chicago (https://en.wikipedia.org/wiki/Metropolitan_Correctional_Center,_Chicago) are two good examples.

Perhaps the most prominent of the new generation prison designs is the **modular design**. These are also known as pod prisons. These facilities allow for direct supervision of the inmates and their living quarters. The design typically has several features improving the ability to watch inmates. One of the noteworthy features is the use of plexiglas panels in place of bars or secure doors. Advanced technological equipment is used to monitor behavior, to open and close cell doors, and to control access to areas of the facility, such as toilets and cafeterias. Many of these institutions are built from individual cells or pods, which were constructed off site and then attached to one another at the institution's location. This method allows for easier expansion of facilities as needs arise. An example of this design is the Golden Grove Prison Facility on St. Croix in the US Virgin Islands.

Each prison has certain features that make it more suitable for particular categories of offenders. Once an inmate is sentenced to prison, personnel from the corrections department usually conduct an initial classification review in which the needs and risk of the offender are evaluated to determine the best placement of that individual within the prison system. Common topics evaluated in this assessment are the danger posed by the prisoner, the length of sentence, any gang affiliation, physical or mental health needs, and whether treatment programs are available and considered important for the prisoner. Based on this assessment, prisoners are sent to an institution that is classified by its security type.

Prison Security Levels

Most American jurisdictions have three to five different types of prisons that are distinguished by their security level. **Supermax prisons** are generally reserved for the most violent and dangerous offenders. Forty-four states have supermax prisons; they are found in the larger jurisdictions and represent the most restrictive and secure prisons in the country (Mears 2005). These prisons can be stand-alone facilities or separate units as part of other prisons. They are extremely high-cost operations and have strict limitations on the number of prisoners they can hold. Inmates in these facilities are confined to their cells except for very brief periods of exercise. Supermax prisons utilize the most sophisticated security systems and most rigorous safety procedures.

Maximum-security prisons represent the next highest level of security. Stephan (2008) notes there are 355 state maximum-security prisons housing almost 500,000 prisoners in the United States. These facilities typically hold the most violent and disruptive prisoners in those jurisdictions without supermax facilities. Movement within the prison is very restricted by numerous checkpoints and gates. These facilities are often surrounded by high fences or high walls (18–25 feet) with gun towers placed at strategic intervals. Inmates are housed in individual cells that rise in tiers. Shops or industries are often operated within these institutions where inmates produce goods used by state agencies. There may also be schools and other treatment programs designed for inmate rehabilitation. It is important to note that the primary purpose for confinement in maximum-security prisons is incapacitation, deterrence, and/or retribution, not rehabilitation. Services for feeding, clothing, and meeting health needs of inmates are provided. Around 40 percent of the US prison population is housed in institutions like this.

A third security classification known as **close security** is used in some jurisdictions and is between a maximum- and medium-security prison. Such facilities may be used for disruptive inmates who do not pose as great a physical threat to inmates or staff and for individuals convicted of violent offenses who do not require a maximum-security setting.

A total of 438 **medium-security prisons** house a diverse population of inmates (approximately 550,000 prisoners or 43% in the US state prisons) (Stephan 2008) and are built in any number of architectural styles. They are usually enclosed by chain-link fences topped with barbed wire. Industries operating within these facilities are more modern than in maximum-security prisons and may include computer programming, television repair, or other technical skills. Generally, only offenders who have been carefully screened for low risk of escape or assault will be assigned to a medium security institution. Inmates may have some degree of movement within the institution during certain times of the day and participate in a range of activities, so there is some relative freedom of movement. However, the specifics of inmate life and the amount of security can vary considerably, even within different prisons of the same jurisdiction.

Finally, **minimum-security prisons** represent the most-open and least restrictive type of institution. There are over 900 state minimum-security prisons housing almost 250,000 prisoners in the United States (Stephan 2008). In general, these facilities do not have fences and the security around the perimeter is relaxed. It is easier for inmates to escape from these prisons as there are no armed guards, no gun towers, no barbed wire, and no electronic devices to make sure inmates stay confined. The grounds generally resemble a school campus and a nearly normal lifestyle is experienced by staff and inmates alike. Family visits are quite leisurely and take place more frequently in comparison to the higher-security level prisons. Housing is usually like a college residence hall with semiprivate or even private rooms. There is a wide range of programs for residents of these facilities including vocational training, academic education, psychiatric treatment, counseling, and drug/alcohol treatment. Work release and study release programs are encouraged whereby inmates are allowed to travel away from the institution to attend school or work. Given these characteristics, it is easy to see why minimum-security facilities can house prisoners convicted of nonviolent offenses, those who pose a minimal security risk, and/or those nearing final release.

Web Activity

A great deal of information and data is available about corrections, prisons, jails, inmates, and other related topics on the Federal Bureau of Justice Statistics website (www.bjs.gov/index.cfm?ty=tp&tid=1). Investigate this site, as well as the Correctional Statistical Analysis Tool (CSAT): Prisoners (www.bjs.gov/index.cfm?ty=nps).

Some jurisdictions also have specialized prisons that mostly house offenders with attributes that pose unique challenges to institutions such as sex offenders, drug addicts, mentally handicapped or psychiatric prisoners. These facilities offer treatment programs or services that are tailored to meet the needs and risks posed by these populations. Each jurisdiction typically has a facility dedicated to housing prisoners with severe psychological disorders because of the unique problems such inmates present to the operation of an institution.

FEDERAL CORRECTIONS

Federal corrections can be traced to 1891 and the passage of the **Three Penitentiary Act**. This act authorized the construction of three federal prisons to hold those convicted of federal offenses. Prior to this act, federal prisoners were housed in state prisons. The growth in the number of federal inmates necessitated the construction of additional facilities and led to the establishment of the Federal Bureau of Prisons (BOP) within the US Department of Justice in 1930. Beyond prisons, the BOP operates detention centers, prison camps, halfway houses, community correctional centers, reentry centers, and other facilities, as well as contracting with several private prison companies (Bureau of Prisons [BOP] 2018b).

Federal prisons have a smaller number of offenders than found in local and state institutions. This is largely due to the fact that most criminal laws are state-based and not federal, thus there are fewer federal criminal offenders. Federal criminal law deals primarily with offenses that cross state lines, involve interstate commerce, and are mostly serious felonies outlined in federal law. Currently there are over 181,000 inmates in 111 federal facilities (BOP 2018b) compared to over 1.1 million inmates in roughly 1,800 state facilities (Kaeble and Cowhig 2018; Stephan 2008).

Web Activity

The BOP provides access to a wide range of data and information on its operations. Visit www.bop.gov/about/statistics and investigate information on inmates, facilities and staff.

Types of Federal Prisons

Federal facilities are separated into five security categories similar to that of state prisons. Minimum-security facilities have little security (and possibly no perimeter fencing) and inmates live in a communal, dormitory setting. These facilities are generally known as **Federal Prison Camps** (FPC). There are seven FPCs housing 17 percent of the federal inmates (BOP 2018a). The inmates in these facilities are involved in work and other programs to address their individual situations and needs. These institutions have a relatively low staff-to-inmate ratio.

The second facility category, low security **Federal Correctional Institutions** (FCI), includes forty-two facilities and 38 percent of the federal inmates (BOP 2018a). These facilities are characterized by double-fenced perimeters. Inmates live in cubicles or dormitories and participate in work and other programs. The staff-to-inmate ratio is higher than in the minimum-security facilities.

Forty-seven FCIs are medium-security facilities in the federal system and contain three out of every ten inmates (30%) (BOP 2018a). Medium-security correctional institutions typically house inmates in cells and have double fencing with electronic security systems. The institutions offer a range of treatment programs as well as work opportunities. There is a higher staff-to-inmate ratio and a higher degree of control exercised.

High-security institutions are known as **US Penitentiaries** (USP). There are seventeen USPs holding 12 percent of the federal prisoners (BOP 2018a). High-security institutions have strong perimeters of reinforced fencing or walls. Inmates live in cells and their activity is closely monitored and controlled. These institutions have the highest staff-to-inmate ratios.

The final classification is Administrative Facilities. These facilities generally handle specific types of offenders, such as those in pretrial detention, individuals with specific medical conditions or are very dangerous or violent. One of these Administrative Facilities is a supermax facility located in Colorado.

There are BOP facilities beyond those that fit under the above categories. First, there are Federal Correctional Complexes that address a variety of needs and inmates. These may include elements from many security levels. In some instances they are a true complex of buildings located near one another with each adhering to different security levels. The idea is that the different buildings/facilities can share resources and services for efficiency. Second, the BOP contracts with private organizations for prison services. There are eleven BOP prisons that are under contract with private companies. (These will be discussed later in this chapter.)

Growth in Federal Corrections

The federal prison population has experienced great growth since the 1980s. The **Sentencing Reform Act of 1984** eliminated parole and set tougher sentencing guidelines that mandated imprisonment in many cases. Along with other mandatory sentencing and three-strikes laws, the changes in the late 1980s and early 1990s helped to increase the federal prison population over sevenfold to more than 180,000 inmates today.

The absence of parole in the federal system has led to the establishment of **residential reentry centers** (RRC). These are half-way houses that serve as pre-release centers for inmates nearing the end of their sentence. The centers offer a range of services including financial management help, employment assistance, housing assistance, mental health care, and substance abuse treatment (BOP 2018b). The BOP contracts with 162 RCCs with almost 9,000 available beds.

The BOP is not the only federal agency involved in the incarceration of prisoners. The **US Immigration and Customs Enforcement Agency** (ICE) runs or contracts with seventy-five detention facilities mainly to handle illegal immigrants. These facilities include detention centers, correctional centers, jails, prisons, and processing centers (Immigration and Customs Enforcement 2018). The average daily detainee population in November 2017 was 39,322. This number includes both adults and youths. Most of these individuals were in private facilities under contract with ICE (Cullen 2018). The immigration debate and enforcement action on the border with Mexico during 2018 has led to more detainees and the opening of temporary holding facilities.

PRIVATE PRISONS

Another feature that can distinguish corrections programming and institutions is whether they are privately operated or managed and staffed by a jurisdiction's own personnel. Historically, it has not been uncommon for some degree of private interest to be involved in the operation of correctional interventions, including jails and prisons. Community agencies have long been involved in providing treatment, rehabilitation, and assistance to offenders. Probation and parole rely on a wide array of programs and interventions offered by non–criminal justice system agencies. One prime example is substance abuse treatment. Another example is contracting with colleges and vocational training programs to provide classes, degrees, or vocations skills to offenders.

Since the advent of the modern prison around the turn of the nineteenth century, American correctional systems have had a variety of relationships with private for-profit businesses and nonprofit agencies. During the twentieth century, however, the funding and operation of most American prisons has primarily been the responsibility of the public sector. The push for increasing privatization of government services began in the 1980s and since then American jurisdictions increasingly contract out some of their correctional services. For example, treatment services, community service, and smaller residential programs are more commonly privatized than major prisons.

Privatization of the correctional system was influenced by increasing incarceration rates, prison overcrowding, and escalating operating costs during the 1980s. Thus, governments became attracted to alternatives that could increase the cost-effectiveness of correctional budgets. Although the term "private prison" is often used to indicate a correctional facility that is managed and operated by a private corporation, the privatization of correctional services can take any number of forms. Typically, the authority to operate these facilities is granted through a contract awarded by a jurisdiction's government. There is considerable debate about the validity of incorporating a profit motive in the punishment of offenders. The first contracted prison was in 1984 in Tennessee. Today there are three major companies contracting with local, state, and federal agencies to run prisons or other correctional services. CoreCivic (formerly Corrections Corporation of

America) is the largest of the three running 139 facilities, of which thirty-seven are nonresidential (CoreCivic 2018). The GEO Group manages or operates 139 facilities, including prisons, detention centers, and community reentry facilities (GEO Group 2018). The third company, Management and Training Corporation (MTC) has twenty-four facilities (twenty-one correctional facilities and three detention centers) (Management and Training Corporation 2018). The BOP contracts with all three companies for a total of eleven prisons (BOP 2018a). Since 2000, the number of federal and state adults held in private facilities has increased from just over 87,000 (Guerino et al. 2011) to over 128,000 in 2016 (Carson 2018).

There are also real questions about whether private prisons are actually more cost-effective than their public counterparts, and if the quality of services provided at those institutions is better or worse than those in government-run institutions. Another issue is the question of liability for actions in private prisons. Who is liable? The company? The individual guard? The government agency contracting for the services? All three? The legal questions are an ongoing issue in private facilities. Despite the issues and concerns with private corrections, punishment is a major for-profit enterprise and several states and the federal government have private prisons that are used in conjunction with state-run facilities.

Web Activity

You can view an informative video on private prisons at http://www.pbs.org/now/shows/419/video.html.

SUMMARY

The challenges facing corrections have meant major changes over the years, as demonstrated by the varied jails and prison structures in the past and the new organizational arrangements in recent years. The changes are not restricted to the physical structures; they also appear in realm of probation, parole, community corrections, and juvenile institutions. This will be demonstrated further throughout the coming chapters. We now turn to a discussion of the varied goal and philosophies underlying both the physical designs and the programmatic makeup of corrections.

KEY WORDS

campus model	Federal Correctional	maximum-security
close security	Institutions	prison
courtyard design	Federal Prison Camps	medium-security prison
detention centers	intermittent surveillance	minimum-security prison
direct supervision	jails	modular design

new-generation jails	Sentencing Reform Act	Three Penitentiary Act
(NGJs)	of 1984	US Immigration and
radial design	skyscraper design	Customs Enforcement
residential reentry	supermax prison	Agency (ICE)
centers	telephone pole design	US Penitentiaries

DISCUSSION QUESTIONS

1. The local news has just reported on the conviction of several offenders and everyone assumes prison time will be in the future for the convicted individuals. Explain what the different possibilities are in place of incarceration.
2. You are asked about how jails are organized. Provide an answer that compares and contrasts different designs and layouts of jails.
3. The state is looking at constructing a new correctional facility, and debate has begun on design. You have been asked to provide an overview of different designs. List different types of designs and briefly explain what is unique about each.
4. There is a need for additional prison beds but the state claims that the cost of a new prison is prohibitive. A private company offers to build and run a prison under a contract with the state. What are the pros and cons of such an arrangement?

SUGGESTED READINGS

Harding, R. (2001). "Private Prisons." In *Crime and Justice: A Review of Research*, vol. 28, edited by M. Tonry, 265–346. Chicago: University of Chicago Press.

Kurki, S., and Morris, N. (2001). "The Purposes, Practices and Problems of Supermax Prisons." In *Crime and Justice: A Review of Research*, vol. 28, edited by M. Tonry, 385–424. Chicago: University of Chicago Press.

Johnston, N. (2000). *Forms of Constraint: A History of Prison Architecture*. Urbana: University of Illinois Press.

Williams, J., D. Rodeheaver, and D. Huggins (1999). A comparative evaluation of a new generation jail. *American Journal of Criminal Justice*, 23(2), 78–89.

Zupan, Linda L. (2002). "New Generation Jails." In *Encyclopedia of Crime and Punishment*, edited by D. Levinson, 1089–1091. Thousand Oaks, CA: SAGE.

REFERENCES

Applegate, B. K., R. Surette, and B. J. McCarthy. (1999). "Detention and Desistance from Crime: Evaluating the Influence of a New Generation Jail on Recidivism." *Journal of Criminal Justice* 27: 539–548.

Austin, J. (2014, April 5). *Key trends in national crime, arrests, and jails*. [Video file, Center for Evidence-Based Crime Policy website, George Mason University]. Retrieved from https://www.youtube.com/watch?v=kAKat5OPA18.

Bureau of Prisons. (2018a, November 8). "About Our Facilities." Federal Bureau of Prisons website. Retrieved from https://www.bop.gov/about/facilities/federal_prisons.jsp.

Bureau of Prisons. (2018b, November 5). "About Us." Federal Bureau of Prisons website. Retrieved from https://www.bop.gov/about.

Carson, E.A. (2018). *Prisoners in 2016.* Washington, DC: Bureau of Justice Statistics.

CoreCivic. (2018). "Find a Facility." CoreCivic website. Accessed November 6, 2018. http://www.corecivic.com/facilities.

Cullen, T. T. (2018). "ICE Released Its Most Comprehensive Immigration Detention Data Yet. It's Alarming." National Immigrant Justice Center website. Accessed November 7, 2018. https://immigrantjustice.org/staff/blog/ice-released-its-most-comprehensive-immigration-detention-data-yet.

GEO Group. (2018). "Our Locations." Geo Group website. Accessed November 6, 2018. https://www.geogroup.com/Locations#us-corrections.

Guerino, P., Harrison, P.M., and Sabol, W.J. (2011). Prisoners in 2010 (revised). Accessed November 7, 2018 from https://www.bjs.gov/content/pub/pdf/p10.pdf

Immigration and Customs Enforcement. (2018). "Immigration Enforcement." US Immigration and Customs Enforcement website. Accessed November 7, 2018. https://www.ice.gov/detention-facilities.

James, D. J., and L. E. Glaze. (2006). *Mental Health Problems of Prisons and Jail Inmates.* Washington, DC: Bureau of Justice Statistics.

Kaeble, D., and M. Cowhig. (2018). *Correctional Populations in the United States, 2016.* Washington, DC: Bureau of Justice Statistics.

Management and Training Corporation. (2018). Corrections Services Accessed November 6, 2018. https://www.mtctrains.com/corrections/.

Mears, D.P. (2005). A critical look at supermax prisons. *Corrections Compendium,* 30, 6–7, 45–49.

Stephan, J. J. (2008). *Census of State and Federal Correctional Facilities, 2005.* Washington, DC: Bureau of Justice Statistics.

Zupan, Linda L. (2002). "New Generation Jails." In *Encyclopedia of Crime and Punishment,* edited by D. Levinson, 1089–1091. Thousand Oaks, CA: SAGE.

CHAPTER 3

Correctional Sentencing and Goals

AFTER READING THIS CHAPTER, YOU SHOULD BE ABLE TO:

- Relate how corrections is involved in the sentencing of offenders
- Discuss the paradigmatic tenets of Classicism and how they relate to corrections
- Show how Positivism differs from Classicism and identify types of correctional interventions that fall under Positivism
- Discuss how Classicism and Positivism intersect and give examples of that intersection
- Name six correctional rationales and identify whether they are Classical or Positivistic
- Identify and define the two types of deterrence and relate the assumptions of both.
- Explain how incapacitation is expected to deal with crime and identify different ways to incapacitate offenders
- Discuss rehabilitation as a correctional rationale and give examples of rehabilitation programming
- Show how criminal justice processing is criminogenic and discuss the use of diversion as a response to this problem
- Define restorative justice and explain how it is a rationale for correctional intervention

INTRODUCTION

Correctional intervention can take a wide array of forms: Depending on the offense, it can range from fines to probation to incarceration to the death penalty. Understanding corrections starts at the point of sentencing by the court/judge. The imposition of a specific sentence and correctional placement are influenced by legal statutes and the available correctional alternatives. It also responds to the underlying goals for corrections. These goals are not set by the correctional system. Rather, they are set by society and reflect different and changing assumptions about the individuals and behaviors being sanctioned. This chapter briefly addresses the issue of sentencing before moving on to a discussion of the varying goals/rationales for corrections.

SENTENCING

Sentencing is not typically considered a major topic within correctional discussions. This is because sentences and sentencing fall primarily in the realm of the courts. Indeed, sentencing is the last step in the court process once an individual has been convicted of a crime. The type of sentence is largely determined by the legislature through statutes. The actual sentence can involve a range of possible alternatives, from fines to restitution to community service to probation to jail/prison time (and many other possibilities). Although sentences are typically outlined by the legislature and then imposed by the judge, corrections can greatly influence the sentencing of convicted offenders.

There are several points at which corrections has an influence on sentencing. One of the earliest of these involves the role of correctional personnel in determining the appropriate sentence for the offender. Individuals convicted of offenses that could lead to a period of incarceration typically undergo a presentence investigation (PSI). This investigation is often conducted by probation officers, social workers, or others involved in addressing the needs of offenders. The presentence investigation considers the immediate offense and the individual's offense history, as well as background information on the offender, the offender's family, employment, education, drug use, and other factors. The court uses the PSI when making a final determination of the sentence.

Corrections and those involved in the correctional process also play a role in sentencing when offenders are given an indeterminate sentence. An **indeterminate sentence** is one where the judge imposes (or legal statutes set) a minimum and maximum amount of time to be served. The determination of release is left to the discretion of correctional personnel or another agency (such as a parole board).

The correctional system can greatly influence sentences, even when a **determinate sentence** (one with a fixed term of incarceration or supervision) is imposed by the court. The court typically imposes a sentence and leaves the specific conditions of the sentence to the correctional system. Beyond an indeterminate or determinate sentence, the sentence can be to community or other noncustodial supervision. A sentence involving incarceration does not usually mandate a specific facility or location. Within each institution the type of housing, programming, work assignment, or other considerations are left to the correctional system or the individual facility. Similarly, a community sentence does not typically indicate the conditions of probation or participation in specific interventions. Those particulars are left to the probation department, community correctional agency, or other personnel supervising the offenders.

Web Activity

Sentencing discussions typically look at a wide range of issues besides those presented here. Besides indeterminate and determinate sentences, courts must adhere to sentencing guidelines, blended sentencing, concurrent/consecutive sentences, three-strikes laws, and many other parameters. Further information on these topics can be obtained at https://legal-dictionary.thefreedictionary.com/Sentencing and https://criminal.findlaw.com/criminal-procedure/sentencing.html.

The sentencing decisions, either at the point of sentencing by the court or at the point of determining specific correctional interventions by correctional agencies, are influenced by the varying goals of corrections. In a broad sense, correctional intervention rests on a number of implicit beliefs and assumptions about individuals and the world in which they operate. The underlying **paradigm**, or set of assumptions and beliefs, about why people act the way they do, drives the correctional approach to behavior.

THEORETICAL SCHOOLS OF THOUGHT

Within the study of crime and corrections, the way people regard correction of human misbehavior falls into either the Classical or the Positivist schools of thought. These two perspectives are not antithetical. They share many elements between them, but the differences arise from the ways they view the human condition.

The Classical School

Classicism finds its roots in the writings of Cesare Bonesana Marchese de Beccaria (1738–1794) and Jeremy Bentham (1748–1832). Beccaria was an Italian aristocrat who broke with the ruling classes to condemn the methods of dealing with crime and morals in society. In outlining a new set of criminal and penal practices, he set forth several beliefs about man and the function of society in relation to deviance.

Under **Classicism**, man is viewed as being 100 percent **free willed**. That is, individuals choose to act the way that they do after calculating the pros and cons of an activity. A second important Classicist belief is that individuals are **hedonistic**. Under the *hedonistic calculus* individuals seek to maximize pleasure and minimize pain (Bentham 1948). Individuals choose activities and behaviors based on their determination of the amount of pleasure and pain that will result. Pleasurable behaviors will be undertaken and repeated. Painful activities will cease. Under Classicism, individuals make a conscious, *rational* decision to commit crime based on the expectation of a pleasurable outcome.

These beliefs about free will and hedonism suggest that the solution to crime requires altering the outcome of the hedonistic calculation. That is, increasing pain and reducing pleasure can reduce, and possibly eliminate, deviant behavior. Beccaria and other classicists, therefore, focused their efforts on making laws and setting punishments that would alter the choices of individuals. The classicists believed that individuals cannot make an informed decision to avoid crime in the absence of a clear set of laws and punishments that are generally known by the populace. The emphasis must be on the *offense* and *the legal system*, and not focused on any characteristics of the offender. There must be a set punishment for each crime and the level of punishment must be sufficient to offset any pleasurable consequence of an individual's unlawful behavior.

Classicism seeks to *prevent* and *deter* crime by *punishing* the offender for the offense. Punishment is not meant to be a form of retribution or retaliation by society. Instead, punishment is solely for the purpose of altering the outcome of the hedonistic calculus. Table 3.1 provides important elements of both Classicism and Positivism.

Table 3.1 Major Elements of Classicism and Positivism

Classicism	Positivism
Free will	Determinism
Hedonism	Multiple causation
Rational offender	Emphasize offender/ Situation differences
Emphasis on offense	Medical model – Crime as "symptom"
Legal responses – Clear laws and procedures	Individualized response Rehabilitation and treatment
Punishment for prevention and Deterrence	

The Positivistic School

Advances in medicine, psychology, and sociology in the late 1800s and early 1900s led to a more scientific approach toward explaining and understanding deviance. Simple punishment was not solving the crime problem and the newly emerging sciences questioned the belief that free will was the overriding factor behind behavior. While Classicism and deterrence did not disappear, a new paradigm emerged—it was called Positivism.

Positivism rejects the basic tenets of Classicism, which claim that individuals have free will, choose their behavior, and are totally responsible for their actions. Rather than hold the individual responsible for his actions, Positivists claim that behavior is *determined* (caused) by factors beyond the control of the individual. Altering behavior cannot be brought about through simply raising the amount of pain a person will receive if caught and punished. Rather, changing behavior can only be accomplished by identifying and eliminating the factors that are causing the individual to act in a certain way.

Positivism typically recognizes that there are *multiple causes* of behavior. Deviance may be the result of a single factor, multiple causes, or a series of events or situations occurring over a period of time. Two people committing the same deviant act may be the outcome of totally different causes. Positivism calls for examining each individual case for the reasons behind deviant behavior. The approach used to identify causes follows a *medical model* or uses a *medical analogy*.

Using a medical model, the scientist approaches deviance the same way that a doctor approaches a sickness. Just like a doctor considers coughs and fevers as symptoms of other problems, the Positivist views deviant acts, like burglary and rape, as *symptoms* of other underlying causes or conditions. The Positivist attempts to identify what causes an individual to commit a deviant act and prescribes a tailored response to the person and circumstances. The emphasis in Positivist theory is not on the offense; rather, the emphasis is on the *offender*, the unique *situation*, and the various factors causing the individual to be an offender.

The logical extension of the focus on determinism and multiple causation is the belief in *rehabilitation* and *treatment*. Instead of punishing an individual for his or her actions, the key is to remove the root causes of the deviant behavior. The proper rehabilitation or treatment strategies may be as diverse as the number of clients. For example, one burglar may need financial assistance for his/her family since the offense serves as a means to provide food for the family. Whereas a Positivist may determine that another burglar may require group counseling to address the specific animosity he/she had toward the victim, which ultimately led to the offending action. In the Positivistic view, any intervention needs to be tailored to the circumstances of the individual.

INTERSECTIONS AND CHANGE

The Classical and Positivist schools of thought exist side by side in the modern era. Indeed, correctional interventions exist today that correspond with each school. Positivism seems to have held sway in the twentieth century, especially in academic discussions of crime and criminal behavior and in the rehabilitation emphasis of corrections. At the same time, elements of Classicism persist. The two schools of thought often influence each other. Before turning to specific correctional rationales, we will investigate examples of how Classicism and Positivism have co-mingled and influenced societal responses to behavior.

One cornerstone of Classicism is outlining what constitutes crime, or what activities should be subject to a criminal penalty. Positivistic evidence occasionally shifts those definitions. We speak of offenses as belonging to two distinct categories: *mala in se* (a Latin phrase meaning "bad in itself") and *malum prohibitum* (Latin for "bad because it is prohibited"). The latter category is sometimes regarded as "bad *only* because it is prohibited [by a special interest group]," and thus reflects, and is subject to, changing social mores.

Mala in se crimes are generally recognized as such across ages and cultures. The seven original categories of the Uniform Crime Report's Part I crimes meet this definition: murder, aggravated assault, forcible rape, theft, motor vehicle theft, burglary, and robbery (a combination of theft and assault or threat of assault) are offenses not permitted in any known social or legal system. *Mala prohibitum* crimes, by contrast, reflect specific cultural beliefs or needs, and are subject to change over time. The changing nature of *mala prohibitum* crimes can be examined along several dimensions We will consider changing beliefs about people, substance use, sexual morality, and immigration in the following discussion of the interplay between Classicism and Positivism.

Changing Beliefs about "Person"

Legal changes do not always result from social changes, although changes in the law usually reflect shifts in social attitudes and beliefs. Individual conduct that was once seen as enforcing and reinforcing a proper moral code under the Classical school becomes criminalized as social understandings shift under Positivist influences.

American racial segregation was based on a long-outdated Classical belief in the inferiority of the "Negro" and "Mongoloid" races to the Eurocentric white "race." Activities were forbidden to men and women based solely on the color of their skin, even though the same activities by white Americans were deemed perfectly legal. One example of this in American history was the lynching of African Americans for behaviors that would not even be criticized if engaged in by white Americans. The murder of Emmett Till for allegedly wolf-whistling at a white woman in Mississippi in the 1950s is seared into the memories of Americans of that era. Similarly, the arrest of four African American college students for sitting at a whites-only lunch counter in Greensboro, North Carolina, was another major episode that began to shift Americans' perceptions of their underlying beliefs. The actions against Till and the students violating the "whites-only" policy fit the moral code at the time but presaged and galvanized the social change embodied by the American civil rights struggle of the 1950s and 1960s.

A similar transformation took place in Europe. The Nazi regime in Germany first vilified Jews as "inferior" (based on distorted Classical precepts in the dominant Christian religion). They then systematically attempted to exterminate them, along with others considered "inferior" by the Nazi government (Gypsies, homosexuals, Communists and Socialists). In the post–World War II period, Germany made a concerted effort to atone for those actions, notably opening its borders to immigrants fleeing conflict in the Middle East and Africa over the past two decades.

Comparable, though less fatal, movements have played out in the United States over the last century. Women's right to vote was the first, as denial of the privilege was based on a Classical belief in the inferiority of women. Further, the beating of women was considered legitimate under a belief in a husband's rights and masculine supremacy. Similar actions against a male spouse would have been treated as a criminal offense, yet wife-beating was shrugged off as normal, and even necessary. The status of women has clearly changed, thus prohibitions against women voting no longer exists and the physical control of women is illegal today.

Changing Beliefs on Substance Use

The cultural view of the consumption of alcohol and drugs have also undergone similar shifts. Alcohol had largely been an accepted form of social behavior, at least when used in moderation. Yet the Prohibition era began in 1920 (Cherrington 1920) with the passage of the Eighteenth Amendment, after the Women's Christian Temperance Union (WTCU) convinced the Congress to criminalize the sale and consumption of alcohol. The underlying rationale for the ban was based partly on Classical perspective's religious view (the biblical ban on drunkenness), and partly on observable (and thus Positivist) evidence of the impact of severe drunkenness and alcoholism.

Prohibition was repealed in 1933, when it became apparent that criminalizing the manufacture, possession, and consumption of alcohol had not curbed the underlying problem of drunkenness. Instead, it had both encouraged law-defying behavior and created a large and violent criminal underground that supplied the banned substance to an American public that did not share the WCTU's vision or beliefs. Alcoholism has moved under the Positivist banner in modern times and is now treated as a biological aberration rather than a mere willful defiance of a proper moral code.

Drug use has many parallels, but the biological underpinnings are different. The end of the Prohibition era led to the criminalization of marijuana (a substance also associated more with the African American community than with the white populace at the time). The underground drug culture that emerged in the 1960s brought the drug to a wider audience and led to a comparable Prohibition-style crackdown. Medical evidence on marijuana's effects have defied the propaganda against it and the tide has begun to shift. Marijuana possession and use has been decriminalized in many jurisdictions (although unlawful sales and possession of large amounts remain criminal offenses) and fully legalized in others. Driving under the influence of marijuana, as under alcohol, continues to pose a threat to the safety of others, and remains a criminal offense even in jurisdictions where the possession and use of the drug are decriminalized.

Other drugs, however, do not have the nontoxic effects of marijuana. Many opioids and synthetic drugs create severe addiction problems. Not only do the users suffer, but their deteriorating condition affects others around them, creates potentially hazardous situations on the job and elsewhere, and creates serious and expensive health problems for the users. Followers of the Classical philosophy note that the ill effects of these drugs (including many prescription drugs) are well known, especially their addictive properties, and those who choose to ignore them do so of their own free will when they try them for the first time. Though the sale, possession, and use of such drugs remains criminalized because of their disproportionate negative effects (compared to the social and recreational use of alcohol and marijuana), the Positivist school holds sway in the correctional arena, emphasizing efforts at rehabilitation and reinstating sobriety.

Sexual Morality

Sexual conduct is another form of human behavior that has seen major change over the years. Classical religious aversion to homosexual relations varies according to the faith, but Christianity has long based its opposition in the words of a single biblical verse (see, Leviticus 20:13–15) and an interpretation of the story of Sodom and Gomorrah (in the book of Genesis). While that view persists in the minds of many, increasingly more people have come to accept the Positivist view that homosexuality is an innate part of the human condition for a portion of the human race. Penalties for gay sex and legal barriers to serving the LGBTQ population (lesbian, gay, bisexual, transsexual, and queer) have fallen even in extremely conservative nations (such as India) (Gettleman and Schultz 2018).

The age at which heterosexual relations can begin is also a Classical element for criminal sanctions, but uneven across cultures. United States culture has long criminalized adults having sex with "minors"—persons under the "age of consent" who are not yet able to comprehend the consequences of their actions. That has traditionally meant the age of adulthood, but "adulthood" has varied considerably—it is age thirteen in some religions (the sacrament of confirmation in Christian churches and of the bar and bat mitzvahs in Judaism, for instance) and age eighteen for military service and for voting. There has been a sexual divide as well. Teenage boys who had underage sex were celebrated as "real men," whereas unwed women who conceived and bore children were long subject to shaming, often having to give up their "illegitimate" children for adoption. Scientific evidence indicates vastly different rates of maturity for the biology of puberty and the biology of brain development. Consequently, Classical prohibitions fly in the face of Positivistic revelations underlying behavior.

Immigration Decisions and Policy

A final example of the interplay between Classicism and Positivism involves immigration. Humans have migrated from one area of the globe to others throughout recorded history (and there is considerable evidence in prehistory as well). Migrants seek to escape harsh conditions in their homeland or to find new opportunities for growth. Indeed, the United States, Canada, and Australia are nations founded by such immigrants from Europe. Today, conditions in Africa, Central America, the Middle East, and parts of Asia are creating waves of desperate migration to Europe, the United States, and Australia. At issue for the receiving nations is whether migrations provide cover for the spread of terrorism, whether the migrants will contribute positively to the economy of the receiving nations or be a drain on them, and the threat of foreign influences on the "purity" of the receiving country.

Migrants from South and Central America to the United States are the focus of political concern. Many are fleeing horrendous conditions in their gang- and dictator-controlled home countries. Others are seeking to better their lives and their families' futures. Those who conform to the state-imposed requirements for entry are deemed legal immigrants. Those who cross the border surreptitiously, with or without the aid of smugglers, are considered illegal immigrants. It is a classical mode of thought that there are requirements to be met to conform with the law. Those who choose not to meet them are criminals.

Criminalizing undocumented immigration, however, has proven to be problematic. At least in the short run it has overburdened correctional facilities, led to lengthy delays for court hearings due to heavy caseloads, and exposed a lack of viable options for handling the "offenders." Once declared an illegal immigrant, a person can only be expelled from the country: Experience has shown that many expelled migrants, facing few viable options in their home territories, will attempt reentry to United States until they succeed in avoiding the authorities. The Classical goal of changing future behavior by expelling or criminalizing the violator is not realistic.

The fact that the United States had accepted wave upon wave of immigrants in the past, coupled with the politically divisive use of family separation and rigid legal responses to immigration in recent years has raised calls for more humanistic, less punishment-oriented responses. In essence, simple adherence to legal codes is not effective (or acceptable to many). Recognizing the forces driving immigrants to "illegally" enter a country (a Positivistic view) has led to modifications in the responses.

Intersections and Change Summary

The concept of corrections—of sanctions administered to intervene in bad behavior and shape better behavior in the future—has Classical roots, and assumes that the offender has both a knowledge of the wrong and an ability to do better. As scientific knowledge of the human condition has expanded and society has gained greater understanding of, and appreciation for, the inevitability of social variation, the Positivist school has nudged the field of corrections to expand its approach to some *mala in se* offenses, and has diminished the use of punishments for many *malum prohibitum* acts now regarded as either not amenable to criminal sanction, or ineligible for it.

We now turn to six goals/rationales for correctional intervention. Each tends to lean toward either Classicism or Positivism. The first three—retribution, deterrence, and incapacitation—are primarily Classical in orientation. The remaining three—rehabilitation, diversion, and restorative justice—are Positivistic concepts.

RETRIBUTION

Retribution is perhaps the earliest codified response to undesirable behavior and reflects the tenets of Classicism. The concept of **retribution** has two forms: (1) individual (or clan) response to a perceived wrong, and (2) an action by a state polity for a perceived wrong against the social collective. Although the root word suggests a matter of repayment, the individual form has been perceived as more a matter of vengeance than of "evening the score." It hints at accelerated injuries far exceeding the original slight or injury. In some cases, the state or collective action may be seen in the same light, such as leveling the death penalty for treason, even though no adverse results came of the betrayal. In certain times and places, the case could be made for retribution being an aspect of religious groups as well, although the line between vengeance and deterrence or incapacitation (discussed next) is somewhat blurred in those contexts.

As Chapter 1 has indicated, the idea of "an eye for an eye, a tooth for a tooth" dates back almost to the dawn of recorded history, appearing in the written laws in the Code of Hammurabi. While modern treatment of the phrase sometimes links it to the concept of *lex talionis*, historians regard Hammurabi's code as the first recorded attempt to limit previous practices, where retribution-as-vengeance was often disproportional to the original offense. It also is the first known attempt to subsume what was often personal vindication into a state-controlled form of justice.

The counterpart to "an eye for an eye" is the more humane "do unto others as you would have others do unto you." In the religious sense, that directs primary actions, not secondary reaction, but the concept embodies the idea that retaliatory measures should be proportional to the harm originally inflicted, not worse. Even so, the sardonic recognition that "an eye for an eye leaves the whole world blind" has led to the development of the other philosophies outlined below, and attempts to find a more measured and controlled means of responding to harms inflicted by one person against another, or against the state.

For most of history, and in many societies, retribution was a private matter, focused on the individual harmed, or their families, or their clans. In American history, the most celebrated example is that of the feud between the Hatfields and the McCoys, which illustrated the weakness of the victim-centered interpretation. If there is no mutual recognition of the original wrongdoing—and that is often a matter of biased interpretation of facts—then the first retaliatory measure taken by the victim—the second eye taken for the first eye—is viewed as an offense by the other side. They view the taking of that second eye as the first offense, requiring the taking of an eye from the other side to even the score. The situation merely accelerates: No "eye" taken *ever* evens the score, because there is no agreement about the propriety of the first incident.

Retribution and an eye for an eye are not abstract concepts rooted in ancient history. Law enforcement officials who must deal with gang violence are well aware of its manifestation in modern American life: Any gang slaying will generate another round of retributory violence—usually drive-by shootings that target the original offender's family or his gang associates. They are the modern-day versions of gangland shootings that took place during the Great Depression and the Prohibition eras, and the American clan-based violence typified by the legendary feud between the Hatfields and McCoys.

In countries or regions where militant shariah law is imposed, a similar concept exists. News media have reported incidents where the supposed perpetrator of a crime is brought into public arena, and the means of his execution are handed to the family of the victim. It is left to the family's discretion whether to exact an eye for an eye (or "a life for a life") or to adopt a different means of reckoning.

Modern Western justice systems recognize the limits of the retributory practice. Not every murder (or other criminal homicide) requires the death of the killer, for instance, life imprisonment is now the more prevalent sentence, and many killers are released without serving a full life term (for a number of reasons discussed later in this volume). In most American legal systems, a life for a life requires aggravating circumstances, such as the murder of federal or state officials, murder under circumstances reflecting extreme depravity, or the murder of particularly vulnerable victims.

DETERRENCE

The concept of **deterrence**, another Classical approach, is simple: The threat of punishment, or the actual application of punishment, acts to convince both potential and actual wrongdoers that they should not offend. The centerpiece is impacting the hedonistic calculus of the offender or potential offender. The two categories of deterrence generally spoken of are specific deterrence and general deterrence.

Specific deterrence is the term applied to the punishment of those who have been caught doing something wrong and are punished as a result. The intent of the punishment is partially retributory, of course, but it is also future oriented. The notion is that the severity of the punishment will be so great that the next time the offender is tempted to commit the crime (or another type of crime), they will stop and think: "Do I really want to go through that punishment again?" Effective deterrence will result in an answer of "No, I do not," and cause the potential offender to abandon their plan, conforming their behavior to expected law-abiding limits.

General deterrence is intended to act upon two different groups: those who have not offended (and may in fact be unlikely to offend) and those who may have offended but have not yet been caught. By witnessing (directly, or secondhand) the punishment inflicted on others, the potential offenders or reoffenders ask themselves a similar question: "Do I want that done to me?" Coming to the conclusion that they do not will spur them to maintain, or resume, law-abiding behavior.

As is often the case, attempting to apply a general concept to a broad potential audience is fraught with difficulties. The same penalty may deter one offender but be laughed off by another. It is difficult to know what level of punishment is necessary to deter any given individual, and our social commitment to a broader concept of equal treatment under the law has linked punishments to the type of offense, not to the individual offender.

Statutory definitions and strictures limit the punishments that can be prescribed to the offense rather than to the offender. A long history of prejudicial sanctions has mandated that approach, as "despised" groups throughout history have always been subjected to more-severe punishments than were those in the majority group who committed similar offenses. Punishment in those eras carried the undertone of repression, keeping "those" people "in their place" by threat of legal or extralegal violence, whether formally or informally applied. Legal and extralegal lynchings (executions, usually by hanging) of African Americans for even noncriminal acts constitute the most prominent example: The deterrent sought was not the cessation of criminal action but any attempt to seek equality of treatment. Historically, African Americans have suffered under this approach, of course, but each new immigrant group coming to America has faced similar, if less severe, prejudices both within the legal structure, and just outside it. The separation of children from their undocumented/illegal immigrant parents in 2018 is a recent example.

Beyond the idea of specific deterrence, the concepts of general deterrence through punishment may be overrated. Most citizens decide to conform their behavior to expected norms because they believe that it is right, not because they fear punishment. That said, there is little doubt that seeing punishment inflicted has some deterrent effect. But the abstract question remains regarding whether the average citizen would ever undertake a particular type of offending if they were not aware of the punishment given to others.

Most scholars agree that the **certainty** of punishment and the **severity** of punishment are the two factors that underlie the concept of deterrence. The state (or other entities within it) has the greatest control over the severity of punishment, primarily through legislation. When existing laws seem to have little effect in lowering the crime rate, there is often a general reflex to get tough on crime by increasing penalties.

Increasing penalties for particular crimes to deter the most resistant offenders may result in the over-punishment of those who would ordinarily be deterred by the original lesser sentences. Their original moral culpability tends to void any real concern about their extended exposure to sanctions (in turn, that reflects back to the notion that retribution is more important than deterrence, even if proponents of stronger sentences may not see it in exactly those terms).

Attempts to guarantee severity under the auspices of being fair have emerged in the form of mandatory sentencing statutes. The most notable are "three strikes" laws. These laws typically mandate life sentences for a third conviction for certain crimes, ranging from assaultive behavior to drug offenses. While these laws are meant to increase punishments for all violators, the enhanced penalties often target subgroups of the population due to the predominance of certain groups' participation in certain behaviors. As such, mandatory sentences can raise more concerns over discriminatory punishments than they can deter crime.

The inability to guarantee certainty is the greatest weakness in public policy in this area. Both specific and general deterrence are vulnerable to inconsistent apprehension of offenders and erratic sentencing practices. If a young person considering whether to join a gang-sponsored drug-selling operation sees one person punished severely but notes that twenty more continue to sell drugs and reap large amounts of money with seeming impunity, the deterrence effect of the one punishment is severely undercut. Rationalizations like "he was just stupid" or "she was just unlucky" also can eviscerate any potential deterrent effect.

In similar fashion, individuals who have profited from particular crimes may decide that the occasional criminal penalty that results is just the cost of doing business: weighing that over the long term, they will gain far more than they will lose. Instead of abandoning their criminal ways, these offenders will take steps to try to minimize their risk, quite possibly becoming better criminals in the process.

Moreover, while this is a pattern often observed in profit-motivated crimes like drug sales and burglaries, it does not extend to all types of crimes or all types of offenders. Those who are driven by emotional needs—often manifested in crimes of sex and violence—have little ability to consider the consequences of their actions. As such, they may be impervious to concept of deterrence.

That does not mean that attempts to establish greater certainty of apprehension (and thus punishment) are not made. The concepts of *"hot spots" policing* and *intelligence-led policing* both attempt to direct police resources to areas where crime is more likely, thus increasing either general deterrence or greater levels of apprehension that lead to specific deterrence. The use of closed-circuit TV (and public notice of CCTV usage) is another tool for promoting at least the belief in greater certainty of apprehension.

Asserting severity of punishment in the absence of certainty of punishment generally has not produced the positive results claimed by its champions. In recent times, greater severity has had the adverse effect of creating astronomically increased costs to the taxpayers (in the form of more prisons—including construction costs and staffing costs—as well as lawsuit costs when "severity" breaches the countervailing expectations of dignified treatment of human offenders). Current trends in corrections are defined by a swing of the pendulum back to less punitive, and more cost-efficient means of correcting offenders' behaviors. However, for the most dangerous offenders, the idea of incapacitation still holds considerable appeal.

INCAPACITATION

Incapacitation is a third goal corresponding to the Classical school of thought. In its most basic manifestation, **incapacitation** means "depriving the offender of the ability to continue to offend," and typically appears today through imprisonment. Locking up and physically restraining offenders mitigates their ability to commit another crime or harm another person. In ancient times, the death penalty was often invoked both as an instrument of vengeance (retribution) and as a means of preventing future crimes—at least by that individual. (Punishment by death also merged with the concept of *general deterrence*, particularly with public executions; in the mid-1800s, though, a British judge noted that the execution of pickpockets provided an opportunity for other pickpockets to work the crowd while people's attention was focused on the hangings.)

The concept of incapacitation through imprisonment has replaced the death penalty in most jurisdictions in the Western world. It recognizes that some offenders may not be amenable to rehabilitation or constraint. Under those circumstances, the only way to protect society from offenders is to keep them "under lock and key," in controlled environments that isolate them from society in general. The usual justification for such treatment is a demonstrated history of offending despite the imposition of other less restrictive correctional measures, or a demonstrated proclivity or mental condition that is thought to be impervious to standard correctional techniques.

Sentencing guidelines generally build in accelerated punishments (usually longer sentences) for criminals who offend repeatedly, despite repeated attempts to change or control their behavior. While at one level that meets the definition of increased severity, the goals of the two are similar: create conditions under which the offender will choose no longer to offend. Incapacitation lies at the far end of the increased severity scale, both a warning and a practical closure.

An alternative control measure allows the state the possibility of civil commitment after serving a criminal sentence for those judged to have a mental deficiency that defies standard correctional measures. Repeat sex offenders often receive this as a last resort. While nominally a form of treatment, it constitutes a means of isolating them from their potential victims in the general population.

Incapacitation can also be achieved by way of electronic monitoring of offenders in the community. Home confinement using electronic monitoring has increased substantially since its introduction in 1977 for two reasons. First, the overcrowding of the US prison system and court-ordered release of offenders drove a search for alternatives to incarceration. Second, technological advances led to the development of electronic monitoring tools. From its introduction as a home-telephone-based system, electronic monitoring came to include global positioning system technology using satellites to locate and track persons released into the community. While electronic monitoring technology does not physically restrain an individual, it does limit their behavior by eliminating their freedom from oversight of their movements in the community.

Critical Thinking Exercise

The public's call to get tough on crime largely reflects the idea of punishing offenders. What do you think is the underlying rationale for this point of view? Why do you believe the public holds that view? In your opinion, how effective is that approach in the public's view?

REHABILITATION

The rehabilitation goal/rationale reflect the tenets of Positivism. The need for **rehabilitation**—making the offenders "better"—cuts across all the other concepts and rationales discussed here. It takes the form of a parallel process but has the same goal: To make offenders *better* in whatever ways are needed to eliminate future offending on their part. It has analogs in other social interaction as well, whether it be an intervention to make an alcoholic realize that he or she needs treatment, or a "come to Jesus" meeting to motivate backsliding members of a religious group to mend their evil ways and bring them back into the fold.

Rehabilitation is not a singular intervention. It assumes myriad forms and addresses a wide range of issues. In all cases, the goal is to improve the life of the offender, and to improve their impact on the social group or polity. The means by which that happens varies, according to the needs of the individual offender, but they apply regardless of the correctional framework decreed by the courts. Offenders with deficient education and no real work skills are at risk of returning to crime to support themselves. Ironically, so too are those whose criminal histories deprive them of the opportunity to apply any new education and skills in a proper environment.

The concept of rehabilitation addresses both situations, and it is bounded and promoted by correctional supervision after sentencing. Part of the process could be termed *moral education*, providing a foundation of understanding that might not have been present during the offenders' upbringing. Some of it is practical, working to provide education (often basic literacy) and/or job skills that improve the offenders' marketability.

Rehabilitation may involve efforts to address substance abuse. Alcoholics Anonymous and Narcotics Anonymous are common programs used with convicted offenders. For more youthful offenders, programs to address peer pressure are offered. Cognitive-behavioral therapy that works to alter the decision-making process of individuals and helps them to identify prosocial responses is a proven technique for changing individuals. All of these efforts can take place both in jail and in prison environments and when an offender is in community supervision on probation or parole.

While we tend to think of these efforts as a matter of state action, it is important to realize that many private citizens understand the need for second chances. Some actively seek to employ a certain number of ex-offenders to help them regain their footing. Others are tolerant of employees with criminal histories, even though they do not actively seek them out. All work actively to support and encourage the offenders to help them readapt to law-abiding behavior. Because they are not representatives of the state, these citizens and corporations are a vital link in the chain of restoring an offender to a law-abiding life.

DIVERSION

Diversion is a relatively modern Positivistic addition to the goals of corrections. It stems from recognition of the detrimental effects of system processing. The argument is that subjecting a person to system intervention is **criminogenic**, that is, participation in the criminal justice system leads to increased criminal behavior. This argument rests on what is called the labeling theory. **Labeling theory** argues that giving someone the label of "criminal" often produces the opposite of deterrence. Instead of discouraging criminal behavior through a moral imperative, it far too often has the unintended effect of encouraging future criminality. The label limits certain opportunities, may lead to exclusion from participation in conforming activities, and can change the way other citizens interact with the offender. The offender is referred to as a criminal and eventually accepts the label and begins to act in accordance with it— "Well, if they're going to treat me like a criminal, I might as well be one" is the shorthand version of the individual's reaction.

Diversion programs first gained traction with juvenile offenders, as our broader understanding of human development recognized that at certain ages, youngsters will test society's (or family) limits by engaging in behaviors that they know are illegal or antisocial, to see what results. Since the 1890s, society has recognized that most youth will quickly (or eventually) abandon such antisocial conduct in favor of being accepted into the larger, law-abiding community. The first level of policy changes separated juvenile delinquency from adult crime, and afforded all citizens a second chance, a "fresh start," when they reached the age of majority.

Diversion attempts to avoid even the initial application of a label, in this case, "delinquent." Although the formal meaning of delinquent means "behind," or "lagging," it has come to bear the meaning of "underage criminal." When first-time offenders are placed into a diversion program, they are given a chance to avoid that label as well. Juvenile offenders are afforded the chance to wipe the slate clean well before their birthday into adulthood. By giving up some of their free time and participating in structured, supervised activities that have some benefit to the larger community, they earn their way back into the good graces of the community. The positive actions counterbalance the negative ones.

Diversion at both the juvenile and adult levels can involve an array of different programming. Generally, it involves community-based alternatives often run by non-system agencies or organizations. The types of programs focus on rehabilitation and treatment. First-time offender programs, informal adjustment, referral to counseling or educational/vocational training, or community service activities may be used in lieu of formal system processing.

One diversion approach that has grown in recent years is the concept of drug courts. Drug abuse is recognized as a special problem, beyond the control of the offender in many cases, and requires a different response besides simply shaming and labeling Drug courts represent a coalition of prosecutors, police, probation officers, judges, treatment professional, social service agencies, and other community groups working together to get the offenders off drugs and keep them off drugs (Drug Courts Program Office 2000). The emphasis is more on the good that the offender can do (and be), and less on the bad behavior that brought them before the court. Where regular criminal courts pass judgement on behavior, drug courts do more to encourage, by focusing on what the offender can become rather than on their offense.

Pragmatic persons understand that not every individual will respond positively to diversion programming, but in terms of reduced future offending, research has indicated that far more respond to positive treatments than do those who are simply penalized. The notion of "respond" ideally means no future offending, but it also encompasses the recognition of longer delays before relapsing into criminal behavior, and less serious behavior in the future. The diversion process is recognized as a longer-term investment, not a "one time fits all" cure for the problem. Initial results suggest that these programs successfully reach a broader group of offenders than do traditional punishments, which has an overall beneficial effect for society.

There are many complicating factors that attend the practical application of diversion, especially with respect to youths. Most important, the first apprehension may not be the first offense. Another factor is that we have learned that juveniles are very much aware of the automatic fresh start that comes with their turning age eighteen or twenty-one, and some are tempted to continue their offending because they expect their record as a delinquent to disappear. The same argument can be made for "first-time" adult offenders in relation to their expectation of a fresh start.

RESTORATIVE JUSTICE

The most recent development in correctional thinking is that of restorative justice. As opposed to retributive justice, which focuses on the lawbreaker and the imposition of sanctions for the purposes of deterrence, vengeance, and/or punishment, **restorative justice** seeks to repair the harm that was done to both the victim and the community. Additionally, there is an underlying assumption that the offender can benefit or be "repaired" by participating in the restorative process. Crime has traditionally been seen as a dichotomous relationship between the state and the offender. The citizens who were victims of crimes were relegated to a minor, supporting role as witnesses in support of the state's case. Under restorative justice victims and citizens become an integral part of addressing antisocial behavior.

Restorative justice practices vary but have a common theme and practice of bringing together a range of interested parties in a nonconfrontational setting, including the victim and the offender, as well as family members or friends, criminal justice system personnel, and members of the general community. The participants, as a group, seek to understand the actions that led to the criminal or antisocial behavior, reveal the feelings and concerns of all parties, negotiate or mediate a solution agreeable to everyone, and assist in implementing that solution (Bazemore and Maloney 1994).

Restorative justice reflects the basic tenets of Positivistic interventions. The underlying theoretical explanation for restorative justice is Braithwaite's (1989) reintegrative shaming. As with labeling, **reintegrative shaming** rests on the assumption that typical criminal justice system processing of offenders serves to isolate the offender and stigmatize him or her. Restorative justice seeks to repair the harm to the victim, community, and offender and to reintegrate the offender into society. Part of that process is using shame in a positive way to help with the reintegration.

An important concern with restorative justice is the ability of the meetings to achieve consensus on a solution and whether the parties carry through with the agreement. Before that can even be assessed it is important to note that participation in the programs is voluntary. Both victims and offenders must agree to the meeting and dialogue. This is especially true for victims, although offenders can also opt out of the process in many places. The fact that the program is voluntary may mean that only those individuals who are more amenable to the process to begin with are included in the programs.

An additional problem is that not every type of crime is amenable to restorative justice. Advocates have pushed for dialogue in even serious personal crimes, arguing that it is in those situations that the understanding of consequences—in personal terms rather than legal ones—is most important. Offenses such as spouse abuse, sexual assault, aggravated assault, murder, and similar crimes, however, are relatively rarely addressed. Some research indicates that restorative justice programs may be too ambitious in their attempt to solve very complex societal problems (Kurki 2000). Simply gathering common citizens together to talk about a problem and to brainstorm possible solutions is only the beginning of a much more complex process to address major social forces that may cause crime. Many problems involve long-standing interpersonal disputes that may not be amenable to simple mediation or conferencing.

Critical Thinking Exercise

Investigate a correctional facility or program in your state or community. What is the primary rationale under which the facility or program operates? Does it incorporate more than one rationale? If so, what are they and with which offenders and crimes does each apply?

SUMMARY

Corrections responds to a range of goals and takes its lead from legal statutes and sentences imposed by the courts. The concept of corrections—of sanctions administered to intervene in bad behavior and shape better behavior in the future—has Classical roots, and assumes that offenders had both knowledge of the wrong and the ability to do better. Seeking retribution for what the offender did, trying to deter future behavior by imposing punishment on offenders, and incapacitating offenders so they cannot harm anyone else are all rationales stemming from Classicism. As scientific knowledge of the human condition has expanded and society has gained greater understanding of, and appreciation for, the inevitability of social variation and the causes of behavior, the Positivist school has nudged the field of corrections to expand its approach. Rehabilitation, in its many forms and programs, has grown to be almost synonymous with corrections today. There is an overriding belief that offenders can be helped to become non-offending members of society. Part of this is due to the belief that punishment has failed and that participation in the criminal justice system can exacerbate criminal behavior. Both the diversion and restorative justice rationales build on these beliefs and help to address the causes of crime.

Critical Thinking Exercise

The range of goals and rationales for corrections have influenced different correctional practices over the years. The goals often appear contradictory. This is particularly evident when you consider the different assumptions of Classicism and Positivism. Is it possible to use/implement competing correctional approaches at the same time? What could be the implications of doing so?

KEY WORDS

certainty
Classicism
criminogenic
determinate sentence
deterrence
diversion
free willed
general deterrence

hedonistic
incapacitation
indeterminate sentence
labeling theory
mala in se
mala prohibitum
paradigm
Positivism

rehabilitation
reintegrative shaming
restorative justice
retribution
severity
specific deterrence

DISCUSSION QUESTIONS

1. Which of the two major schools of thought (Classicism and Positivism) do you believe is the most appropriate approach to understanding and addressing crime? Why? Would your response differ if you were considering youthful delinquency?
2. What societal changes have most influenced current correctional approaches? What specific correctional changes have occurred? How have the societal changes led to the modern correctional practices?
3. Retribution and deterrence both involve punishment but for different goals. If the correctional action (e.g., incarceration) is the same, is it important to differentiate between the goals? Why or why not?
4. The Supreme Court has ordered your correctional system to reduce the number of prisoners due to overcrowding. Simply releasing prisoners is not acceptable. You are the director of corrections for the state and are tasked with building support for correctional changes and funding. What goals will you promote and why?
5. Restorative justice has received a great deal of attention in recent years as an alternative to traditional correctional interventions. You are tasked with advocating for a restorative justice correctional approach. How will you appeal to those who advocate retribution, deterrence, rehabilitation, and other correctional goals?

SUGGESTED READINGS

Cullen, F. T., B. S. Fisher, and B. K. Applegate. (2000). "Public Opinion about Punishment and Corrections." In *Crime and Justice: A Review of Research*, vol. 27, edited by M. Tonry, 1–79. Chicago: University of Chicago Press.

Duff, A. (1995). "Penal Communications and the Philosophy of Punishment." In *Crime and Justice: A Review of Research*, vol. 20, edited by M. Tonry, 1–97. Chicago: University of Chicago Press.

Kurki, L. (2000). "Restorative Community Justice in the United States." In *Crime and Justice: A Review of Research*, vol. 27, edited by M. Tonry, 235–303. Chicago: University of Chicago Press.

REFERENCES

Bazemore, G., and D. Maloney. (1994). "Rehabilitating Community Service: Toward Restorative Service in a Balanced Justice System." *Federal Probation* 58:24–35.

Bentham, J. (1948). *An Introduction to the Principles of Morals and Legislation*. New York: Hafner.

Braithwaite, J. (1989). *Crime, Shame and Reintegration*. Cambridge, UK: Cambridge University Press.

Cherrington, E. H. (1920). *The Evolution of Prohibition in the United States of America*. Westerville, OH: American Issue Press.

Drug Courts Program Office. (2000). *About the Drug Courts Program Office*. Washington, DC: US Department of Justice.

Gettleman, J., and K. Schultz. (2018, September 7). "For Gay Indians, Landmark Ruling Is Just the Beginning." *New York Times*. Retrieved from https://www.nytimes.com/2018/09/07/world/asia/india-gay-rights-ruling.html.

Kurki, L. (2000). "Restorative and Community Justice in the United States." In *Crime and Justice: A Review of Research*, vol. 27, edited by M. Tonry, 235–303. Chicago: University of Chicago Press.

CHAPTER 4

Institutional Corrections

AFTER READING THIS CHAPTER, YOU SHOULD BE ABLE TO:

- Understand how and why inmate subcultures are formed
- Explain the importance of the total institution in relation to prisonization
- Distinguish life in prison prior to the 1970s to current experiences
- Compare and contrast the deprivation and importation models of prison
- Discuss the similarities and differences between male and female inmates' adaptation to life in prison
- Trace the history and the implications of the prisoners' rights movement
- List different special offender populations
- Discuss the problem of HIV/AIDS in prison
- Point out issues and responses to an aging prison population
- Discuss the problem of handling inmates with mental illness
- Summarize the duties and types of correctional officers
- Identify the arguments for and against women as correctional officers
- Demonstrate how Gilbert's four types of correctional officers function
- Detail the structured conflict between inmates and correctional officers
- Explain the challenges occurring in prisons and their implications, including how technological advances have affected the operations of prisons and jails

INTRODUCTION

Inside prison walls, two social realities coexist—(1) the official reality where persons convicted of crimes are supervised by correctional staff under the management of correctional administrators in a secure setting, and (2) the inmate world. For the most part, those who work and live in correctional settings adhere to the formal rules that govern the institution, but whether inmate or officer, the informal adjustments needed to navigate and adapt to a stressful, yet monotonous interpersonal environment create a social system that is unique toprison. This chapter explores these two realities through a historical lens to examine present situations as they relate to future challenges.

LIFE BEHIND BARS

You are sentenced to prison or jail. You live with others, but not because you chose to do so. You not only live with others involuntarily you also share space in tight quarters. Aside from your bed, nothing is truly "yours" and you have limited privacy. You are an inmate.

For well over sixty years, social scientists have examined the prison setting and consistently, researchers confirm that prison is a social entity and inmates encompass a unique social group. A **social group** is a collection of individuals who share similar characteristics and circumstances and in interaction with one another become united. Typically, we use the term "subculture" to refer to the social grouping of inmates. Research suggests that the unique nature of prison life results in a distinct subculture within prisons. The prison subculture arises out of the informal inmate world whereby, through their shared experience of being incarcerated, they learn to navigate the official structure of the rules, policies, and procedures of the facility that are enforced by prison staff.

Subcultures can help us understand the socialization of inmates, can help us determine how they are adapting to the prison environment, and can provide insight for correctional officers to control the prison environment. Before inmates had full access to the courts to have their custodial concerns heard before a judge (i.e., the **prisoners' rights movement**, which is discussed in more detail later in this chapter), prisons were more homogeneous, and every inmate suffered the same deprivations (Sykes 1958). After the prisoners' rights movement, many deprivations were weakened. For example, inmates are able to move around facilities more freely, and this liberty can lead to more cohesiveness among inmates. In the mid-1970s, life within the prison walls began to look like life on the outside: racially, politically, and religiously divided (Carroll 1974; Irwin 1980).

The traditional subculture of inmates versus correctional officers became inmates versus inmates. The black population became politically and religiously centered on the rally of white oppression and racism, often divided across racial and ethnic identities. Whites, on the other hand, only looked out for number one when it came to surviving in prison (Carroll 1974). These events broke the solidarity-in-numbers factor inherent in the traditional inmate subculture. In addition, gangs began to enter prisons, which made it easier for new inmates to adapt to prison life when their gangs were already established within a facility (Irwin 1980). See Table 4.1 to learn the characteristics of the six major prison gangs affecting US prisons today.

Adapting to the Prison Life prior to the 1970s

Being incarcerated can be both taxing and monotonous. Yet, adapting to this environment is essential for an inmate to cope effectively with the strains of imprisonment. Adaptation to prison is a complex process known as **prisonization**. During prisonization, new inmates learn the ways of the prison setting and what is expected of them. One concept that is learned is the *inmate code*, which is a set of rules that dictate how inmates are to behave toward one another and toward the correctional officers. In most correctional facilities, the inmate code goes like this:

- Don't inform on another convict.
- Do your own time.
- Don't interfere with inmate interests.
- Don't quarrel with fellow inmates.
- Don't weaken.
- Don't trust guards or the things for which they stand.
- Respect inmates who have been imprisoned for a long time, they are the real "cons."
- Deal with your own problems, do not pull in staff.

Table 4.1 Characteristics of Six Major Prison Gangs in US Prisons

Gang	Date & Location of Origination	Racial/Ethnic Composition	Common Identifiers	Rivals	Way of Life
Aryan Brotherhood	1967 in San Quentin State Prison, CA	White	Swastikas, shamrock clover leaf, initials "AB," numbers "666," double lightning bolts	Black Guerrilla Family, Crips, Bloods, El Rukns	Holds white supremacy ideologies; introduce contraband, drugs; shirk rules and regulations while in prison; works with Mexican Mafia
Black Guerrilla Family	1966 in San Quentin State Prison, CA	Black	Cross sabers and shotgun, black dragon overtaking prison or prison tower, antiauthority mentality shown by display of "BGF" initials	Aryan Brotherhood, Texas Syndicate, Aryan Brotherhood of Texas, Mexican Mafia	Most political of prison gangs, works with La Nuestra Familia; black street gang members are recruited upon imprisonment; history of violent acts
La Nuestra Familia	Mid-1960s in Soledad Prison, CA	Mexican American/ Hispanic (traditionally rural, young)	Red rags, large tattoos often on their backs, initials "NF," "LNF," "ENE," "F," number 14 for "N" standing for Norte or Northern California, sombrero with dagger symbol	Mexican Mafia (primary rival), Texas Syndicate, Mexikanemi, F-14s, Aryan Brotherhood	Started to protect members from Mexican Mafia; membership extends beyond prison, drug trafficking, extortion, and pressure rackets
Mexican Mafia	Late 1950s at Duel Vocational Center (young offender facility), CA	Mexican American/ Hispanic	"EME" initials, eagle and snake with "EME," black single hand print, "MM" or "M" initials, EME symbol of eternal war	La Nuestra Familia (primary rival), Northern Structure, Arizona's New Mexican Mafia, Black Guerrilla Family, black street gangs	Ethnic solidarity and supremacy; drug trafficking; most active gang in federal prisons; extortion and pressure rackets; will kill to punish or gain respect
Neta	1970 Rio Pedras Prison, Puerto Rico	Puerto Rican American/ Hispanic	Red, white, and blue, sometimes black for blue are colors; wear beads, clothing, rags, and other items in these colors; Puerto Rican flag, have Neta identification cards, emblem of heart pierced by two crossing Puerto Rican flags and a shackled right hand with middle and index fingers crossed	Latin Kings, Los Solidos	Started to halt violence between inmates in the Rio Pedras Prison, claim to be a cultural organization, very patriotic, call for independence of Puerto Rico, view themselves as oppressed, not willing to be governed by US authorities; keep low profile; drug trade and extortion; known danger to staff and inmates
Texas Syndicate	Early 1970s, Folsom Prison, CA	Mexican American/ Hispanic	Tattoos with "TS" located on back of right forearm or outside neck, chest, or calf areas	Aryan Brotherhood, La Nuestra Familia, Mexican Mafia, Mexikanemi, Mandingo Warriors	Started to protect native Texas inmates from CA prison gangs, Membership increasing, considered to be a security threat in prisons due to violent acts, drug trafficking, extortion, and pressure rackets

Inmates even use a unique vocabulary to communicate. This language, so to speak, is termed "prison argot" and some terms can differ from prison to prison as argot is usually driven by the interactions of the prisoners with one another, the staff and administration, and the institution itself. Terms consistent across many prisons are as follows.

- Badge or the Man = correctional officer
- Cellie = cellmate
- Fish = a newly arrived inmate
- Free worlder = any person who is not an inmate
- Front = pretend to be tough
- Ink = tattoos
- Jamming = fist fighting
- Joint = prison or jail
- Hard stuff = heroin or opioids
- Mule = a person who is not incarcerated who transports contraband to and from the prison
- Railroad = getting blamed for an act one didn't do
- Rat/Snitch = an inmate who squeals on other inmates to the prison administration
- Schooled = knowledgeable in the ways of prison life
- Throw down = fight

Whatever the specifics of a given institution's subculture, it is important that a prisoner become socialized into this environment by learning the norms or expectations of behavior and various techniques to cope and adapt to this environment. Personal safety and dealing with the violence that can occur within an institution are two major concerns of most inmates. One mechanism for adjusting, really surviving, to life behind bars is to become part of the prison subculture. Most of the research on prison subculture tends to be from the study of maximum-security prisons. There is reason to believe that elements of a unique prison subculture exist even in less secure facilities, however. Two models have been used to explain the formation of prison subcultures and adaptation to the prison environment: (1) deprivation model and (2) importation model.

Based on the premises of the **deprivation model**, the nature and impact of an individual prison's culture over its residents will vary across prisons and among residents. In his seminal work, *The Society of Captives*, Sykes (1958) identified several characteristics of prison life that contribute to the development of the prison culture and individual responses to imprisonment. These *pains of imprisonment* included the loss of liberty, deprivation of goods and services, the barring of heterosexual relations, limitations to a prisoner's autonomy, and concerns over personal security. These pains are thought to be central features of prison life and require adaptations by individual prisoners if they are to cope with their new environment in any positive manner. Inmate subcultures originally developed out of these pains of imprisonment.

The first pain, the deprivation of liberty, refers to the fact that inmates were confined to the total institution and within the institution and this first deprivation drives the other five. The concept of the "**total institution**" was developed by Erving Goffman in the 1960s. In his formative work titled *Asylums*, he set forth what he meant by "total":

> First, all aspects of life are conducted in the same place and under the same single authority. Second, each phase of the member's daily activity is carried out in the immediate company of a large batch of others, all of whom are treated alike and required to do the same things together. Third, all phases of the day's activities are tightly scheduled with one activity leading at a pre-arranged time into the next, the whole sequence of events being imposed from above by a system of explicit, formal rulings and a body of officials. Finally the various enforced activities are brought together into a single rational plan purportedly designed to fulfill the official aims of the institution (1968, p. 17).

Critical Thinking Exercise

What other places do you think capture Goffman's idea of the "total institution?" Defend your selection. How do the places you listed compare to the prison as a total institution? Are some institutions more "total" than others? Why?

The second pain was that of the deprivation of goods and services in which inmates deprived not only of individual dress, but also of amenities such as televisions, radios, and favorite foods. The third pain is that of the lack of heterosexual relationships, which inmates experience a loss of identity. The fourth pain noted by Sykes was the deprivation of autonomy or the lack of freedom to make choices for oneself. The final pain is that of the deprivation of security in which inmates housed together with the violent and the nonviolent, constantly living in fear of victimization. Today, many of these deprivations exist to some degree. In a total institution like the prison, inmates are living together under the charge of prison staff and administration who control where they sleep, what they eat, where and when they work, and what activities and programs are available. In theory, life in prison is designed to be uniform for all inmates, but the reality is, not all inmates will experience these pains of imprisonment the same within and across institutions.

Since Sykes's (1958) publication of *The Society of Captives*, the degree to which inmates experience these deprivations has changed. Some deprivations, such as the deprivation of goods and services have been lessened somewhat with the opportunity to purchase some goods in the commissary. The deprivation of heterosexual relationships can be attenuated if prisoners are allowed conjugal visits with significant others. For example, some women's facilities have provided family "homes" in which their family members can visit with their wife/mother over a couple days. These facilities, while still located on prison grounds, are usually set apart from the general prison population. This opportunity is a privilege not a right; therefore, corrections officials can withhold these visits from inmates in order to gain compliance to directives.

Researchers also believe that individual characteristics, as opposed to the characteristics unique to the prison as detailed in the deprivation model, will affect a particular prisoner's ability to adjust. The **importation model** suggests that the skills, experiences, and attributes that individuals bring with them into a prison environment affect the prison culture and the ability of an individual to adjust to that environment. The main support for the importation explanation is that the values and norms found in the prison subculture are similar to the ones we often find on the streets. The newly incarcerated will rely on these previously developed beliefs and behaviors to adapt to life as an inmate.

It is likely the interaction of individual attributes with the unique physical and social dynamics of a given institution (i.e., the situational factors) will determine the nature of the prison culture and how inmates adapt to the prison environment. Irwin and Cressey (1962) described three subcultures that have guided prison adjustment research for decades. First is the **convict subculture**, which characterizes people as those who have spent most of their lives in some form of institution such as foster homes, juvenile correctional facilities, jails, and prisons. Second is a first- (and only) time offender who normally lives by the conventional rules in society and wants to stay out of trouble while serving time. This is the **straight subculture**; the third is that of the **thief subculture**. These professional criminals tend to keep to themselves while incarcerated.

Additional characterizations by which inmates adapt to the prison environment and function within the inmate subculture by following a particular **prison lifestyle** have also been described. Below are five main types:

1. *The Mean Dude* Some inmates adjust to prison by starting fights with anyone willing to engage; they receive high numbers of write-ups for infractions and find themselves in solitary confinement. The prison subculture opens itself up to "mean dudes" by the expectation that inmates are supposed to be tough in order to survive. Toughness for the mean dude is expressed through aggressive interactions with fellow inmates and correctional staff.

2. *The Hedonist* The "hedonist" takes advantage of the few perks of incarceration such as, smuggling contraband like cell phones, drug running, gambling, and other behaviors that are officially banned in the prison. Individuals who adapt to prison as a hedonist figure out ways to increase their pleasure during their time of "pain."

3. *The Opportunist* These inmates follow the adage of "make the best out of a bad situation" and participate in whatever vocational, educational, counseling, and other self-improvement programs they can while they are incarcerated. Their adaptation style is said to be that of **gleaning** or taking advantage of the prisons' offerings so they can succeed. The "opportunists"

are the model prisoners—the "do-gooders"—and are appreciated by the correctional staff. Their fellow inmates, however, do not trust them and avoid interacting with an opportunist because of their model prisoner status.

4. *The Retreatist* Inmates adapting to prison as a "retreatist" find life behind bars as harsh and demanding, and fear being victimized by inmates and correctional staff. They cope by abusing alcohol and drugs, or attempting suicide. Mental illness is common in the retreatist along with psychotic episodes in which protective custody and counseling often becomes necessary.

5. *The Colonist* - For these inmates, prison is their home as they have spent many years being "raised" by the state from foster care to juvenile detention to prison. Since "colonists" have been institutionalized most of their lives, they understand how prison works and have social connections. These experiences often mean that other inmates respect them which enables them to hold positions of power and influence within the inmate subculture. Their mode of adaptation to prison is "jailing," (i.e., spending their lives as an inmate), and prefer to stay incarcerated than be released. Some will even recidivate after release just so they can return to prison.

Critical Thinking Exercise

Of the lifestyles above, which would most closely support the deprivation model? The importation model? Think of some famous (or infamous, as they might be) offenders. What subculture do you think they would fall under and why?

Many inmates, however, adapt to prison by just "doing time," which means that they prefer to serve out their sentences by abiding by the inmate code, participate in activities, and do whatever is necessary to survive. They want to experience as little discomfort as possible given their current living arrangements.

Web Exercise

Go to: https://www.congress.gov/bill/115th-congress/senate-bill/1524/text. What provisions are included in Senate Bill 1524, The Dignity for Incarcerated Women Act of 2017? Pick a state and compare what, if any, similar pieces of legislation have been introduced and/or passed into law. What do you think should and should not be included in acts like these?

Prison Life in the Late Twentieth, Early Twenty-First Centuries

During the **mass incarceration** era, which refers to the exponential increase in the number of persons incarcerated over the past forty-plus years, the composition of the inmate population has become more diverse. Today, over 2 million people are incarcerated or housed in jails. In the late 1970s, early 1980s, that number was a little over half million. The traditional inmate subculture of "us" versus "them" (i.e., prisoners vs. the correctional officers) would change and the "them" could be any number of groups and sometimes individuals. This erosion of the traditional prison subculture was driven by changes in arrest and sentencing policies and practices, such as mandatory-minimum sentences for drug crimes, which affected racial minorities disproportionately with larger numbers of blacks and Hispanics being sent to prison compared to whites. The problem of disparity arises when the nonwhite incarcerated populations are out of line to the percentage they make up in the overall US population. To illustrate, if one group represents 40 percent of the prison population, but that group only makes up 15 percent of the US population, this would be considered a disparity. These circumstances would have a noticeable effect on the composition of general prison populations across the country. And it did, mostly in the form of gangs affiliated by race/ethnicity to carry out illicit activities in prison in competition with one another, with the drug trade being the most common operation both inside and outside the prison walls (Kreager and Kruttschnitt 2018). In some ways, the illicit market created an informal system of inmate governance that replaced the traditional inmate code some prisons (Skarbek 2014).

Two other groups also changed the dynamics of the inmate subculture. First, the United States saw an influx of individuals with mental illness who, after the closing of long-term residential mental health facilities, would go from being labeled "patient" to "inmate," which led to more problems and more stratification of the inmate population (Irwin 1980). Second, the policies that set in motion the mass incarceration era resulted in more individuals over the age of fifty-five being housed in US prisons today compared to their numbers several decades s ago. Prisons were not built to provide the medical, emotional, or physical care older inmates have such as limited mobility, changing dietary needs, and increased risk for diseases. These challenges have led to problems with adjustment to the prison environment for some inmates and have changed the dynamics for prison staff in the management of the facility. These special offender populations and others are discussed in more detail later in this chapter.

Web Activity

Go to https://www.earhustlesq.com/episodes/2018/3/14/firsts and listen to the *Ear Hustle* podcast on inmates' experiences when they first entered prison. What were some common themes throughout this podcast? How does the idea of the total institution affect the San Quentin inmates' experiences?

Women and Prison Life

Most of the research on inmate subcultures and prisonization has focused on male inmates, and while the two sexes are exposed to similar environments and experiences during incarceration, there are some differences between the two groups. Most notably, women's adaptation to prison appears to be more difficult compared to their male counterparts and this has been a consistent theme in the past and today. There are three main reasons for this: (1) Women tend to value privacy at a greater extent compared to males, so they have a harder time adapting to the shared life, spaces, and rules of prison; (2) Sometimes women do not get as much support from their significant others outside the walls; and (3) They are often fearful that after their release from prison that they will be abandoned and not know how to cope with the loneliness and vulnerability that some ex-inmates face after confinement. Complicating the prisonization process is that about two-thirds of incarcerated females are mothers. To deal with these challenges, imprisoned women tend to form **pseudofamilies**, where inmates organize into quasi-family structures with women taking on roles as parents and children in order to compensate for the loss of emotional support, intimacy, and social ties they once had in free society.

While on many levels, men and women enter into similar prison worlds with the same rules, restrictions, loss of autonomy, and limited freedoms, women have unique health needs that men do not. Some women enter prison pregnant or having recently given birth within the last year. These circumstances present unique challenges to the prison administration as these women require different medical care, nutrition, services, resources, and programs. Prenatal care and parenting classes are inadequate in some prisons leading to additional stressors on the inmate and her baby. Probably the most controversial and concerning practice has been the use of waist and leg restraints (i.e., shackling) when women are going through labor and delivery. Currently, only a few states have forbidden the use of restraints and eighteen have limitations on their use. At the federal level, a bill known as the Dignity for Incarcerated Women Act of 2017 or Senate Bill 1524 was introduced to provide protections and regulate the treatment of female prisoners on several areas, including pregnancy, healthcare, and prohibiting shackling. To date, it has been referred to the Committee on the Judiciary for consideration.

Web Activity

To hear some personal stories about life in prison for women, watch *20/20* ABC "A Nation of Women Behind Bars: A Diane Sawyer Hidden America Special": https://www.dailymotion.com/video/x4uloac.

Prosocial Adjustment to Prison Life

Prosocial opportunities exist in the majority of prisons that can assist inmates in adjusting to life as an inmate. With the exception of the highest security prisons, most prisons offer programs that are promoted as helping with offender rehabilitation and increasing the structure and activities involved in an inmate's daily routine. The number and types of programs will vary across different institutions and jurisdictions. In many facilities, inmates can receive good time credits (i.e., days reduced from their sentence) by productively participating in approved activities. In some states, participation in certain programs improves inmates' chances of an earlier release from custody. The categories of programs offered typically fall under the headings of education, vocational, mental health/substance abuse treatment, religious, and recreation. Specific programs under the education and vocational headings that might be available in some facilities include: GED classes, literacy, parenting, postsecondary education classes and carpentry, welding, electronics, computer programming, and landscaping training, respectively. Religious programs include scriptural studies, access to prison chaplains, weekly spiritual services, and prison fellowships. Exercise courses, intramural athletics, open gym, outdoor yard, and music and band, and other leisure activities would fall under the recreational program category.

Web Activity

Explore some prison programs being offered across the country and create one presentation slide based on what you learned about one of the options below, or find one offered by your state's department of corrections.

- **Offender Change Washington State** https://www.youtube.com/watch?v=CRK hlhi7Rj0&app=desktop
- **Wild Horses Rehab Program** https://fusion.tv/story/4996/rehabilitation-program-pairs-prisoners-with-wild-horses-its-life-changing/
- **Substance Abuse Program for Female Offenders** https://www.youtube.com/watch?v=y-042I7NeD8&app=desktop
- **Arizona Corrections Prison Programs** https://www.youtube.com/watch?v=yUh_TAag3qc&app=desktop
- **Pathways to Rehab Solano Prison** https://www.youtube.com/watch?v=Wwgb CeTEipY&app=desktop
- **Prison Inmates Train Dogs for Disabled** https://www.youtube.com/watch?v=zvyTw37Alzg

---

At a minimum, in many institutions, inmates are given a work assignment that constitutes a major part of their day. Many basic prison operations such as food service, laundry, and grounds keeping are carried out by prisoners with varying degrees of staff supervision. Involvement in other prison programs, like those noted in the previous paragraph, are voluntary and are available in some prisons for interested and eligible inmates. Funding for such programs, however, tends to be a relatively low priority even when many scholars and practitioners consider these types of activities as important in helping prisoners cope with the stresses of prison life and improving a prisoner's likelihood of successful reentry after release.

INMATE RIGHTS

History and Background

Prior to the middle of the twentieth century, appellate courts took a **hands-off approach** to the problems and grievances of those incarcerated. The reasons for this hands-off approach were threefold. First, the courts felt that they should not interfere with the operations of the prisons. Second, the judiciary offered a type of checks and balances. And last, the judiciary could not possibly understand the problems of prison administrators because judges lacked working knowledge on the specifics of prison life. In 1941, the Supreme Court ruled in ex parte *Hull* (312 U.S. 546) that the Fifth and Fourteenth Amendments to the Bill of Rights granted everyone, even inmates, access to the courts. However, it was not until 1964 that the courts really begin to lift the hands-off policy with the *Cooper v. Pate* (378 U.S. 546) decision.

Most prisons were homogenous institutions in which strict control, sometimes rehabilitation, and structure were the rule until the mid-1960s (Sykes 1958). With the arrival of the civil rights movement, many groups began to seek legitimacy for their grievances and remedies to solve their problems through the use of court decisions (i.e., **fundamental democratization**). As a result of the prisoners' rights movement (PRM), courts' doors opened for inmates and granted them access to address their grievances similar to that which other marginalized groups in society were given. Inmates went from not having access to having their concerns heard to being able to pursue litigation once the courts took a **hands-on approach**.

Types of Inmate Litigation

Mainly, three types of lawsuits are brought to the courts by inmates. When inmates feel that their guarantees and protections under the Bill of Rights to the US Constitution have been infringed, they can ask the courts to step in and determine if there was a civil rights violation. Historically, the grievances brought forth by inmates under the PRM have been related to the following amendments:

> First Amendment Religious freedom; freedom of speech, particularly in relation to inspection and censure of mail;
> Fourth Amendment Unreasonable searches and seizures of cells and self;
> Eighth Amendment Prohibits cruel and unusual punishment such as living in overcrowded, unsanitary conditions; being subjected to corporal punishments by correctional officers looking to gain compliance;
> Fourteenth Amendments Unequal treatment based on race/ethnicity, gender, or socioeconomic status such as having equal access to law libraries or legal assistance.

Since the PRM, inmates can also bring forth habeas corpus cases where they challenge the fact that they are confined and/or the length and circumstances of their incarceration. In these cases, the government must prove why an inmate should serve time to prison/jail. Finally, in cases where inmates are injured by another person, such as a correctional officer, while incarcerated, they can seek assistance from the courts through cases known as *torts* where the judge determines if the injury was a result of negligence by correctional staff or the administration.

Implications of the Prisoners' Rights Movement

Despite the significance of the PRM, there are limitations to inmates' access to the courts. In 1966, Congress passed the Prison Litigation Reform Act (PLRA), which restricts the number of lawsuits against state correctional officials that challenge the conditions of the facilities they operate, such as excessive force or harassment by correctional officers, overcrowding, poor food quality, or limited medical treatment. These suits fall under federal statute Section 1983 of the Civil Rights Act of 1871, which permitted people to sue the government for civil rights violations. Under the PLRA, if inmates' previous three cases were not heard because they were considered frivolous or trivial, then they cannot file additional lawsuits.

A second PLRA was passed in 1996 as some federal policymakers believed that inmates were filing too many meritless cases with the courts. This version created additional restrictions for inmates to have their grievances heard in court. First, inmates must now have their case heard through the grievance procedure established in the correctional facility where they are housed before they can file their case in federal court. After moving through the internal prison process, only then can a case can be filed with the federal courts. Second, inmates must pay for their court filing fees in full either up front or in monthly payments. Prior to the passage of the PLRA 1996, inmates could ask to have these fees waived. Third, if the judge finds three suits to be frivolous, malicious, or without a proper claim, the inmate cannot file subsequent lawsuits unless the full court fee is paid in advance. And last, inmates must establish that they experienced a physical injury, not just an emotional or mental one.

In addition to having access to the courts similar to free citizens, the hands-on approach to inmate rights also led to a number of the pains of deprivations being lessened. The PRM led to the establishment of certain privileges that were not available previously. For instance, inmates now could buy televisions or radios, wear what they wanted in some prisons, or could have visitors bring in the amenities they desired. Consequentially, this led to a situation of the "haves" versus the "have nots" in which the "have nots" would burglarize or victimize the "haves" to obtain what they wanted. Relative to the philosophies of corrections, these circumstances can undermine the goal of incapacitation because crime is going on in the prison. Recall, that the purpose of utilizing correctional facilities for incapacitation is to prevent offenders from committing any further crimes. If crime continues in the prison, the goal of incapacitation is no doubt more difficult to achieve.

Another result of the PRM is increased freedom of movement and the elimination of the requirement that inmates must participate in treatment programs. Lack of structure means idle time for some inmates, which occasionally leads to violence (Wooldredge 1994). Some inmates will experience a more arduous time in prison compared to others because they are being victimized. Hence, the philosophy of retribution is undermined in that no longer will punishment for similar crimes be the same for all inmates. Rehabilitation as a goal may be impossible to meet because inmates must be able to concentrate on their treatment and if they are constantly worrying about being victimized, they cannot actively participate in their own reformation. Deterrence, or the idea that imposing severe punishments will incite enough fear that the costs outweighing the benefits the commission of crime would prevail, may also be undermined because some offenders will be victims and some will be offenders. To complicate these matters, correctional officers have been known to ignore some infractions because they do not want to attract the attention of the administration that is primarily concerned about the effective control of the prison.

SPECIAL OFFENDER POPULATIONS

Similar to the general public, the prison population is composed of individuals with substance abuse problems, mental illness, physical disabilities, and diseases. There has also been an increase in the number of aging offenders in correctional institutions due to the "get tough" sentencing policies adopted and implemented during the 1980s. Inmates are a unique population in that they are one of two groups in society that are entitled to medical treatment based on decisions handed down by the US Supreme Court. The other group is the military. Although there are services available in society to deal with these issues and problems, the prison, its officials, and its "guests" are often forced to deal with such a wide variety of problems. It is important to become better acquainted with special offender populations.

Inmates and HIV/AIDS

Since the 1980s, the prison population, like the general population, has witnessed an explosion of individuals diagnosed as HIV positive or with AIDS. Today, there are approximately 24,000 inmates in state and federal prisons who are HIV positive, and one-quarter of that number have confirmed cases of active AIDS (Maruschak 2004). Prior to 1999, it was estimated that prisoners were seven to nine times more likely to have confirmed cases of AIDS than was the general population. The good news is that, since 1999, the number of inmates who have HIV/AIDS is decreasing. Despite this, AIDS is a leading cause of death in prison.

The number one method of transmission of HIV in the United States is through the sharing of needles or other equipment used to ingest illegal substances. The increase in mandatory-minimum sentencing practices arguably led to an increase of substance users in prison, many of whom had already been exposed to HIV. In secure facilities HIV is most often spread through sexual contact between inmates who were most likely exposed prior to their incarceration via unclean drug-taking methods.

Correctional administrators and staff across the country have implemented several approaches to decreasing the number of new cases within the prison. Some institutions focus on education in terms of how the disease is contracted and the treatment options available. A few institutions have provided condoms for those inmates engaged in sexual activities; however, this option is controversial, as sex between inmates is usually prohibited. Voluntary or mandatory testing to determine who is infected with HIV has been used, as well asspecial housing for inmates at different stages of the disease. It has been proposed that, at a minimum, infirmaries should be established where inmates already confirmed to have AIDS can be held to protect them from airborne infections such as tuberculosis and pneumonia.

Many state corrections systems have been proactive in collaborating with public health agencies to increase the knowledge about how to take care of not only HIV/AIDS in the prison but also other sexually transmitted diseases and tuberculosis, which are widespread among correctional populations disproportionate to the general population (Hammett 1998). Considering that many inmates will eventually be released into society and given the gravity of these communicable diseases, there is a definite need to provide appropriate treatment, prevention, and post-release programs to curb further transmission of these conditions. Thus, it would be remiss to ignore what goes on in the prison merely because the population affected is made up of offenders.

Inmates and Substance Use

Approximately one-half of offenders housed in jails and prisons across the United States admit to having been under the influence of alcohol or drugs when they committed the current offenses that led to their incarceration. Drug and property offenders are more likely than other types of offenders to engage in crime to acquire money to feed their substance addiction. Those with mental illness are more likely to be under the influence at the time of their offenses than those who are not. Overall, approximately 70–80 percent of incarcerated offenders report that they have used drugs in their past. Younger offenders, particularly those who are first-time or minor drug offenders, make up a significant proportion of jail populations. Since the war on drugs in the 1980s, the United States has seen unprecedented increases in incarceration rates for drug crimes that carry longer sentences than was typically the case prior to "getting tough."

Given that breaking the cycle of addiction is difficult for those seeking treatment in the general population and their success rates are low, the environment of the prison often complicates effective service delivery for inmates to rid themselves of their substance addictions. Treatment in correctional facilities can involve counseling, therapeutic communities, detoxification, and twelve-step programs such as Alcoholics Anonymous or Narcotics Anonymous. Of these treatment options, recent research shows that in-prison therapeutic community interventions (TCI), especially if coupled with continued treatment after participants are released from prison, are especially effective (Galassi, Mpofu, and Athanasou 2015). Some institutions also provide aftercare services for released inmates to prevent relapse. The introduction of drug courts as alternatives to incapacitation since the late 1980s has provided yet another avenue for handling offenders with substance abuse problems.

Overall, some treatment programs have been found to be ineffective in reducing recidivism. It is important to note, however, that only about 20 percent of inmates in secure confinement actually participate in alcohol or drug-treatment programs that are offered, but over 70 percent of inmates in state prison have substance abuse with and without co-occurring mental health disorders (James and Glaze 2006). The probability of engaging in recidivist behaviors is two to four times higher for those individuals who abuse drugs or alcohol compared to those who do not, so providing and encouraging completion of effective treatment programs while incarcerated increases the probability of higher success rates postrelease (Bennett, Holloway, and Farrington 2008).

If inmates do participate, they usually do so during the last six months of their sentences. The length of time in treatment could be one of the hurdles standing in the way of reducing recidivism. In fact, a review of the literature demonstrates that programs that do work are intensive, last nine to twelve months, focus on offenders who are younger and more at risk, and maintain services upon and after release. Some programs actually work quite well and save money, too. Several recent studies have observed that offenders who participate in treatment programs both in prison *and* in the outside community have fewer occasions of drug relapse and criminality (see McCollister et al. 2004).

Aging and Elderly Inmates

One prominent issue in the United States over the past ten to fifteen years has been a surge in the percentage of the population over the age of fifty-five. News reports and politicians have often highlighted this fact with an emphasis on government programs in need of reform such as Social Security and Medicare, long-term care, and prescription drug costs. Special housing, such as assisted-living communities and retirement communities, has been a significant moneymaker for construction companies, investors, and real estate developers alike. Few cities over 50,000 residents are without such properties.

It is often noted that what happens in the general society soon occurs inside the prison walls. With the mandate to provide medical treatment for inmates, the costs and unique problems posed by an aging prison population is an ever-pressing dilemma for an institution that traditionally held convicted offenders between the ages of eighteen and forty-nine. The number of state and federal prisoners aged fifty-five and older is growing at twice the rate of their younger counterparts. Between 1980 and 2010, inmates fifty-five plus increased by nearly 1400 percent. According to Chettiar, Bunting, and Schotter of the American Civil Liberties

Union (2012), if this rate of growth continues, the population of prisoners fifty-five and older will have increased 4400 percent from 1980–2030, which means that one-third of the US prison population will fall under the label of **elderly inmate**. There is no epidemic of older persons committing crimes, rather, the increase in this age group in our nation's prisons is a result of longer sentences, life-without-parole sanctions, and mandatory-minimum provisions. As a result, state and federal corrections systems need to allocate three times the expenditures to care for aging inmates compared to their younger counterparts (Faiver 1998). Some state prisons have created special wings that are essentially nursing homes to provide for their population of older prisoners.

When people age, in or out of prison, they change physically, socially, and mentally. For offenders who are aging behind bars, however, many of the issues associated with aging are aggravated and heightened. Although aging inmates are entitled to healthcare, the quality of that care may not be sufficient to take care of many of the problems associated with old age, such as dementia. In addition, older inmates may not be able to take care of themselves if they are harassed or assaulted by younger inmates.

Possible solutions to the above-noted problems involve early release on medical parole, also known as compassionate release, sentences served in the community for older offenders who do not pose a significant risk to the community, increases in funding to serve aging inmates, and the creation of geriatric units within existing and proposed facilities. Certainly, the former two alternatives would be the most cost-effective for the administration of corrections, considering that offenders serving their time in the community are responsible for their own housing, medical treatment, and daily care. Government allocation of more funds to correctional budgets would be helpful, but not practical or economical based on recent fiscal crises over the past several years. In general, most states spend more on corrections than on education and other social programs.

Creating geriatric units and even geriatric prisons are becoming the major approaches for dealing with the aging inmate population. These facilities look like mini-hospitals that are staffed with registered nurses and equipped with appropriate medical devices, which are more readily available than they would be in the typical prison infirmary. Some states have developed prison hospice facilities. Similar to hospice facilities in the community, prison hospices care for terminally ill inmates who are not eligible for or who were denied medical parole. Certainly, as the prison population continues to gray, different approaches, programs, and facilities will be needed to house this population, especially if other back-door options are not available.

Inmates and Mental Illness

Historically, asylums held society's misfits, whether they were insane, poor, or criminal. In nineteenth-century America, asylums were institutions where the mentally troubled were held until a cure for their sickness could be found. Once tranquilizers became available, asylum patients were often sedated into a stupor.

Essentially, this practice continued into the twentieth century. Long-term institutionalization in a secure hospital setting became the primary method of care in the United States until the early 1970s. Family members of patients confined in mental hospitals were requesting lengthier periods of confinement for them. Something had to be done.

With the passage and implementation of community mental health acts by states across the country, patients housed in the asylums who were no longer considered to be a threat to themselves or others were released into general society due to advent of new medications that were believed to effectively control symptoms of mental illness, a process called **deinstitutionalization**. Soon, many city streets in America were occupied by thousands of mentally ill ex-hospital patients, many of whom were unable to function in ways that were deemed appropriate law-abiding behaviors. Most jurisdictions responded to the problem by confining these "offenders" in correctional institutions. This process is known as **transinstitutionalization**; the mentally ill were first placed in secure confinement in a hospital setting, then they were released, and then they were reconfined, this time under the auspices of the criminal justice system.

Today, it is estimated that 15–20 percent of inmates housed in jails or prisons can be classified as having a mental disability (Pollock 2004; Torrey et al. 2014). Symptoms of mental health disorders most commonly observed in jails and prisons are mania, followed by major depressive disorder, and psychotic disorder. Nearly all the state public and private correctional facilities in the United States have reported that they provided some sort of treatment to cover inmates' mental health needs (Beck and Maruschak 2001). Treatment forms range from therapy or counseling services to psychotropic medications and separate care units within the facility.

Inmates with mental disabilities are often most at risk for victimization—both physically and psychologically. These inmates are also found to be difficult for staff to control because many correctional officers do not have the training or educational background to deal with the compounded problems inmates with mental illness face in correctional facilities—especially when officers must give inmates orders of compliance to maintain security and control within the institutions. For example, correctional officers may be required to distinguish between those inmates who truly do not understand the orders that they are given, and as a result act out irrationally, from those who understand the expectations but become upset because they do not want to comply (Pollock 2004).

Dual-disorder inmates are also becoming a major concern for management issues in the nation's prisons and jails, and then for communities, post-release. These inmates are those who can be classified as having both substance abuse and mental health problems. These inmates are especially problematic for jails, since most of these offenders are purportedly arrested more frequently for less serious offenses (Alemagno et al. 2004). In addition, some of these dual-disordered individuals may seek treatment in a traditional psychiatric center for their mental illness, but they are often turned away because some centers or programs prefer not to deal with patients who also have drug addictions. Whatever the reason, many individuals will return to the community still needing treatment to improve their chances for successful reentry. Further complicating matters, offenders with mental illness are more likely to be homeless, jobless, and alcohol or drug dependent during the year preceding their offense (Ditton 1999).

CORRECTIONAL OFFICERS

Rank and Responsibilities to Ensure Safety and Security

As a general rule, the **paramilitary model** is followed to ensure security in most institutions for those residing and/or working in them. In practice, this means that the correctional officers (COs) wear uniforms and badges and go by a hierarchical list of titles such as sergeant, lieutenant, captain, and major. Terms that are common in the military such as "company," "mess hall," "drill," and "inspection" are used. There is also a clear separation between the higher and lower ranking officers. Even the methods and organizational structures used to control inmates follow a militaristic style. In fact, for many years, inmates marched to the dining hall and to their daily assignments. Standing at attention when the warden appeared or removing one's hat in the presence of a captain was commonplace.

Today, life in prison, while still quite regimented and military-like, does not adhere so strictly to the aforementioned practices. At the top of the administrative food chain is the warden who oversees every aspect of the prison from security to budgeting. Associate wardens typically come next and are essentially responsible for custody and operations, which basically means that they need to know where inmates are at all times. Although few in number, guard captains follow and are usually in charge of administrative tasks or are commanders of the COs under them. Guard captains will often designate duties to other COs to supervise various units in the prison such as laundry, library, programming, or to chair disciplinary committees.

Under the guard captains are the guard lieutenants, who are the troubleshooters in the facility. They are involved in such activities as quelling volatile incidents or removing problem inmates from the general prison population and then placing them in segregation. Next come the guard sergeants, who like their army counterparts, manage specific units in the institution, such as cellblocks, the hospital, or mess hall. Another duty of the guard sergeant could be to supervise other COs.

Regardless of type of correctional facility or rank of officers, persons who work in these secure residential settings have important responsibilities in order to maintain the safety and security of the institutions, the inmates, staff and administration, and the general public. They have to operate orderly facilities under three general headings. One, they must make sure that inmates follow the institution's rules and procedures, which are typically given in written form and communicated verbally with inmates upon admission. Second, officers must be on the lookout for, identify, and uncover illicit items that could be disruptive and affect the security of the institution. Finally, corrections personnel must keep the facility free from **contraband**, or items that inmates are not allowed to have in their possession, such as drugs, cell phones, and other items that would disrupt the orderly operation and welfare of those who live and work there.

Types of Correctional Officers

There are at least five general types of COs and their duties are dependent upon the units in which they work. There are

1. **Housing unit officers**: These officers maintainsecurity where the inmates are housed, open and close steel-barred doors, take frequent inmate counts, distribute medicine, mail, and laundry, oversee maintenance activities, and supervise inmates showering.
2. **Work detail supervisors**: Inmates work in any number of areas in a prison such as the kitchen or laundry. Some prisons even have gardens where some of the facility's food is grown. Work detail supervisors monitor the inmates while they are working in these capacities.
3. **Industrial shop and school officers**: These COs are responsible for watching over inmates while they are working in industrial areas or sitting in academic or vocational courses.
4. **Yard officers**: Inmates spend time in recreational activities daily. These COs function to make sure that there is order and safety during these sessions.
5. **Perimeter security officers**: Conventional prisons are usually surrounded by towers positioned along the high wall surrounding the perimeter of the institution. Perimeter security COs sit in these towers and act as watch guards. In prisons built more recently, these officers actually walk or drive along the outside of the facility to maintain security and prevent escapes.

Women as Correctional Officers

For the most part, COs in male prisons have been, and currently are, males. Not until the passage of an amendment in 1972 to Title VII of the Civil Rights Act of 1964 were women as COs welcomed in men's prisons. This piece of legislation prohibited sex discrimination in government employment. Three major criticisms have been issued arguing against having women function as COs in male institutions. First, some have argued that women should not be COs because they are not strong enough, are too easily corrupted by male inmates, or are weak backups for fellow officers in trouble. Second, some contend that women can have a disruptive influence because inmates might refuse to follow their orders or compete for their attention. Third, some critics allege that having female COs violates prisoners' privacy, particularly if women work in shower areas or conduct strip searches. Are there any bases to these claims?

Several studies have been conducted on this topic and they have compared male and female COs on the variable of job performance. Overall, the majority of these studies reported that there is no difference between males and females on this factor. However, some studies also noted that women and men are not necessarily equal on all tasks. For example, male COs may be more effective in handling physical assaults, while female COs are more successful in defusing incidents before they turn violent. Females have also been found to be more treatment oriented than male COs. In addition, observations were noted that women tend to supervise inmates in a more personal style compared to their male counterparts. For example, women are more likely to ask inmates to do something rather than commanding them to comply with an order.

Problems Faced by Correctional Officers

Regardless of sex, today's COs face many of the same problems guards of the past confronted. Being employed as a CO means you are working in a dangerous environment, are not satisfactorily compensated in this low-status position, and your role expectations are confusing. On the one hand, COs must perform custodial functions, much like a security guard. On the other hand, COs need to develop relationships with the inmates in order to change the offenders' behavior in a constructive manner; indeed, "they routinely assume numerous essential yet sometimes contradictory roles (e.g., counselor, diplomat, caretaker, disciplinarian, supervisor, crisis manager) often under stress and dangerous conditions" (Josi and Sechrest, 1998, p. 11). Perhaps Hans Toch, the respected prison scholar, put it best when he wrote in 1981, which still rings true today that

> Prison guards are truly imprisoned. They are not physically confined but are locked into movie caricatures, into pejorative prophecies (sometimes self-fulfilling), into anachronistic supervision patterns, into unfair civil service definitions, into undeserved hostilities and prejudgments of their actions. Officers are imprisoned by our ignorance of who they are and what they do, which is the price they pay for working behind the walls. (Foreword to Lucien X. Lombardo, Guards Imprisoned, New York: Elsevier, p. xiv.)

On many levels, COs are between a rock and a hard place—they are the lowest level workers in the institution but have the greatest amount of responsibility in managing and supervising inmates. Failure to follow the policies, rules, and procedures of the administration can lead to reprimands, suspensions, or firings. Following these same policies, rules, and procedures to the letter can also be problematic in attempting to gain inmate compliance. Some rules can be broken, such as allowing some drug use to go on in the prison as a quid pro quo for gaining obedience from the CO's charges. To cope with this role conflict and daily tasks, COs, like police officers, have developed certain work styles. A great comparison of these working ideologies was postulated by Gilbert (1997) who extended the work of the well-known Muir police officer typology descriptors. Muir's work as cited in Gilbert (1997) refers to four role types: (1) the Professional; (2) the Reciprocator; (3) the Enforcer; and (4) the Avoider. Table 4.2 provides a general description of each of the types of officers and then a comparison of how police officers and COs behave relative to that role (Gilbert, 1997, 54–55).

Table 4.2

Professional Role of Police Officers	Professional Role of Corrections Officers
• Develops the beat	• Develops the housing unit
• Takes educated risks	• Takes educated risks
• Provides citizens advice on law and government	• Provides inmates advice on rules and regulations
• Increases pressure over time to correct behavior	• Increases pressure over time to change behavior
• Uses arrest as a last resort	• Uses the "write-up" as a last resort
• Tries to preserve the dignity of citizens using nondemeaning behaviors and attitudes	• Tries to preserve the dignity of inmates using nondemeaning behaviors and attitudes
• Views offenders as not much different from self	• Views offenders as not much different from self
• Empathizes with the human condition of citizens and offenders	• Empathizes with the human condition of inmates
• Allows for exceptions in his/her own behavior and that of others	• Allows for exceptions in his/her own behavior and that of others
• Uses coercion and force judiciously	• Uses coercion and force judiciously
• Calm and easygoing	• Calm and easygoing
• Articulate and open	• Articulate and open
• Focuses on attaining justice for individuals	• Focuses on ensuring the due process and decency in security and control tasks
• Views most other officers as being enforcer oriented	• Views most other officers as being enforcer oriented

The Reciprocator Police Officer	The Reciprocator Corrections Officer
• Allows local "roughs" to keep citizens in line, a mutual accommodation	• Allows inmate leaders to keep die unit quiet, a mutual accommodation
• Uses clinical/social work strategies to help people "worthy" of assistance	• Uses clinical/social work strategies to help inmates "worthy" of assistance
• Rationalizes situations	• Rationalizes situations
• Attempts to educate, cure, or solve the citizen's problems	• Attempts to educate, cure, or solve the inmate's problems
• Low tolerance for rejection	• Low tolerance for rejection of offered assistance
• Easily frustrated	• Easily frustrated
• Often does not use coercion when it should be used	• Often does not use coercion when it should be used
• Inconsistent job performance	• Inconsistent job performance
• Irrational behavior by citizens stymies the officer	• Irrational behavior by inmates stymies the officer
• Often displays a superior attitude toward others	• Often displays a superior attitude toward others
• Highly articulate	• Highly articulate

Table 4.2 *(continued)*

THE ENFORCER POLICE OFFICER	The Enforcer Corrections Officer
• Aggressive law enforcement	• Aggressive rule enforcement issues many "tickets"
• Makes many arrests	
• Actively seeks violations	• Actively seeks violations
• Frequently uses force or excessive force	• Frequently uses force or excessive force
• Tends to view order maintenance and service functions as not part of police work	• Tends to view treatment functions as what "others" do with or for the inmates
• Strict enforcement orientation, limits service and order maintenance duties	• Strict security and control orientation, limits service delivery duties
• Little or no empathy for the human condition of citizens/offenders	• Little or no empathy for the human condition of inmates
• Citizens often complain about this officer's behavior	• Inmates often submit grievances over this officer's behavior
• Rigid, rule bound, makes few exceptions even when appropriate	• Rigid, rule bound, makes few exceptions even when appropriate
• Maintains a dualistic view of human nature (good/bad, cop/criminal, strong/weak)	• Maintains a dualistic view of human nature (good/bad, officer/inmate strong/weak)
• Dislikes management	• Dislikes management
• Postures for effect	• Postures for effect
• Crazy/brave "John Wayne" behaviors, takes unnecessary risks	• Crazy/brave "John Wayne" behaviors, takes unnecessary risks
• Views other officers as "soft" or "weak" if not like him/her	• Views other officers as "soft" or "weak" if not like him/her
• Views officers like him/her as being the majority of officers	• Views officers like him/her as being the majority of officers
The Avoider Police Officer	**The Avoider Corrections Officer**
• Often leaves situations as quickly as possible	• Often leaves situations as quickly as possible
• Tends to view most functions as not being "real" police work or part of the job	• Tends to view human communications with inmates as not being part of security and control
• Uses the patrol car to reduce contact with citizens	• Uses the mechanical aspects of security and control to reduce contact with inmates
• Often the last to arrive in response to an emergency	• Often among the last to arrive at an emergency scene
• Likely to seek refuge from the street in the patrol car	• Likely to select tower duty/isolated positions away from inmates
• Plays the "phony" tough and frequently backs down	• Plays the "phony" tough and frequently backs down
• Tends to blame others for avoidance behaviors or inadequacies	• Tends to blame others for avoidance behaviors or inadequacies
• Structures the work to reduce chances of offenses and use of coercion	• Structures the work to avoid observing infractions and use of coercion
• Avoids confrontations and interactions	• Avoids confrontations and interactions with inmates

The Professional is calm, easy going, open, and nondefensive. When warranted, he/she will make exceptions, and prefers to gain compliance by using interpersonal communication skills but will use coercive tactics and force if necessary. The Reciprocator is also calm and easygoing. He/she wants to help people and assist them in resolving their troubles by using social work strategies whenever possible but tends to be inconsistent in making exceptions. He/she does not like to use coercion or force even when justifiable.

Critical Thinking Exercise

Imagine you are a CO in a maximum-security prison and you notice some contraband coming into the facility. The group of inmates bringing in the drugs typically do their time and do not cause problems, that is, until now. Take each of Gilbert's adaptations of Muir's personality types (see Table 4.2) and detail how each one would handle the situation. Which one do you think would be most effective given what you know about the prison world?

The Enforcer officer, however, is rigid, a go-by-the-book person who aggressively enforces the rules/laws. He/she actively seeks out violations and rarely makes exceptions to the rules/laws. Enforcers have little empathy for others and see situations and people as either good or bad. He/she takes unreasonable risks to personal safety and is quick to use threats, verbal coercion, and physical force. Finally, the Avoider is described as a nervous officer who minimizes contact with offenders. Often, this officer chooses to not see certain actions as offenses even when they are. He/she does not use coercion and avoids confrontation. The interpersonal components of the job are not seen as being necessary to carry out his/her responsibilities. The Avoider is inconsistent in work behaviors, backs down when confronted, and blames everyone else for his/her problems.

Relationships between Correctional Officers and Inmates

The descriptions noted above offer a glimpse of how COs might interact with inmates based on the four work style preferences. The relationship between COs and inmates has often been described as one of structured conflict. The COs must function according to the organization's subculture but must also be cognizant of the inmate subculture. After all, COs are responsible for preventing disciplinary problems within the institution. When you couple this charge with the policy changes that have afforded inmates more rights, the frustration levels of COs tend to be high. The point here is to note that while alterations in policies were intended to protect inmates from abuses from correctional staff, COs tend to see these protections as harmful to their own safety interests and welfare because they view the granting of certain rights as compromises to their authority. This scenario leaves COs fearful and agitated as now they must deal with inmates more formally.

For many COs, this means that they have developed a more defensive posture and a more negative attitude toward inmates.

Despite these broad generalizations, there is a certain level of understanding that coexists among COs and inmates. Many COs do try to help inmates when problems arise, but they are more likely to do so within the confines of the guidelines established by the prison administration. Above all, COs cannot be perceived as being too lenient with inmates. Thus, they must follow ethical standards and perform their duties with integrity. One way COs have transitioned from a more informal, more interpersonal style of supervision is to not get caught up in personal dialogues with inmates.

Inmates are notorious for playing games with COs who fail to maintain a professional association with their charges. A common mistake made by COs is talking to inmates about their own personal lives, only to find the information used against them when trying to to gain compliance from prisoners. Regardless of how friendly a relationship between COs and inmates may be, inmates still see COs as the "police" and are quick to compromise the position of COs to get what they want. For example, using personal information to weaken the solidarity among the staff is a tactic employed by some inmates to achieve their objectives, be it more recreation time or to avoid being written up for an infraction.

Fortunately, research has shown us what seems to work for COs when working with inmates. Officers who are fair and friendly and relate to inmates as fellow human beings are often liked and obeyed. Officers who were consistent, fair, and flexible in the enforcement of the rules are considered effective COs. The same goes for officers who can develop a rapport of respect with inmates. Further, COs who have higher levels of job satisfaction and adopt a less punitive or custodial orientation toward inmates are more successful in gaining inmate compliance than officers demonstrating other interpersonal authority roles.

PRISON ISSUES

Crowding

Crowding in prisons has been a pervasive problem for several decades. One reason for this overcrowding is due to the practice of confining and managing large numbers of offenders since other philosophies of corrections, as was discussed in Chapter 3, other than rehabilitation, have been more readily followed. The second reason, is that we have more punitive sentencing policies in place such as mandatory-minimum sentences, longer prison terms, and limited use of release on parole. Finally, as a result, we have widened the number of offenses eligible for incarceration. For example, it is estimated that 44 percent of the prison population can be accounted for due to the war on drugs (Blumstein 1995) with more people imprisoned for drug crimes today compared to the total number of persons incarcerated for any crime in 1980. The rise in prison populations is indicative of the trends that can be attributed to judges and prosecutors in convicting more persons and sending them to prison. In general, prison populations will vary according to how many people are sentenced to prison, how long offenders are sent to prison, and the rate at which they return. The US inmate population is being affected by all of these influences at arguably an alarming rate.

Crowding leads to a number of problems within the institution, such as elevated blood pressures, more trips to clinics, difficulty sleeping, suicides, homicides, and other types of assaultive behaviors (Harer and Steffensmeier 1996). In addition, crowding adds to the uncertainty, apprehension, and cognitive overloads of inmates negatively experiencing crowded conditions—in essence, fear for their own physical and emotional safety can result from living in crowded facilities. These struggles can interfere with treatment efforts where available because inmates need to concentrate on their reformation if they are to be helped. Further, crowding can undermine any rehabilitation efforts going on in that classification of inmates into appropriate housing, programs, and the like are made more difficult when there is only so much space and so many cells available. In some facilities, the prison gym has become makeshift living quarters. Dense prison populations also deplete resources, leaving some inmates to be placed on treatment waiting lists or resulting in the cancellation of programs altogether.

In addition, the philosophy of incapacitation, which is followed today, can be undercut when early release mechanisms are relied upon to reduce crowded conditions. Thus, inmates will be released sooner and may return to crime due to shorter sentence lengths that do not enable inmates to take advantage of treatment efforts where available. Inmate crowding can also weaken the goal of general deterrence because would-be offenders would see that crowding has led to no space in facilities, which means that they may not be sent to prison at all. Crowding could also abate the objectives of specific deterrence as affected inmates have to reside in harsh living conditions when prison environments are overpopulated. Finally, crowding could negatively affect retribution because no two sentences will be served equitably since some inmates will adjust better to the surroundings while others will fare worse.

Prison Violence and Prison Discipline

Violence, or at least the threat of violence, is a common concern among both inmates and staff. After all, prisons tend to be filled with people who have already demonstrated a willingness to engage in violent or otherwise unlawful acts. Knowledge about violence within prisons is limited by concerns over the validity and reliability of prison records and the limitations of other methodologies used to study prison violence. The level and extent of violence will greatly vary from prison to prison and for different prisoners. Different features of the prison, such as its architectural design, inmate freedom of movement, and group and individual dynamics, can affect the level of prison violence (Adams 1992; Bottoms 1999).

Research suggests that most prisons are not characterized by the systematic and rampant violence often portrayed in the popular media (Bottoms 1999; Edgar, O'Donnell, and Martin 2014). Of course, there have been and continue to be prisons and prison systems that are plagued by higher levels of violence. Coercion and the threat of violence appear to be more common than actual physical assaults. Coercion may be used by physically dominating inmates to obtain items such as food, money, personal services, and sex. This threat of violence, including sexual assault, is very real to inmates. In fact, 4 percent of state and federal inmates and 3.2 percent of jail inmates who participated in the National Inmate Survey ($N = 92,449$) reported being victims of some type of sexual assault by either another inmate or staff while incarcerated (Beck and Stroop 2017). While there is no sure way of preventing all crimes of sexual violence in correctional facilities, the federal government passed the Prison Rape Elimination Act (PREA) that requires the Bureau of Justice Statistics to collect data and report annually on incidences of prison rape. It also established national standards to prevent, detect, reduce, and respond to sexual victimization of incarcerated persons.

Furthermore, prisoner assaults on staff and other prisoners do occur and can result in serious injury or death. Female prisons tend to have less explicit violence than male prisons, though violence and the threat of violence are clearly a reality in women's prisons as well. Similar to male prisons, there tend to be female "convicts" within any given institution who are more willing to use instrumental violence and cause disruptions within the facility (Johnson 2002).

Prison officials have a number of tools to deal with violence and other violations of institutional rules. For violations that are criminal offenses, administrators can refer the matter for criminal prosecution. However, the difficulty in obtaining a conviction in many of these cases and the logistical problems involved often discourage such attempts (Jacobs 1982). A more common response is to use one or more of the sanctions that prison officials have at their disposal. One popular form is placing inmates in isolation from the rest of the prison population in **solitary confinement**, also known as segregation, and falls under the umbrella term of **restrictive housing**. Other terms for restrictive housing include disciplinary or punitive segregation, administrative segregation, and protective custody. Solitary confinement has been in use for years, and recall that it formed the basis for the Pennsylvania system, which was covered in Chapter 1. More recently, there has been a movement to decrease its practice since it has been shown to be used disproportionately against persons of color, young inmates, and those suffering from mental health disorders (Digard, Vanko, and Sullivan 2018). Research has also shown it to be psychologically and physically damaging for inmates confined under such control (Haney and Lynch 1997; Haney 2018).

With solitary confinement, an inmate is secured in a cell that will hold only the inmate for twenty-two to twenty-four hours a day. All meals are served within the cell and freedom of movement and interaction with others are highly constrained with inmates only receiving about one hour per day outside the cell for recreation. Even then, the recreation area is tightly controlled, and in many prisons, there is not much else for the inmate to do but walk alone in a small fenced-in area outside. Some prisons, known as *supermax* prisons, are comprised of multiple single-cell units made mostly of concrete and solid walls with few options for natural light. Some have argued that restrictive housing is necessary as some inmates are violent and too difficult to control in the general prison population.

Other disciplinary options corrections official use include the loss of certain privileges such as visitation or a change in the inmate's classification status or location (Jacobs 1982). Prison officials may also have the discretion to reduce an inmate's good-time credit. In jurisdictions with indeterminate sentencing, parole officials will examine an inmate's behavior and may reject a parole application if an inmate has a history of disruptive behavior while incarcerated.

Critical Thinking Exercise

Should solitary confinement be abolished? Do you see any value to the practice of restrictive housing? Assuming solitary confinement is not going away, what types of inmates do you think it is appropriate for? What is the maximum length of time someone should be allowed to stay segregated? Justify your responses.

INSTITUTIONAL CORRECTIONS AND TECHNOLOGY

Technology is a large part of society, from smartphones, smartwatches, handheld computers, and fitness bands. Technology keeps us in touch with friends, relatives, and even businesses. It is constantly changing and upgrading in any number of settings, including institutional correctional facilities. Two types of technology that are becoming more prevalent in correctional facilities are full-body and handheld scanners and video conferencing and visitation.

Full-body scanners used by the Transportation Security Administration to screen passengers entering the departure gates at airports are being used by correctional facilities to detect contraband, such as cell phones and weapons, and to confiscate these items from visitors or inmates before they enter the general prison population. These scanners were banned from the airport for the flying public because their real-life nude images displayed on the screen violated privacy rights. In correctional facilities, however, inmates' constitutional rights and privacy protections are much more limited. Since the primary responsibility of a correctional facility is to maintain safety and security, inmates are often subjected to screening and scanning like the body scanners. Body scanners are effective at detecting objects individuals have hidden under their clothing, but they are expensive and typically do not detect objects that are not made of metal, like credit cards or handmade knives or other blunt objects made of wood or plastic. Handheld scanners, similar to the metal detector wands used at airports, are less costly and can detect both metal and nonmetallic objects (Bulman 2009).

Video conferencing and video visitations is another type of technology that is becoming increasingly common in correctional facilities, especially jails, because it has the potential to increase security, save money, and decrease recidivism. During the past decade, video technology has become popular in prisons and jails. Inmates can use video technology to talk to family members, friends, lawyers, probation officers, and the court. Courtroom appearances for many persons held in jail during pretrial proceedings such as the initial appearance are often done by videoconferencing over the Internet, which is similar to communicating via FaceTime or Skype between the defendant and the judge. Video technologies such as videoconferencing can save money because jail staff are not needed to transport inmates between the jail and court, and related physical transportation costs are avoided.

Videoconferencing, especially between the court and inmates, has been around for about a decade. A more recent application of video technology is video visitation where, again, like FaceTime or Skype, inmates can communicate with family and friends via the Internet. Another model of video visitation is an on-site, no-contact visitation, where visitors speak with the inmate via video systems at the jail. This is commonly called a central video visitation. A fee is charged for a twenty- to thirty-minute visit, ranging from $20 to $30, and the jail receives a certain percentage of the revenue from the company installing the system ("Video Visitation" 2014).

Web Activity

Explore the positives and negatives of video visitation by watching this video: https://www.youtube.com/watch?v=RlG9qA3OO4Q. Should this practice be prohibited by law? Why or why not?

The benefits of video visitation are numerous. First, allowing inmates to have more contact with visitors can reduce prison infractions and facilitate prosocial ties with outside family and friends who can help them upon release as social supports, employment prospects, housing, and finances (Berg and Huebner 2011; Duwe and Clark 2011). Second, if done from a remote location such as the visitor's home, it reduces the travel time and costs for family members and friends, thereby allowing for more-frequent visits. Prior to Internet video visitation, family and friends had to commute to a correctional facility, and depending on where the institution was located, this could range from a tank of gas to multiple tanks of gas, an overnight stay at a hotel, and/or bus or train tickets. Third, once arriving to the facility, visitors avoid the logistical issues of finding parking, passing through screening and metal detectors, standing in line to check in, and standing/sitting in crowded waiting rooms for a visit.

For jail and prison administration and staff, video visitation is also advantageous, especially in regard to monetary and time expenditures. One, fewer staff are needed and less staff time is devoted to scanning and searching inmates and visitors entering and exiting visitation areas. Two, video visitation reduces the opportunity for drugs, weapons, and other contraband from entering the facility and reaching the inmate population. Third, fewer staff are needed to monitor and provide security for inmates and visitors while in the visitation room.

There are also disadvantages to video visitation. First, there are still costs associated with the remote visit that the visitor is required to pay. Depending on the fee, which varies by facility, some inmates' friends and family members might not be able to afford to have many more visits than they would have had in person. Second, some facilities restrict video visitation sessions for shorter time periods than is common with in-person visits. Third, personal visits are preferred by inmates and visitors alike, and there is growing concern that video visits will replace in-person visits in some facilities ("Video Visitation" 2014). Finally, there are some ethical concerns surrounding the profit motive of the facilities that receive a percentage of the fees accrued from the video visitation company.

Web Activity

To explore video visitation further, go to https://www.prisonpolicy.org/visitation/report.html and view the report. Should the prisons and jails profit from video visitations? Why or why not?

SUMMARY

The practice of using prisons and jails to punish offenders has been in operation for over 200 years. We have rationalized our use of secure facilities based on the philosophies of incapacitation, retribution, deterrence, and rehabilitation, with the focus being more on the first three for the past forty years. There are many challenges, however, to achieving any one of these philosophies given that each inmate's experience behind bars is different. Some individuals will adjust to incarceration more readily than others, depending on their age, gender, physical and mental health status, their past histories, where they are incarcerated, the programs and services available there, and how they handle communal living, crowded spaces, and risk of victimization. The types of correctional officers and how they seek compliance and work with offenders will also affect how inmates will spend their time imprisoned. Whether inmate or officer, adapting to and navigating this unique social environment that is often routine, yet at the same time threatening, will have an impact on how those who live and work are "doing time."

KEY WORDS

contraband	elderly inmate	hands-off approach
convict subculture	fundamental	hands-on approach
deprivation model	democratization	housing unit officers
deinstitutionalization	gleaning	importation model

industrial shop and school officers
mass incarceration
paramilitary model
perimeter security officers
prison lifestyle
prisonization
prisoners' rights movement
pseudofamilies
restrictive housing
social groups
solitary confinement
straight subculture
thief subculture
total institution
transinstitutionalization
work detail supervisors
yard officers

DISCUSSION QUESTIONS

1. Imagine you were serving time in prison prior to 1970, during the 1970s, and then today. What would be your biggest challenges in adapting to life in prison over these eras? Why? Now imagine you are a correctional officer working in a prison prior to 1970, during the 1970s, and then today. What would be your biggest challenges in ensuring order is maintained in the facility over these time periods? Why?

2. Which of Sykes's deprivations would be most difficult for you to handle? Why? Which of the five deprivations would bother you the least? Why?

3. A new policy has been adopted by the State Department of Corrections that requires the prison administration and staff to eliminate pseudofamilies in all state correctional facilities. You are a guard sergeant in your unit and are tasked with the responsibility to carry out the directive while working with the correctional officers under your supervision to obtain inmate compliance with the policy. What do you foresee being major hurdles for you and your staff? For the inmates? Why? What ideas do you have to overcome them?

4. Which of the special offender populations do you think will have an easier time adapting to the prison environment? The most difficult? Defend your selection.

5. Would you have preferred to be a correctional officer before or after the prisoners' rights movement? Why?

SUGGESTED READINGS

Alexander, M. (2012). *The New Jim Crow: Mass Incarceration in the Age of Colorblindness*. New York, NY: New Press.

Kerman, P. (2011). *Orange Is the New Black: My Year in a Women's Prison*. New York, NY: Spiegel & Grau.

Rothman, D. J. (2017). *Conscience and Convenience: The Asylum and Its Alternatives in Progressive America*. New York, NY: Routledge.

Senghor, S. (2016). *Writing My Wrongs: Life, Death, and Redemption in an American Prison*. New York, NY: Convergent Books.

Slate, R. N., J. K. Buffington-Vollum, and W. W. Johnson. (2013). *The Criminalization of Mental Illness: Crisis and Opportunity for the Justice System*. Durham, NC: Carolina Academic Press.

Sykes, G. M. (2007). *The Society of Captives: A Study of a Maximum Security Prison*. Princeton, NJ: Princeton University Press.

REFERENCES

Adams, K. (1992). "Adjusting to prison life." In M. Tonry (Ed.), *Crime and justice: A review of research* (pp. 275–360). Chicago: University of Chicago Press.

Alemagno, S., Shaffer-King, E., Tonkin, P., and Hammel, R. (2004). *Characteristics of arrestees at risk for co-existing substance abuse and mental disorder.* Washington, DC: National Institute of Justice.

Beck, A. and Maruschak, L. (2001). *Mental health treatment in state prisons, 2000* Washington, DC: Bureau of Justice Statistics.

Beck, A. and Stroop, J. (2017). *PREA Data Collection Activities, 2017.* Washington, DC: Bureau of Justice Statistics.

Bennett, T., Holloway, K., & Farrington, D. (2008). "The statistical association between drug misuse and crime: A meta-analysis." *Aggression and Violent Behavior, 13*(2), 107–118.

Carroll, L. (1974). *Hacks, blacks, and cons.* Lexington, MA: Lexington Books.

Berg, M. T., & Huebner, B. M. (2011). "Reentry and the ties that bind: An examination of socialties, employment, and recidivism." *Justice Quarterly, 28*(2), 382–410.

Blumstein, A. (1995). "Crime and punishment in the United States over 20 years: A failure of deterrence and incapacitation?" In P. Wikstrom, R. Clarke and J. McCord (Eds.), *Intergrating crime prevention strategies: Propensity and Opportunity.* Stockholm, Sweden: National Council for Crime Prevention.

Bottoms, A. (1999). "Interpersonal violence and social order in prisons." In M. Tonry and J. Petersilia (Eds.), *Prisons* (pp. 205–282). Chicago: University of Chicago Press.

Bulman, P. (2009). "Using technology to make prisons and jails safer." *NIJ Journal, 262.*

Carroll, L. (1974). *Hacks, blacks, and cons: Race relations in a maximum-security prison.* Lexington, MA: Lexington Books.

Chettiar, I. M. and Bunting, W.C. and Schotter, G. (2012). *At America's Expense: The Mass Incarceration of the Elderly.* Retrieved May 17, 2018 at https://www.aclu.org/files/assets/elderlyprisonreport_20120613_1.pdf.

Cooper v. Pate, 378 U.S. 546 (1964).

Digard, L., E. Vanko, and S. Sullivan. (2018). *Rethinking Restrictive Housing: Lessons from Five U.S. Jail and Prison Systems.* New York: Vera Institute of Justice.

Ditton, P. M. (1999). Special report: Mental health and treatment of inmates and probationers. *Washington, DC: US Department of Justice, Bureau of Justice Statistics.*

Duwe, G., & Clark, V. (2013). "Blessed be the social tie that binds: The effects of prison visitation on offender recidivism." *Criminal Justice Policy Review, 24*(3), 271–296.

Edgar, K., O'Donnell, I., & Martin, C. (2014). *Prison Violence: Conflict, Power and Vicitmization.* Routledge.

Ex parte Hull, 312 U.S. 546 (1941).

Faiver, K. (1998). *Health care management issues in corrections.* Lanham, MD: American Correctional Association.

Galassi, A., E. Mpofu, and J. Athanasou. (2015). "Therapeutic Community Treatment of an Inmate Population with Substance Use Disorders: Post-release Trends in Re-arrest, Re-incarceration, and Drug Misuse Relapse." *International Journal of Environmental Research and Public Health* 12, no. 6: 7059–7072.

Gilbert, M. J. (1997). "The illusion of structure: A critique of the classical model of organization and the discretionary power of correctional officers. *Criminal Justice Review, 22*(1), 49–64.

Goffman, E. (1961). "On the characteristics of total institutions: The inmate world." *The prison: Studies in institutional organization and change*, 15–67.

Goffman, E. (1968). *Asylums*. Harmondsworth, England: Penguin.

Hammett, T. (1998). *Public Health/Corrections collaborations: Prevention and Treatment of HIV/AIDS, STDs, and TB*. Washington, DC: National Institute of Justice.

Haney, C., and Lynch, M. (1997). Regulating prisons of the future: A psychological analysis of supermax and solitary confinement. New York University Review of Law and Social Change, 23, 477–570.

Harer, M. and Steffensmeier, D. (1996). "Race and prison violence." *Criminology*, 34, 323–355.

Irwin, J. (1980). *Prisons in turmoil*. Boston: Little, Brown & Company.

Irwin, J., & Cressey, D. R. (1962). "Thieves, convicts and the inmate culture." *Social Problems*, 10(2), 142–155.

Jacobs, J. (1982). "Sentencing by prison personnel: Good time." *UCLA Law Review*, 30, 217–270.

James, D.J., and Glaze, L.E. (2006). Mental Health Problems of Prison and Jail Inmates. Washington, DC: U.S Department of Justice, Bureau of Justice Statistics.

Johnson, R. (2002). *Hard time* 3(3rd ed.). Belmont, CA: Wadsworth.

Josi, D., & Sechrest, D. (1998). *The changing career of the correctional officer: Policy implications for the 21st century*. Boston, MA: Butterworth-Heinemann.

Kreager, D.A. & Kruttschitt, C. (2018). "Inmate Society in the Era of Mass Incarceration." *Annual Review of Criminology*, 1, 261–283.

Lombardo, L. X. (1981). *Guards imprisoned: correctional officers at work*. New York: Elsevier.

Maruschak, L. (2004). *HIV in prisons, 2001*. Washington, DC: Bureau of Justice Statistics.

McCollister, K., French, M., Prendergast, M., Hall, E., and Sacks, S. (2004). "Long-term cost effectiveness of addiction treatment for criminal offenders." *Justice Quarterly*, 21, 559–679.

Skarbek, D. (2014). *The social order of the underworld: How prison gangs govern the American penal system*. New York, NY: Oxford University Press.

Pollock, J. (2004). *Prisons and prison life: Costs and consequences*. Los Angeles, CA: Roxbury Publishing Company.

Sykes, G.M. (1958). *The society of captives: A study of a maximum security prison*. Princeton, NJ: Princeton University Press.

Torrey F.E., Zdanowicz M.T., Kennard A.D. et al. (2014, April 8). *The treatment of persons with mental illness in prisons and jails: A state survey*. Arlington, VA, Treatment Advocacy Center and National Sheriff's Association. Retrieved from http://tacreports.org/ storage/documents/treatment-behind-bars/treatment-behind-bars.pdf.

N.p. "Video Visitation a Growing Trend, but Concerns Remain." *Prison Legal News*. (2014, March 14). Retrieved from https://www.prisonlegalnews.org/news/2014/mar/15/ video-visitation-a-growing-trend-but-concerns-remain/.

Wooldredge, J. D. (1994). "Inmate crime and victimization in a Southwestern correctional facility." *Journal of Criminal Justice*, 22, 367–381.

CHAPTER 5

Community Corrections

CHAPTER OUTLINE

Introduction

Probation

History and Foundations

Presentence Investigation Process and the Probation Decision

Probation Conditions

The Probation Officer Role

Probation Caseloads

Clients with Mental Health and Substance Use Disorders

Intermediate Sanctions

Intensive Supervision Probation

Home Confinement

Electronic Monitoring

Halfway Houses or Community Residential Centers

Day Reporting Centers

Boot Camps

Other Community Sanctions

Economic Sanctions

Fines

Community Service

Determining the Appropriate Sanction

Principles of Effective Classification

Intermediate Sanctions and Widening the Net

Summary

AFTER READING THIS CHAPTER, YOU SHOULD BE ABLE TO:

- Discuss the history and foundations of traditional probation
- Detail the contents of the presentence investigation report
- Summarize the factors that affect the granting of probation
- Describe probation conditions and distinguish which ones are utilized for risk and which ones are utilized for change and motivation
- Differentiate between the varying roles probation officers play in the supervision of their clients
- Define the five types of case assignment models in probation
- Distinguish between community corrections and intermediate sanctions
- Summarize the reasons why intermediate sanctions emerged and their purposes, both stated and unstated
- Identify the common types of intermediate sanctions discussed in the chapter and their effectiveness
- Reference other types of community sanctions
- Understand the elements of the principles of effective classification and their role in community corrections
- Recognize the different types of net widening and be able to provide examples of how they occur and their consequences

INTRODUCTION

Not all sentences are served in a secure facility or institution, as was covered in Chapter 4. In fact, most offenders are serving their sentence outside the prison walls. This chapter explores the more commonly recognized forms of community corrections of probation and parole as well as halfway houses, house arrest, and other fairly recent innovations in corrections outside jails and prisons. **Community corrections** are punishments convicted offenders can be sentenced to serve outside of prison or jail. They range from fines to probation to community-based correctional facilities. Traditional forms of community corrections include probation, fines, and parole. Options that lie somewhere between regular probation and prison are known as **intermediate sanctions**. Figure 5.1 below displays the number of persons under community supervision, probation, and parole from 2000–2016.

PROBATION

History and Foundations

Probation is a conditional sentence granted by the court of a convicted defendant whose behavior is controlled in the community instead of prison. In some jurisdictions, probation also goes by the term **community control**. It is considered "conditional" because the sanction assumes offenders will follow certain rules and

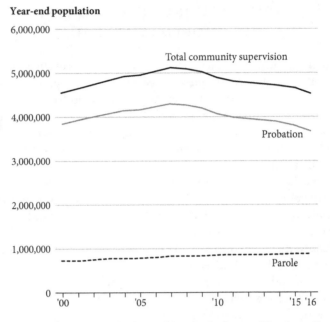

Figure 5.1 **Adults under Community Supervision, Probation, and Parole on December 31, 2000-2016.**
SOURCE: Kaeble, D. (2018). *Probation and Parole in the United States 2016*. https://www.bjs
.gov/content/pub/pdf/ppus16.pdf

not commit additional crimes, but if there is a violation, probation can be revoked, and the offender can be incarcerated. It is the most widely used form of correctional supervision in the United States. In fact, recent figures demonstrated that more than 80 percent of offenders under some form of community supervision are on probation (Kaeble, 2018).

There are several reasons why probation is in such great use. First, it costs over $20,000 less than imprisoning an offender for a year, and in some jurisdictions, probationers pay fees to cover a portion to all of their supervision thereby leading to additional savings for the courts. Second, probation has often been considered a more positive alternative to incarceration for three primary reasons: (1) Offenders avoid exposure to learning more about the criminal lifestyle, which could lead to an increase in recidivism upon release; (2) Probation sanctions allow offenders to stay employed or seek employment, remain with their family, and stay involved with children; and (3) Inmates come out of prison with a record that makes it difficult for getting a job and securing housing so in many ways, they are worse off relative to their probation counterparts. Finally, probation is considered one of the more effective sanctions with many studies showing that probationers have lower recidivism rates compared to those serving time in jail.

The practice of probation in the United States began in 1841 when a shoemaker living in Boston, Massachusetts, John Augustus, as introduced in Chapter 1, attended court and convinced the judge that he would take care of a defendant answering to criminal charges for public drunkenness and even posted his bail. Augustus thought that persons who had problems with alcohol could be rehabilitated if they were assisted outside of prison, so he brought the defendant to his home. Three weeks later, the defendant reappeared in court sober with a change in appearance and demeanor such that he could be considered a law-abiding member of society and free from court supervision. Augustus took in other persons after evaluating them for their suitability for what he would later term "probation." He felt that first-time offenders of less serious crimes should be given a second chance and could be treated successfully outside of prison if they had help finding housing and employment.

By the time of his death in 1858, Augustus had posted bail and served as a volunteer probation officer for 1,946 men and women and only 10 failed to complete their probation sentence. In addition to the practice of probation, the presentence investigation, intake, and supervision processes where detailed evaluations and notes were kept on each offender before imposing and during the sentence of probation are also attributed to John Augustus. No wonder he is considered the "Father of Probation."

Presentence Investigation Process and the Probation Decision

We still use many of Augustus's processes when determining if someone should be considered eligible for probation. One of the first steps after a defendant is found or pleads guilty is for a probation officer (PO) or similar representative of the court to complete the **presentence investigation report (PSI)**. (See Box 5.1 for a sample of a PSI.) In this document, the PO prepares a written report of what is learned after investigating and consulting various sources about the offender's criminal history, known associates, physical and mental health status, family situation, employment and educational background, circumstances surrounding the current offense, risk to the community, and other factors. In most jurisdictions, victims can also share information about how the offense affected them such as any physical, emotional, or financial damage they experienced. This is known as a **victim impact statement**. This information guides the PO when making a sentence recommendation for the judge to consider after reviewing the PSI. The PSI also helps inform the type of supervision and programming needs an offender should have whether sentenced to prison, probation, or other sanction. The judge reads the PSI and, typically, studies show that judges go along with the PO's sentencing recommendation 80–90 percent of the time. Other factors that affect the granting of probation are

- the geographic area where the court is situated due to varying political and social attitudes in rural and urban jurisdiction, crowded court calendars, and jail/prison crowding problems;
- judge's feelings toward the particular offender or the offense;
- age and rehabilitation potential of the defendant;
- defendant's criminal record, including indications of professional criminality, organized crime, and crimes of violence;

═══ **Box 5.1** ═══

Sample Presentence Investigation Report

COUNTY PROBATION DEPARTMENT
223 COUNTY BUILDING
YOUR TOWN, YOUR STATE 43403

PEOPLE OF THE STATE OF _____   )
)
)
v.   )   PRESENTENCE
)   REPORT
)
NAME:_____   )   CASE NO.
_____   )

PERSONAL/IDENTIFYING INFORMATION

NAME: ALIASES:

ADDRESS:

AGE: DATE OF BIRTH: PLACE OF BIRTH:

HEIGHT: WEIGHT: EYE COLOR:

HAIR: MARITAL STATUS: DEPENDANTS:

COURT HISTORY OF CASE

DATE OF OFFENSE: TOTAL DAYS IN JAIL:

OFFENSE/CHARGES: These are the formal charges to which the defendant has to answer in court whereby a verdict of guilty or not guilty would result either via plea or trial.

CIRCUMSTANCES OF THE OFFENSE:
This is the official version of the offense by police and prosecutor.

STATEMENT OF DEFENDANT:
This is where the PO would summarize any discrepancies between what the defendant states about the offense and how it differs from the official version.

STATEMENT OF VICTIM:
Physical, emotional, and/or financial impacts crime had on victim or if victims were murdered, can use family members' or close friends' versions are discussed. Victims also offer a recommendation as to what they believe is an appropriate sentence for the defendant in this section.

MENTAL OR EMOTIONAL PROBLEMS:
Items to make note of would be mental breakdowns, abnormal ways of relating, periods of treatment/hospitalization, personal problems, communication skills.

ARREST HISTORY

JUVENILE RECORD:

ADULT RECORD:

DATE OF OFFENSE: PLACE OF OFFENSE:

CHARGE: DISPOSITION:

FAMILY HISTORY

FATHER: Name   MOTHER: Name

ADDRESS: ADDRESS:

OCCUPATION: OCCUPATION:

NARRATIVE:
Note any problems related to family history (e.g., abuse, attitude of parents, early misbehavior, main influences on defendant, siblings and birth order, family climate, birthplace). Other areas to note here are: school adjustment, truancy, or other misbehavior in school, highest grade completed.

SUBSTANCE ABUSE HISTORY:
Use of alcohol and drugs, type, duration, intensity, when last time used, substance defendant prefers, and substance(s) that seems to create the most problems for the defendant.

EMPLOYMENT HISTORY:
Items to detail include: history of employment from present position back to first work experience, reasons for leaving job, patterns and trends of employment, periods of unemployment, work skills and training participation, work attitudes and aspirations, relationship to criminal behavior.

RECOMMENDATION
This section summarizes the most significant factors from what the PO gathered and noted above from the investigation, including factors contributing to criminality and capacities and strengths from personal history. A recommendation of the sanction for this defendant is presented that is based on the preceding summary. If probation is recommended, ideas for residence, employment, type of supervision required, treatment, training, education, or other options as appropriate are sometimes suggested. If confinement is recommended, special problems and needs of offender while in custody, if any, could be noted. Alternative sentencing options may also be offered in this section.

- defendant's relationship with his/her family;
- evidence of any deviant behavior such as drug abuse or sex offense;
- the attitude of the community toward the particular offense and the particular offender;
- whether the defendant shows remorse;

- whether probation was promised to the defendant to induce him/her to plead guilty;
- whether placing the defendant on probation will enable the defendant to provide the victim with restitution;
- whether granting probation will facilitate support and care for his/her family.

Critical Thinking Exercise

What else do you think should be reported when completing a PSI? How important do you think a victim's impact statement should be in determining the sentencing recommendation?

Probation Conditions

Those who are placed on probation usually have conditions attached to their sentence, which are designed to control the individual's current behavior and modify it in the future. There are many different types of conditions and when possible, conditions are tailored to the offender. Examples include

1. no association permitted with known criminals,
2. no possession of weapons allowed,
3. no use of alcohol or drugs,
4. no leaving the jurisdiction,
5. mandatory drug/alcohol testing or treatment,
6. education or employment requirements,
7. no possession of weapons allowed,
8. community service,
9. no association permitted with known criminals,
10. payment of fines,
11. restitution to the victim.

Conditions one through four are utilized for control such that risk to the community while the offender is under supervision is minimized. The remaining conditions seek change and are intended to motivate conforming behavior once the probation sentence has ended. If probationers violate a condition, they can have their probation revoked. This violation is termed a **technical violation**. If probationers commit a crime while on probation, this is termed a **new crime violation**. Both types of violations can lead to the probation sentence being transformed into a sentence of confinement, which will be determined by the court during a **revocation hearing**. Revocation hearings are held where the offender's probation officer presents all relevant evidence to a magistrate or judge (depending on the jurisdiction) who then decides to withdraw the probation sentence or allow the probationer to remain on probation. If the former occurs, the judge then decides whether to resentence the individual by sending him/her to prison or to impose additional conditions on him/her. Similar revocation hearings are followed if the probationer commits a crime while under the court's supervision.

Web Activity

Go to https://www.uscourts.gov/services-forms/substance-abuse-treatment-testing-abstinence-probation-supervised-release-conditions. What types of conditions do the United State Courts impose on federal probationers? What considerations and interventions are implemented? Do you think these are reasonable? Can they be effective?

Web Activity

Search the web for a famous offender and complete the PSI form above. A good place to start is https://www.crimemuseum.org/. Select a person and read about him/her. Complete what you can of the PSI from the information on the site, and then start a larger web search for additional information.

The Probation Officer Role

In general, probation involves some control and surveillance whereby the probation officer (PO) needs to keep track of the offenders', often termed "clients," whereabouts. Typically, this entails the clients making visits to the probation office. Services delivered by the PO to the client are numerous. The PO helps the offender to adjust and to become reintegrated into a law-abiding life in terms of employment, family, and the use of free time. POs also will provide counseling in the form of brokering where the client is referred to appropriate community services and resources. Job assistance and placement into educational programs also fall under the duties of the PO. Thus, at any given time, POs carry out multiple work roles as they supervise probationers. Sometimes, one role takes precedent over another depending on the risks and needs of the probationers and their placement in the community. Some of these roles include

1. Carrying out the role of *Detector* is when the PO determines by observation when probation clients or the community is at risk of harm.
2. *Broker* or "Referral" role involves telling clients about services and programs in the community that could benefit them.

3. Being an *Advocate* is when POs remove barriers that may be in the way of their clients who are accessing the benefits and resources they need to be successful on probation.

4. The PO *Evaluator* role consists of gathering information about their clients' personal or community challenges, exploring options available for their clients, and making decisions that are the most appropriate given what the PO has learned.

5. The *Mobilizer* role involves preventing problems before they occur by making sure the right resources are made accessible for their clients or creating structure for their clients to ensure compliance with probation conditions occurs.

6. Taking on the role of the *Enabler* is when the PO provides support to their clients as they assist them with making changes in the behavior patterns, habits, and perceptions their clients may have that are blocking their path to a law-abiding life.

7. POs also take on the role of *Information Manager* as they collect, classify, and analyze data that is generated within the community their probationers reside. For example, if a service provider's new program only takes clients who are parents, the POs must not refer clients who do not have children to that provider.

8. The *Mediator* role is when the PO takes the Broker role a step further by acting as a go-between working with their clients and resource systems that are available for them.

9. POs also teach their clients how to develop skills by conveying information and knowledge to them through various mechanisms, such as one-on-one talks or sharing brochures about programs in the community. This is the *Educator* role.

10. The *Community Planner* role is an important one for the probation department, the POs, and the clients. In this role, POs participate in and assist neighborhood, community, or government planning agencies in the development of programs that are matched with clients' needs.

11. The *Enforcer* role is when the POs must use the authority of their office to start the revocation process if clients are not following the conditions set forth by the court or have violated a law.

What this lengthy list of roles demonstrates well is that POs must balance their **dual role** of authority figure and counselor while protecting the community and informing the court of any deviation from rules and regulations their clients might incur. This dual role of serving the interests of the community and their clients can often result in different primary emphases in supervision. Some POs might use constant threats of revocation to obtain compliance from their clients. Other POs focus on casework and counseling to manage probationers. Recent research has found that POs often combine both styles in their positions (Miller 2015), which makes sense given the trend toward a less punitive focus to more treatment-based policies and practices in the criminal justice system.

Web Activity

A program that is often used with probationers, as well as other offender populations, is Thinking for a Change. For a great introduction to this cognitive skill–based
treatment program, go to https://vimeo.com/125686180 and begin at time marker
8:23. Find out if your probation department uses Thinking for a Change.

Web Activity

Explore what life on the job is like for a probation officer by watching this video:
https://www.youtube.com/watch?v=LPT8MFjgo2s. What surprised you about Officer Peebody's responses to the questions he was asked? Would you consider
seeking a position as a PO?

Probation Caseloads

POs are given what is called a **caseload** of clients to manage. Determining the ideal
number of clients per PO is difficult given the varied nature of the communities
and clients being served. There are five types of case assignment models that have
commonly been followed. The first one is the **conventional model** in which clients
are randomly assigned to available POs in the department. The **numbers game
model** involves balancing the number of clients for each PO such that each PO has
about the same number under supervision. Another model is the **conventional
model with geographic considerations**, which was more popular when POs made
more frequent client house visits. This model considers whether clients live in
urban, suburban, or rural areas since visiting too many clients in a rural area would
be challenging given the driving distance between probationers. As such, a PO with
many clients in a rural area would have a smaller number in his/her caseload. For
the general population of probationers who are considered low risk for violating
their conditions or committing a new crime, they would typically come to the probation department to visit with their PO instead of the PO going to visit them.

The fourth type is the **specialized caseloads model**, which takes into consideration the expertise of the PO in handling clients who have certain characteristics. For example, clients with a history of drug abuse and/or mental illness might
be assigned with POs in the department who have the most experience with these
cases. Finally, the **model system**, also known as the "workload" model, has been
adopted by a sizeable number of departments across the country (American Probation and Parole Association 2018). This system classifies clients based on how
many hours per month a PO will need to spend on the client related to their risks
and needs to determine the total caseload size. Thus, higher-risk cases required
four hours per month so a PO would have 30 clients in the caseload; lower risk
client have lower priority so they might only require one hour per month and POs
could have a total caseload of 120 clients.

POs often have large caseloads due to a shortage in staffing and resources. It is not uncommon for POs to have upwards of 200 clients or more. While there are varying positions on what is the ideal caseload, some professionals and scholars state that it should be thirty-five to forty felony offenders per PO in order to achieve effective surveillance and supervision—an ideal that even caseloads that require more intensive supervision find difficult to achieve. Research from the American Probation and Parole Association (2006) recommended that cases that require intensive supervision, which will be discussed later in this chapter, should have a client-to-staff ratio of 20 to 1; for caseloads of moderate to high risk clients, that ratio should be 50 to 1; and the client to staff ratio for low risk offenders should be 200 to 1.

So, does caseload size matter? Yes, it does in that smaller caseloads mean reduced recidivism. Findings from a multisite study showed that there are benefits to smaller caseloads (Jalbert et al. 2011). When POs have fewer clients to manage, they can make more-frequent contacts. During those contacts, POs can spend more time with their clients. Smaller caseloads also mean that POs can utilized effective correctional interventions that are based on evidence-based practices, thereby leading to further reductions in repeat offending.

Clients with Mental Health and Substance Use Disorders

Manageable caseloads are especially salient for probationers dependent on drugs and alcohol and/or having mental health disorders. Probationers (and/or parolees) are four to nine times more likely to have substance use disorders (SUDs) compared to individuals in the general population (Fearn et al. 2016). Clients with mental illnesses have higher probabilities of probation revocation and recidivism and have difficulty following their probation conditions because they do not understand the rules (Van Deinse et al. 2018). In addition, probationers with both substance use *and* mental health disorders are significantly more likely to be at risk for violent behavior (Balyakina et al. 2014; Peters, Wexler, and Lurigio 2015). Given the potential for such adverse outcomes, programs are being used in some counties and at the federal level to address SUDs and mental health disorders. One program where supervision similar to probation is used is **mental health court**. For a thorough look at the mental health court model and to hear from judges and participants in the program, check out the Web Activity box below.

Web Activity

Mental health courts (MHCs) were developed in 1997 in several states. Today, there are around 300 of these specialty courts that researchers have found to be promising in reducing recidivism and getting clients into necessary treatment. To learn more, go to https://www.youtube.com/watch?v=kkTJ208Jh7w. The Council of State Governments Justice Center created this video to explain the MHC model and its impact. Is there an MHC in your area? When did it start? Can you find reports on how many people are diverted there each year? Is that number increasing or decreasing?

The primary aim of these programs is to reduce the likelihood of recidivism and increase clients' abilities to meet the conditions of their probation and be held accountable for their behaviors. Many programs utilizing substance abuse treatment programs observe reductions in recidivism for probationers in the treatment program compared to control group subjects (Fearn et al. 2016; Hollis, Jennings, and Hankhouse 2019). In addition, smaller caseloads can also provide increased opportunities for POs to provide the support needed for probationers to find and maintain employment (Barnes-Proby et al. 2018). One innovative probation program in Sacramento County, California, linked prospective employers with the probation department to facilitate job opportunities and training for probationers. To learn more about the Career Training Partnership program and outcomes, go to the link in the Web Activity box.

Web Activity

The Career Training Partnership (CTP) program in Sacramento County, California, focused on assisting probationers learn about working in the construction industry and then get connected with the local labor union to seek jobs in the trade. To learn more about this program, why it was started, and its outcomes, go to https://www.rand.org/content/dam/rand/pubs/research_reports/RR2100 /RR2179/RAND_RR2179.pdf. What other industries do you think could be explored to set up similar programs in your county probation office? What elements of the CTP would you keep? Change?

INTERMEDIATE SANCTIONS

Since it began, traditional probation has been one of the most popular sentences for many offenders, especially those who are convicted of misdemeanors and less serious, nonviolent felonies (e.g., some drugs crimes). However, since some offenders require more than probation, but their current offense(s) and criminal history are not severe enough to impose imprisonment, something in between the two sanctions is needed—enter intermediate sanctions. It is important to note that intermediate sanctions do not necessarily imply community corrections. The best way to view intermediate sanctions is on the punishment ladder, as shown below. Intermediate sanctions allow judges to fit the punishment to the crime without resorting to a prison sentence, yet still have a punitive edge since intermediate sanctions are increasingly severe as we head up the punishment ladder. In addition, as we go up the ladder, freedom and autonomy decrease. Further, so does contact with society.

Punishment Ladder

- Death penalty
- Prison/Jail
- Boot camps

- Split sentences
- Community residential centers/Halfway houses
- Electronic monitoring
- House arrest
- Intensive probation
- Restitution
- Traditional probation
- Community service
- Fines

Reasons for the emergence and adoption of intermediate sanctions in the early to mid-1980s were threefold. The most important reason was due to increasing jail and prison populations. States were (and continue) facing high numbers of offenders receiving sentences of incarcerations with few available beds in their facilities. As a result, alternatives were needed that would ameliorate the crowded institutions but would still be considered punishment. Intermediate sanctions seem to fit the bill. Second, and related to the first reason, was the rising costs of institutional corrections. Today, depending on security classification and state, expenditures range anywhere from $25,000 to $60,000 a year to house just one inmate in prison. Community corrections options cut those numbers by at least half, more likely by two-thirds. Finally, a call for more humane and effective methods of dealing with offenders was made in the 1960s. Corrections in the community as a step up from traditional probation appeared to be a viable option to incarceration.

As with any alternative to customary ways, proponents had to convince policy makers and the public that intermediate sanctions can be just as effective and punitive as correctional facilities but more penalizing than regular probation. These advocates stated four primary purposes to intermediate sanctions:

1. Intermediate sanctions will save taxpayers money by providing cost-effective alternatives to incarceration for prison and jail-bound offenders.
2. Intermediate sanctions can deter offenders (specifically) and the public (generally) from crime.
3. Intermediate sanctions can protect the community by exerting more control (compared to traditional probation) over offender behavior.
4. Intermediate sanctions show promise in rehabilitating offenders as they rely upon mandatory treatment requirements, which are then reinforced by mandatory substance abuse testing and the swift revocation of violators.

Indeed, intermediate sanctions were sold to the public and officials with much enthusiasm, particularly when we look back and recognize that there were other purposes of intermediate sanctions that likely drew more support for reliance upon and development of these alternative sanctions. First, intermediate sanctions created an "appearance" of correctional reform. Rehabilitation efforts within the prison setting were deemed ineffective by the 1970s so people were looking for other options, particularly alternatives that did not carry the price tag that institutional corrections did. Intermediate sanctions were sold as a way to punish yet still offer treatment—the best of both worlds. This led to the second unstated purpose—intermediate sanctions helped to institute a mechanism for reclaiming limited correctional resources for probation and parole. Probation was often seen as too lenient to offer any real hope of offender reform or punishment. Parole, or supervised release after spending time in prison, which will be covered in Chapter 6, was also viewed as being too soft on criminals. In this vein, the sentiment was that if we are going to send offenders to prison, then they should stay there until they serve their entire sentence. Parole provides inmates an early release valve, which to some members of the public and policymakers is of questionable utility and could be downright dangerous if the wrong (read: persons who go on to commit an even more serious crime after release) inmates are paroled. Finally, and perhaps driven by the first two unstated purposes, intermediate sanctions could provide probation administrators and legislators with an effective response to the more punitive orientation of the public.

Over the years, there have been several different kinds of intermediate sanctions. The ones most commonly found in many jurisdictions include intensive supervision probation, home confinement, electronic monitoring, halfway houses (also known as community residential centers), community-based correctional facilities, day reporting centers, and boot camps. One statement on intermediate sanctions that has been substantiated in most studies on their effectiveness is: They may not work any better than traditional forms of punishment, but they certainly are not any worse—and they are cheaper.

Intensive Supervision Probation

Intensive supervision probations (ISPs) were created in the 1970s and 1980s by probation departments that were under the provisions of state community corrections acts. The primary goals of these acts were to divert prison-bound offenders into correctional services in the community. ISPs generally select offenders who would be considered higher risk compared to those individuals assigned to traditional probation. ISPs are often considered as "probation plus," in that they are similar to regular probation but with added security and controls. ISPs rely on a great degree of client contact by the probation officer (PO) and the POs' roles will be numerous such that many we discussed earlier in this chapter will be carried out on a regular basis. Many systems also use specific conditions to control clients' behaviors. For example, mandatory curfew, employment, drug testing, and community service are often employed. These aspects are necessary since the main objectives of ISPs are to protect the community while providing supervision, surveillance, and services.

There are seven elements of ISPs. First, in order to accomplish the above-noted objectives, POs' caseloads must be small. In traditional probation, it is not uncommon for some POs to handle upwards of 150 clients whereas in ISPs, ideally POs should handle between 25 and 50 offenders. These reduced caseloads are necessary as there are more frequent contacts between the PO and his/her clients; this is the second element. Third, there are periodic performance reviews whereby the

PO assesses the progress of his/her clients in meeting the conditions of their sentence such as finding and maintaining employment, showing up at scheduled meetings with the PO, and participating in treatment-oriented programming. Fourth, there are more restrictions placed on offenders and more use of curfew and house arrest for those serving their sentence in an ISP compared to regular probationers. Fifth, drug and alcohol testing is much more frequent for ISP clients. Sixth, POs often work in teams to ensure that the goals of increased supervision, surveillance, and services are being met. Finally, there is more-frequent use of revocation, which is the process whereby clients who violate a condition of their sentence (e.g., break curfew, use drugs) or commit a new crime are brought before a judge to determine whether he or she should remain on ISP or should be incarcerated for the remainder of the sentence.

Early ISPs, while still focused on supervision and surveillance, were more committed to rehabilitation purposes. Current programs are much more control-oriented, similar to the idea of prison without walls (i.e., great restrictions on movement within the community). ISPs of the past also were not as retributive as they are today. Many clients sanctioned to ISPs today find themselves paying restitution and even serving short stints in jail. Further, today's ISPs often require offenders to pay fees for the services of the program.

Evaluation studies demonstrate that ISPs have higher failure rates than regular probation. However, most of the failures are due to the higher number of technical violations (i.e., violating the conditions of the sentence but not committing a new crime) because ISPs clients are under intense surveillance so even the smallest transgression is more likely to be noticed. ISPs, however, have the support of some correctional administrators, judges, and even prosecutors since there is a heavy reliance on behavioral control via enhanced supervision. ISPs have also given traditional probation more credibility as a viable punishment since POs have demonstrated through ISP programs that they can enforce strict rules, get offenders to maintain employment, and support treatment. In fact, ISPs that have a treatment component increase the probability that the sanction will be more successful at reducing recidivism for some clients.

Home Confinement

The sanction of **home confinement** (HC) began in 1971 as an alternative to housing juveniles in detention facilities. It was believed at this time that the use of HC could serve the goals of (1) rehabilitation and reintegration of offenders into the community; (2) humanitarian purposes such as keeping the family intact; (3) preventing offenders from being subjected to the destructive environment of incarceration; and (4) cost-reductions in that confining offenders to their homes would be cheaper than placing them in correctional facilities.

By the mid-1980s, the main reason to sentence offenders to HC was the need to control overcrowding jail and prison populations. During this period, the states of Florida, Oklahoma, and Michigan were the first of what would soon become tens of thousands of HC programs operating in the United States. This rapid implementation of HC was believed to be driven by five factors. First, states would save costs associated with sentencing offenders to prisons. Second, offenders could remain safe from the abuses often experienced in institutions. Third, the individual needs of offenders could be met with community resources. Fourth, as noted above, offenders could keep their ties with their family and remain employed within the confines of the community. Fifth, the labeling effects related to traditional incapacitation could be avoided because offenders would remain in their own homes in their respective communities.

The HC sanction can range in severity from requiring offenders to remain in their own homes at all times, which would be the strictest exercise of HC, to an evening curfew, which would be the least restrictive form. The varying degrees to which the use of HC is implemented, in terms of constraining the freedom of offenders also varies in intrusiveness. For example, requiring evening curfews is less intrusive on offenders' daily lives, whereas requiring them to remain in their homes at all times with only limited exceptions for specific activities is the most intrusive.

HC, though similar to ISPs, differs in several ways. First, HC was developed to curb prison crowding and was designed to serve those offenders who would have been sent to prison had HC been unavailable. Second, the sentence of HC is usually imposed by the court rather than by administrators of probation. Third, HC programs are supposed to be more restrictive and punitive than ISPs (hence the HC placement on a higher rung of the punishment ladder). Finally, the use of electronic monitoring devices, which we will explore next, has increased for the HC offender population. This last difference between HC and ISP is due to the need to increase the accountability of offenders within the community.

There are a number of advantages HC programs. Certainly advantageous is HC is typically less expensive than incarceration. The savings in costs come from requiring offenders to pay for their confinement, and many programs require offenders to be employed in order to be eligible for a HC sentence. States also save money by abating the need to build more prisons and housing offenders in correctional facilities. Another major plus of HC is that of its flexibility. It can be implemented in a variety of ways to meet different risks and needs of offenders. As was noted earlier, some HC offenders will only be required to meet an evening curfew. For those who require more stringent monitoring, they can be sentenced to HC twenty-four hours a day. Home confinement can also work well with work release programs and can be a gateway sanction for offenders being released from prison as a reintegration method.

Unfortunately, while HC programs may be cost-effective, the disadvantage of **net widening**, or sentencing offenders to an intermediate sanction who normally would not have been sent to prison anyway, arguably overshadows the benefits. Recall that HCs, like most of the intermediate sanctions, were designed to prevent new jail and prison admissions. Some studies, however, have observed that HCs can actually increase institutional admissions, primarily since HC, like ISPs, have stricter conditions and requirements that are more readily noticed because HC offenders are supervised more closely. In addition, judges have been known to place offenders in institutions whenever there is a bed available even when their jurisdiction has HC options. In these places, HC is not seen as being as attractive as a form of punishment compared to prison even when a convicted offender would be a good risk for HC. This weakness of home confinement needs to be overcome before HC can truly meet its diversionary goal. In addition to changing judges' perceptions of seeing secure correctional facilities as the only places of viable confinement, proponents of HCs would be wise to convince the judiciary that the home can also be confining and restrictive. Probation departments should also recommend the sanction of HC for the appropriate clients more often in order to realize the positive impact it can have on offenders.

Web Activity

Go to https://www.flmp.uscourts.gov/home-confinement and https://www.okep.uscourts.gov/standard-conditions-probation-and-supervised-release. Compare and contrast the conditions for those offenders under home confinement to those on standard probation. Do you think one set of conditions is more onerous than the others? Why or why not?

Electronic Monitoring

Electronic monitoring (EM) is not really a sanction type per se, but rather an addition to home confinement; similar to how ISPs are probation plus, coupling HCs with EM is like HC-plus. Electronic monitoring systems were designed to allow continuous surveillance of offenders through computer signals transmitted from offenders' homes to the control station. Now, not all HC programs employ EM. The technology is merely a means of monitoring the client's adherence to the terms of the HC sentence. Think of the EM–HM relationship like this: HC can be employed without EM, but EM cannot be without HC. In general, there are two types of EM devices: (1) passive monitor systems that respond only to inquiries, such as when an offender is called from the probation office and is required to place the EM device on a piece of receiving equipment such as a phone or computer; and (2) active devices that transmit continuous signals to a receiver worn by the offender. Any break in the signal indicates that the offender is not where he or she is supposed to be—or equipment failure; it is infrequently the latter. Global positioning systems have also emerged on the EM scene. Early use of GPS monitoring equipment was utilized with paroled sex offenders rather than as part of the original sentence. Today, smartphones are beginning to play a large role in monitoring offenders serving their sentence in the community.

Characteristically, sanctions that employ EM are typically short term, ranging from a few weeks to six months. Offenders often must pay for their supervision and equipment costs. The advantages and disadvantages are nearly duplicates of the ones aforementioned for HC. The major red flag with EM is that using technology to monitor the whereabouts of offenders will only enhance our ability to detect failures such that more violations will be observed. More violations mean more revocation hearings, and in turn, this often means that offenders are sent to a secure facility to serve the rest of their sentence. When this happens, the goals of cost savings and reductions in crowded institutions are not met.

The reliability of EM devices has come into question over the years. Some offenders have become quite savvy in figuring out how to remove the monitors. Some offenders have even been arrested while committing a crime even though the monitoring system indicated that they were at home. Further, certain types of crimes, such as child abuse, drug sales, and assaults, can still be committed under both HC and HC with EM. Thus, it becomes imperative that inappropriate types of offenders are not sentenced to these sanctions. However, as more and more jurisdictions are faced with tightening budgets and technological advances become more established (read: cost effective, better surveillance techniques, and fewer problems with equipment), the use of EM is likely to increase.

Web Activity

Go online and search for electronic monitoring equipment. Compare and contrast three devices. How much do they cost? Which one would you choose if you were in charge of a probation department? Why?

Halfway Houses or Community Residential Centers

Halfway houses (HHs) or **community residential centers** (CRCs) as they are often referred to today are a more restraining type of intermediate sanction. HHs are different from other sanctions in that they serve as a residential facility for offenders who are being monitored or supervised on some form of early release. For example, probationers might serve some portion of their sentence in a HH. Parolees can be assigned to HHs after release from prison. In general, the length of stay for offenders ranges from eight to sixteen weeks with an average term of ninety days. While residing in the HH, offenders are expected to follow restrictive rules but are still given the opportunity to work outside the home or go to educational, vocational, and/or treatment programs. Residents are required to check in and out as they arrive and leave the HH. Drug testing, counseling, household chores, and recreational activities can be a part of the HH program.

There are a few variations that deserve mentioning when it comes to detailing HHs. First, some programs are operated by private corporations, private but nonprofit organizations, and state or local governments. Second, the kinds of facilities that are used differ. Some HHs function out of large houses, which is the typical picture people get when HHs are mentioned. Other HH programs might be managed in apartment complexes or renovated hotels. Research has demonstrated that the particular form of facility does not seem to be related to offender success.

The significant factor that has been found to be relevant to the effectiveness of HH programs is that the structures should be as "homelike" as possible. Finally, HHs are often categorized as HH-out or HH-in programs. HH-outs serve to gradually integrate residents back into society after serving time in prison. Offenders residing in HH-ins are sent there in lieu of going to a correctional institution with diversion being the primary aim.

Similar to HH-in, the state of Ohio has been innovative in its use of what are called **community-based correctional facilities** (CBCFs). These are short-term residential facilities where there is a focus on rehabilitation and reintegration after release for individuals convicted of nonviolent felonies. Offenders must first be screened by staff at the CBCF to determine if they would be an appropriate candidate for the programs and services offered there. If the criteria are met, the CBCF staff notifies the sentencing judge who then makes the final decision whether to sanction the offender to the CBCF. Once admitted, CBCF offenders, who are now called residents, spend about six months engaging in cognitive behavioral therapy, social and coping skill development, community service, work placements, and taking classes to complete their high school diploma equivalency (i.e., the GED). CBCFs have generally found to be effective alternatives to incarceration.

Day Reporting Centers

Day reporting centers (DRCs) were developed in England in the 1970s but came on the American scene in Massachusetts in 1986. DRCs are often used in conjunction with probation, parole, and pretrial release as a mechanism of surveillance and control. Offenders live at home and report to the DRC each day. While there, they fill out a twenty-four-hour itinerary for what they will be involved in the following day. Offenders denote where they will be at all times and how they will get from place to place. Drug and alcohol testing is also a part of the DRC program. Proponents of DRCs argue that these programs can meet nearly all the goals of corrections, even rehabilitation, as many probationers and parolees are already participating in treatment activities. One recent study demonstrated promise in the effectiveness of DRCs in reducing recidivism by finding that in one DRC approximately 20 percent of participants were incarcerated one year after program completion (Williams and Turnage 2001).

Boot Camps

The renowned boot camp became quite popular in the 1980s for young offenders. The boot camp sanction was iconic in the "get tough" political climate. **Boot camps** also go by the name **shock incarceration**. In brief, boot camps are typically housed in a unit of a larger medium- or maximum-security prison. Mostly young, nonviolent offenders who have not served time in prison on a previous felony conviction are eligible for boot camp. Some boot camps, however, do accept older offenders and/or those who are not first timers. Juvenile boot camps have also been popular.

In terms of selection processes, some offenders are selected by judges to participate, some are selected by the state Department of Corrections, some volunteer, or some are chosen by parole commissions. The content of each boot camp program differs greatly in terms of the number of hours devoted to physical training, work, education, and counseling.

But do boot camps work?

1. Do they reduce crowding?
    a. They can if they shorten the time period offenders are in prison.
    b. They can if they reduce recidivism for new convictions or violations of conditions.
2. Are they cost-effective?
    a. They can be less costly compared to imprisonment if they shorten the duration of confinement for persons who would have otherwise gone to prison.
3. Do they change the offender?
    a. No, strong evidence is lacking in this regard.
    b. Few research studies report lower recidivism rates among boot-camp participants and prison inmates.
4. Can boot camps be considered constructive punishment?
    a. They can if programs involve treatments known to be effective.
    b. Not if they continue to merely provide strict discipline and military regimentation as their modus operandi.
5. What is the impact of boot camps on staff?
    a. There are higher staff turnover rates in boot camps than in prisons.
    b. Staff burnout rates are higher for boot camps.
    c. Boot camps are high-stress environments for all involved.
6. What are the legal ramifications?
    a. There is potential (documented) for injury for staff and inmates, which puts states at risk for lawsuits.
    b. There are issues related to equality of eligibility in terms of who gets an opportunity to shorten their prison term through boot-camp participation.

A number of jurisdictions across the country have closed their boot-camp programs due to numerous studies demonstrating the above-noted issues and problems. Despite the negative observations, however, boot camps will probably remain in some shape or form for years to come due to their presumed public appeal and familiarity.

Critical Thinking Exercise

Watch *Shock Incarceration New York* by going to https://www.youtube.com /watch?v=wExF5aAqcKs. Do you think some states made the right decision to close their boot-camp programs? Defend.

OTHER COMMUNITY SANCTIONS

The three other types of community sanctions that are covered in this section are often added to probation, prison, and intermediate sanction sentences. In fact, fines are the most common noncustodial punishment in the United States, followed by fees and assessments, and can be the only sanction convicted defendants receive from the judge depending on seriousness of the crime. In many ways, community corrections are flexible options for POs to consider when making recommendations to the judge and then for the judge to impose when making the sentencing determination.

Economic Sanctions

Under the heading of **economic sanctions**, a convicted offender's punishment might include probation *and* an economic penalty, of which there are three major categories. First, there are **service fees**. These are fees for the use of a public defender, for costs associated with preparing the presentence investigation report, and for drug testing or evaluations for drug/alcohol abuse. The second category includes **special assessments**, which are monies that may be levied to support a number of general funds such as Crime Stoppers, criminal justice planning fees, and victim compensation. This type of economic sanction does not necessarily relate to the offenders' crime(s). The **broad category** is the third sort of economic sanction. It includes court costs and restitution.

Fines

While it may seem as if fines should fall under economic sanctions, fines are actually under separate consideration. **Fines** are one of the oldest and most widely used punishments in the American criminal justice system. There are generally two types of fines: fixed-sum fines and day fines. The former is set by law according to the seriousness of the crime committed; this is the traditional kind of fine with which most people are familiar. The day fine is a European development and it operates as follows: The court sentences the offender to a certain number of day-fine units according to the gravity of the offense, but without regard to offender's means (i.e., how much money they earn). Then, the value of each unit is set based on a proportion of the offender's daily income. Thus, the fine as punishment will place an equivalent financial burden on both poor and wealthier offenders who are convicted of similar offenses. To illustrate, a person earning $50,000 a year with a day fine of ten units would pay $5000 whereas a person making $5,000 a year sentenced to the same number of units would pay $500.

Community Service

Some experts once hailed **community service** as the fastest growing industry in the United States. While still a popular sanction for minor offenses, community service as the lone punishment is not all that common. Oftentimes, convicted offenders will be sentenced to community service along with probation and/or a fine. Essentially, when offenders are ordered to community service, they are required to complete a specified number of work or service hours without pay for a nonprofit organization or tax-supported agency. Libraries, parks, highway clean-ups, homeless shelters, and animal shelters are examples of places where offenders fulfill the terms of this sanction.

DETERMINING THE APPROPRIATE SANCTION

As has been the focus of this chapter, alternatives to incarceration are options, but deciding which offenders would not be at high risk to reoffend if not incarcerated and who would be better served in the community can be a complicated task. During the presentence investigation stage, defendants are usually assessed to determine risk and needs, which are then used to help POs make recommendations on sentencing options to the judge. The key to classifying and placing offenders appropriately is to target the right offenders (i.e., the risk principle) whose criminogenic needs (i.e., the needs principle) are amenable to the sanctioning and treatment options available (i.e., the responsivity principle). Many instruments are in use across the country to assess these elements and those that are most successful follow the "principles of effective classification."

Principles of Effective Classification

As originally developed by Andrews and Bonta (1994), there are three principles of effective classification: (1) risk, (2) need, and (3) responsivity. The **risk principle** states that we should only target offenders who are medium-high to high risk in terms of their propensity to reoffend. Too often, individuals of lower risk are placed in institutions and programs with more-serious offenders. Low-risk, often situational (i.e., first crime committed is likely the last) offenders in these settings will be influenced by the higher-risk individuals in terms of the justifications and rationalizations, "tools and tricks of the trade," so to speak, for behaving in antisocial, criminal manners. In turn, this exposure can increase the chances that the low-risk offenders will engage in future crimes since they could be influenced by their more "experienced" counterparts. In order to reduce the chances of these negative influences on those who are, and will likely be law-abiding, a one-size-fits-all approach is not advised. Lower-risk offenders may be better candidates for traditional probation or other available intermediate sanctions such that we reserve prison sentences for those most likely to recidivate (i.e., those who are high risk).

The **need principle** focuses on two types of needs. One is *general needs.* Think of these as more like deficiencies in conduct or life, such as lack of employment or educational skills, substance abuse problems, and relationship issues. The second category is the **criminogenic needs**, which include antisocial attitudes, antisocial friends, substance abuse, lack of empathy, and impulsive behavior. We will surely see greater failure rates if we do not address the factors that have been shown time and time again to lead to offending. Successful programs will target the individual needs of each offender relative to those variables that influenced their law-violating behaviors. Community corrections sanctions are often better at addressing criminogenic and general needs because there are usually more programs and services available in free society than is the case in prison. In addition, being supervised in the community and accessing services avoids the difficulties of having to readjust successfully to society after release from prison.

Many offenders are assessed for risk and needs, but few are assessed relative to how responsive, or amenable, they will be to any given treatment or programmatic approach, or to correctional placement. In other words, the **responsivity principle** tells us that we should determine how amenable or open a person will be to a specific program or practice before we subject him or her to it. Aspects to consider when addressing responsivity are a person's personality, maturity level, intelligence, psychological state, learning style, cognitive abilities, and other interpersonal qualities. To illustrate, let us assume there is a program for offenders that requires a journaling component, but several of the individuals the probation department would like to place in this program are unable to read or write past a third-grade level. These individuals will likely not be as successful in this type of program and therefore, we will not see promising outcomes for these offenders. Too often, we hear that programs do not work, when, they do work for some offenders but not for others. However, when we compare all the participants to one another, the successes are often masked, or canceled out, by the failures when the program is evaluated. Instruments are available to assess the risk and need principles of effective classification, which include the Level of Supervision Inventory—Revised, Ohio Risk Assessment System, Correctional Offender Management Profiling for Alternative Sanctions, and the Offender Screening Tool. Tools to assess responsivity are Beck's Depression Inventory, Jesness Personality Inventory, Treatment Motivation Scales, Culture Fair IQ Test, External Pressure Scales, and Desire for Help.

Most jurisdictions consider offenders' risk and needs, albeit frequently neglect criminogenic needs, but few assess for responsivity. Additionally, some common problems with offender assessment deserve mention. First, some departments assess offenders but ignore dynamic factors, or those that can be changed through intervention programs and services, and focus too much on static factors, or those that cannot be affected by programming. Examples of dynamic factors include attitudes, substance abuse, negative peer associations, and unemployment. Static factors include prior criminal history and age at first offense. Second, some agencies evaluate offenders but do not differentiate between risk levels such that low risk offenders may be referred to a more restrictive sentence when regular probation may be more appropriate.

Third, regardless of assessment scores, all offenders receive the same treatment or are sentenced to the same sanction. For example, even though some offenders do not have a history of substance abuse, they are required to attend a community drug treatment program just like those who do have issues with addiction because the program is offered regularly in the jurisdiction and there is nothing else available. Finally, sometimes errors in calculations are made when scoring the instrument, and instead of adjusting them, the offender gets assigned a risk score that does not correctly classify their risk and need levels. Assessment instruments assign scores based on responses to the key areas measured. If a PO scores a question higher or lower incorrectly, the total score for the entire instrument could be altered such that an offender who is actually lower risk is placed in a high-risk category or vice versa.

Depending on the direction of the error, offenders who are not suitable candidates for a community sanction could be placed in prison and vice versa. Then, they likely will not receive the appropriate programming to reduce their criminogenic needs effectively, which then could lead to an increase in recidivism. Similar outcomes can happen if staff are not adequately trained in using the assessment instruments or how to interpret the results. These common errors could be addressed through extensive training and utilizing validated instruments, which are important endeavors for departments to pursue, especially given that studies have shown for over twenty-five years, what programs can work, for what types of offenders, and in what types of settings if offenders' risk, need, and responsivity levels are adequately and accurately assessed.

Web Activity

For a good primer on the principles of effective classification, watch Dr. James Bonta in this webinar: https://www.youtube.com/watch?v=H0MF-3-oLUQ. If you were completing a presentence investigation report and making a sentence recommendation and did not have an instrument to assess risk and need, would you find it more or less challenging to appropriately assist judges in the sentencing decision? Explain.

INTERMEDIATE SANCTIONS AND WIDENING THE NET

Intermediate sanctions broaden sentencing options for judges. However, as mentioned under the discussion on the sanction of home confinement, it is important to understand their implications for widening the net of control over individuals who would not have been sentenced to an intermediate sanction when regular probation was the more appropriate alternative to prison. When the growth of intermediate sanctions surged in the mid-late 1980s and early 1990s, we witnessed numerous offenders receiving a correctional supervision sentence merely because judges had something to give them. Thus, net widening occurred.

Critical Thinking Exercise

Since intermediate sanctions often involve more contacts and supervision by court officers, there is a higher probability that sentence violations will occur. These violations might lead to revocation of the intermediate sanction and the sentence will be carried out in confinement in jail or prison, depending on the nature of the violation. Other than incarceration, what options could be used to keep offenders out of prison and in the community if violations occur? Another way to look at this question is, what could officers do to reduce that sentence violations will occur?

There are three primary ways by which net widening extends the reach of criminal justice system control. First, *wider nets* are cast when we see a significant increase in the number of individuals whose behaviors are now being regulated by the government. To illustrate, prior to the emergence of intermediate sanctions, offenders either were sentenced mainly to regular probation, incarceration, or imposed a fine and court costs. Once the menu of intermediate sanctions expanded, defendants who committed crimes for which the court usually imposed a regular probation sentence were now placed under intensive supervision probation (ISP). Under ISP, their behaviors were monitored more intensely and violations could lead to a revocation of the term in exchange for prison time. If one of the main pushes for intermediate sanctions was to divert offenders away from incarceration, casting wider nets is counterproductive. For example, in some states, minor marijuana possession offenses have fines and citations attached to them instead of a supervised sanction. If the legislation was changed and allowed judges to sentence offenders to imprisonment on a second offense for this crime, then more people could be under the control of the criminal justice system. Prior to the reform, these same individuals just would have paid their fine and moved on without any conditions regulating their behaviors regardless of the number of times they violated this law.

The second way is by casting *stronger nets*, which increases the government's capacity to control individuals by granting it more authority over the reach of the criminal justice system. Under stronger nets, more intrusive sanctions are imposed on offenders than they would have typically received had they not been available. To illustrate, judges could add on community service to a regular probation sentence or impose shock incarceration prior to serving a straight probation term.

The final type of net widening is *different nets*. This occurs when reforms are passed that transfer jurisdictional control from one component or agency of the criminal justice system to another. In the example above where a judge could impose a sentence of shock incarceration on an offender to strengthen the reach of the criminal justice system, under different nets, if the offender is not successful in the shock incarceration program, he/she could be under residential control longer than was originally intended by the judge in the court. In this case, the authority of the length and conditions of the sentence was first held by the judge and then transferred to the department of corrections that runs the shock incarceration program.

Another example of different nets that commonly occurs is when judicial authority over the prison term shifts to correctional officials who award inmates good time credits that will reduce the number of days spent in prison. The distribution of these credits essentially means that the department of corrections could ultimately control the time spent incarcerated and not the sentencing judge. If supervised release on parole, which will be covered in the next chapter, is an option for some offenders, control could also be transferred to another government agency with the decision-maker changing yet again. Thus, with different nets, we see different agents of the system having an influence on how and where offenders serve their sentences, and this occurs unchecked in most cases.

Regardless of the ways in which net widening occurs, there are some consequences that should be considered. First, with more sanction alternatives and more decision-makers having input, a greater proportion of people will be under the control of the criminal justice system. Second, typically, when the reach of criminal justice control is expanded, recidivism increases rather than decreases mostly because we are more likely to observe people violating the conditions of their sanction. Third, and related to the first two consequences and illustrated above, net widening leads to increases in formal social control and more restrictive sanctions. If intermediate sanctions are touted as a cost-saving approach, we have to be careful of just how wide, strong, and different the nets are.

Critical Thinking Exercise

What could be done to reduce the negative consequences of net widening and improved implementation of intermediate sanctions? Describe.

SUMMARY

This chapter covered the common alternatives to incarceration that are offered in the community. Particular focus was on the intermediate sanctions with foundational knowledge on probation and the principles of effective classification. The punishment ladder was introduced and explored to place the options available under community corrections in context. The consequences of net widening were discussed and cautions raised.

The future of community corrections, like so many other areas in our lives, will continue to be driven by technological advances in supervision. There are cost and efficiency advantages, but better and more-capable devices could also mean that more offender violations will be uncovered. The goal of decreasing incarceration rates and costs will be difficult to achieve, which is a primary driver for using community correction sanctions. The expanded utilization of smartphones will change the operations of community corrections. Offender location monitoring, check-ins, and appointment reminders can occur automatically, and the use of the video camera function will change the nature of supervision in numerous ways. For example, court officers will be able to conduct virtual home visits, watch offenders take their medication, and verify documentation such as paychecks or completion of paperwork for jobs, education programs, or activity similar prosocial activities. These interactions can be recorded for use later should violations be detected, but they can also be used for positive reinforcement to encourage law-abiding behavior.

KEY WORDS

boot camps
broad category
caseload
community control
community-based correc-
  tional facilities
community corrections
community residential
  centers
community service
conventional model
conventional model with
  geographic
  considerations
criminogenic needs

day reporting centers
dual role
economic sanctions
electronic monitoring
fines
halfway houses
home confinement
intensive supervision
  probation
intermediate sanctions
mental health court
model system
need principle
net widening
new crime violation

numbers game model
presentence investigation
  report
probation
responsivity principle
revocation hearing
risk principle
service fees
shock incarceration
special assessments
specialized caseloads
  model
technical violation
victim impact statement

DISCUSSION QUESTIONS

1. In many jurisdictions today, some probationers report for probation by check-ing in on a kiosk that looks similar to an ATM machine. They do not meet with a probation officer face to face, but rather go through a series of questions on the machine on a designated day or days. Probationers can pay fines through the machine with credit cards, present pay stubs, and be notified to report for a drug test. Some machines even offer probationers a receipt to document the visit. Do you think these kiosks are suitable replacements for face-to-face visits between probationers and their assigned officers? Why or why not?

2. Consider Jolie, twenty-two years old with no high school diploma or equiva-lent. She has been on probation for six months for a shoplifting conviction and has yet to find a job or connect to services. Her records show a history of drug and alcohol use during her teen years as well. Of the probation officer roles in the text, which ones do you think you would need to utilize so Jolie can com-plete probation successfully? Why did you choose these roles?

3. You are promoted to chief probation officer of a felony court located in Z-Land, which serves a county of 370,000 residents and is 581 square miles. You are now in charge of assigning caseloads to the probation officers under your su-pervision. Which caseload model would best work for your office? Why did you select this model compared to the other options?

4. Are economic sanctions an undue burden on offenders? What about fines? Community service? Which one do you think is most effective at punishing offenders? Rehabilitating offenders? Defend your position.

5. Your county is being given a grant for an intensive supervision program to divert clients, who have mental health and/or substance use disorders, away

from secure confinement so they can have access to the services they need in the community. What plans could you put in place to lessen the potential for net widening? Describe.

SUGGESTED READINGS

Andrews, D. A., and J. Bonta. (2016). *The Psychology of Criminal Conduct*. New York, NY: Routledge.

Byrne, J., and D. Hummer. (2016). "An Examination of the Impact of Criminological Theory on Community Corrections Practice." *Federal Probation* 80: 15.

Byrne, J. M., A. J. Lurigio, and J. Petersilia, eds. (1992). *Smart Sentencing: The Emergence of Intermediate Sanctions*. Thousand Oaks, CA: SAGE.

Irizarry, Y., D. C. May, A. Davis, and P. B. Wood. (2016). "Mass Incarceration through a Different Lens: Race, Subcontext, and Perceptions of Punitiveness of Correctional Alternatives When Compared to Prison." *Race and Justice* 6, no. 3: 236–256.

Latessa, E. J., S. L. Listwan, and D. Koetzle. (2014). What Works (and Doesn't) in Reducing Recidivism. Waltham, MA: Anderson.

Morgan, K. (2015). *Probation, Parole, and Community Corrections Work in Theory and Practice: Preparing Students for Careers in Probation and Parole Agencies*. Durham, NC: Carolina Academic Press.

Morris, N., and M. Tonry. (1991). Between Prison and Probation: Intermediate Punishments in a Rational Sentencing System. New York, NY: Oxford University Press.

Petersilia, J., and E. P. Deschenes. (1994). "Perceptions of Punishment: Inmates and Staff Rank the Severity of Prison versus Intermediate Sanctions." *Prison Journal* 74, no. 3: 306–328.

REFERENCES

American Probation and Parole Association. (2006). "Issue Paper on Caseload Standards" (updated). Retrieved from https://www.appa-net.org/eweb/docs/APPA/stances/ip_CSzPP.pdf on September 22, 2018.

American Probation and Parole Association. (2018). Probation and Parole FAQs. Retrieved from: https://www.appa-net.org/eweb/DynamicPage.aspx?WebCode=VB_FAQ#7.

Andrews, D. A., and J. Bonta. (1994). *The Psychology of Criminal Conduct*. Cincinnati, OH: Anderson Publishing.

Balyakina, E., C. Mann, M. Ellison, R. Sivernell, K. G. Fulda, S. K. Sarai, and R. Cardarelli. (2014). Risk of Future Offense among Probationers with Co-occurring Substance Use and Mental Health Disorders. *Community Mental Health Journal* 50, no. 3: 288–295.

Barnes-Proby, D., P. E. Hunt, L. Jonsson, and S. Cherney. (2018). *Bridge to Opportunities: How One Probation Agency Developed a Program Designed to Connect Probationers to High-Wage Jobs*. Santa Monica, CA: RAND.

Fearn, N. E., M. G. Vaughn, E. J. Nelson, C. P. Salas-Wright, M. DeLisi, and Z. Qian. (2016). "Trends and Correlates of Substance Use Disorders among Probationers and Parolees in the United States 2002–2014." *Drug and Alcohol Dependence* 167:128–139.

Hollis, M. E., W. G. Jennings, and S. Hankhouse. (2019). "An Outcome Evaluation of a Substance Abuse Program for Probationers: Findings from a Quasi-Experimental Design."

American Journal of Criminal Justice: the Journal of the Southern Criminal Justice Association, 44, 3, 395–408.

Jalbert, S. K., W. Rhodes, M. Kane, E. Clawson, B. Bogue, C. Flygare, R. Kling, and M. Guevara. (2011). *A Multi-site Evaluation of Reduced Probation Caseload Size in an Evidence-based program setting.* Washington, DC: U.S. Department of Justice.

Kaeble, D. (2018). Probation and Parole in the United States, 2016. US Department of Justice, Office of Justice Programs, Bureau of Justice Statistics.

Miller, J. (2015). "Contemporary Modes of Probation Officer Supervision: The Triumph of the 'Synthetic' Officer?" *Justice Quarterly 32*(2), 314–336.

Peters, R. H., H. K. Wexler, and A. J. Lurigio. (2015). Co-occurring Substance Use and Mental Disorders in the Criminal Justice System: A New Frontier of Clinical Practice and Research. *Psychiatric Rehabilitation Journal, 38*, 1–6. Retrieved from https://psycnet-apa-org.ezproxy.bgsu.edu/fulltext/2015-12225-001.html.

Van Deinse, T. B., G. S. Cuddeback, A. B. Wilson, and S. E. Burgin. (2018). Probation Officers' Perceptions of Supervising Probationers with Mental Illness in Rural and Urban Settings. *American Journal of Criminal Justice 43*(2), 267–277.

Williams, D. J., and T. Turnage. (2001). "Success of a Day Reporting Center Program." *Corrections Compendium 26*(3), 1–3, 26.

CHAPTER 6

Parole and Reentry

AFTER READING THIS CHAPTER, YOU SHOULD BE ABLE TO:

- Detail the predecessors to parole and how they influenced parole practices in the United States
- Define the two meanings of parole
- Distinguish between discretionary release, supervised mandatory release, and expiration or unconditional mandatory release
- Identify the arguments for and against parole
- Characterize parole boards and note what goes into making the decision to grant parole as well as the criteria that are taken into consideration
- Detail the conditions of release, types of parole violations, and the parole revocation process
- Illustrate what parole officers do and how they handle their caseloads
- Summarize other mechanisms of release from prison and sentence reductions
- Demonstrate an understanding of the reentry movement and the concept of reentry and how it came to be
- Analyze the barriers and challenges individuals face post-release
- Discuss reentry programming and services in the context of the 2008 Second Chance Act and evidence-based practices

INTRODUCTION

The word "parole" comes from the French term **"parole d'honneur,"** which means "word of honor" and represented a promise from prisoners of war who were released on the condition that they would not return to battle. The justice-influenced word "parole" is defined as the release of inmates from secure custody before the end of their sentence. As was the case with most practices, there is a history of how parole evolved over time, and like most American criminal justice system processes, England played a sizable role.

Before starting our historical tour and progressing to contemporary post-release options, it is important to note that probation and parole are not the same. Probation hails from the judiciary in that a judge makes the decision to sentence convicted defendants to community control and supervision by probation officers. Parole, while similar to probation in that it has supervising officers and conditions that must be followed, is an early release mechanism that occurs while offenders are incarcerated. The decision whether a person will be released from custody is a discretionary decision made by a parole board.

PREDECESSORS TO PAROLE

Noted previously in this text, an early and frequently utilized method of punishment by England was **transportation**, or removing offenders from prisons, placing them on ships, and transferring them to other territories they occupied, commonly the American and Australian colonies. Transportation, unlike **banishment** where criminals are forced out of their village or town for life, provided a means of labor in the developing lands overseas and helped England alleviate crowding, unemployment, and costs of incarceration. Transported offenders were contracted by the British penal system to ship's captains who could use them on the ship until they arrived at their destination.

Upon arrival to the American colonies, the captain would often auction off these involuntary prisoners in a bidding system where they would become **indentured servants** to their new owner and were no longer under control by the English government. Under indentured servitude, the former convicts would sign a contract (i.e., the indenture or covenant) that listed the conditions of their service, such as working for a specific number of years in exchange for shelter, food, and clothing supplied by their owner. Many indentured servants worked on farms or domestic laborers. After they fulfilled their contracts, the indentured would become free persons. It is estimated that one-fourth of the immigrants from Britain came to the American colonies as transported convicts. After victory in the American Revolution, the colonists refused to accept any more convicts from England.

Australia and Alexander Maconochie
Transportation operated a bit differently in Australia. Transported criminals were under the control of the penal colony governor who was appointed by the British government so by extension, would still be under England's rule. The governor would lend out the transported criminals to work for settlers in the Australian territory, and like their American colony counterparts, would be given basic living needs in exchange for their labor. Once the ex-convicts were pardoned, many stayed in Australia as free settlers. In eighty years, over 160,000 English and Irish criminals were transported to one of Australia's six penal settlements. Of the six, Norfolk Island was well known for being the most horrendous, chaotic, and inhumane of all the penal colonies, until British Naval Captain **Alexander Maconochie** was appointed governor. Some historical documents note that the worst of the worst offenders were sent to Norfolk Island, but like most transported criminals, they were convicted of property crimes. Regardless, Norfolk prisoners faced hard labor with limited food and inadequate shelter; they did not even get forks and knives to eat their meals with while imprisoned. Failure to comply or a show of any disrespect to their keepers (i.e., soldiers of the British military) resulted in torturous punishment like flogging. It was a common occurrence for the prisoners to attempt escape and riot under former penal colony governors.

Web Activity

Go to http://slq.qld.gov.au/resources/convict-queenslanders and select three people from the list of Queenslander Convicts in Australia. What did they have in common? How did they differ? If transportation was not a possible sanction, what sentence recommendation would you have made?

When Maconochie assumed leadership, he implemented changes that laid the foundation for modern parole practice, which is why he is known as the "Father of Parole." Upon his arrival, Maconochie treated the prisoners with respect by getting to know them, banned flogging and chains, built churches and schools, and offered a plan for prisoners to reduce their sentence under the **mark system**. Prisoners worked their way through a series of steps where upon earning marks for work and good behavior they would graduate and eventually earn release with the **ticket of leave**. Upon completion of each step, prisoners would earn more freedom in movement. The first step was the most stringent and included moral and religious teachings on penitence. The second step was where the prisoners would work to earn marks that would fund their clothing, food, and shelter. When the first two steps were accomplished by demonstrating good behavior, prisoners would then move to the stage where they would work together in small groups on joint projects. At this phase, prisoners could move around more freely within a limited area and have greater freedom of movement that mimicked the conditions one would have post-release. The ticket of leave was issued after the prisoners accumulated enough marks, and this ticket allowed them to live without restrictions on location. Some prisoners even returned to England and Ireland. The ticket of leave did not require supervision from any government official, but those released had to notify the police where they were living.

The Irish Penal System and Sir Walter Crofton

Maconochie's practices were seen as too progressive for the British government, so he was removed from his post as the penal colony governor of Norfolk Island in 1840, just four years after he arrived. In 1853, however, the English Parliament did provide for a conditional release for persons sentenced to prison under the English Penal Servitude Act. The ticket-of-leave system did have footing elsewhere in Europe under the direction of **Sir Walter Crofton** who became the director of the Irish Penal System in 1854. Crofton took Maconochie's ideas and expanded their application and further development under the **Irish system** of penal administration, which also went by the name of **intermediate system**. Like the mark system, there were graduated stages that prisoners had to progress through until release. The stages were as follows:

1. **Initial Stage** Prisoners would first serve around eight to nine months in solitary confinement. The first three months would be the most restrictive in that prisoners could not work and they were only given small rations for food. The remaining months were spent engaged in labor, and prisoners were allotted their full food rations. Crofton believed that by limiting what prisoners could do upon arrival that they would be eager to work and earn their conditional release.

2. **Second Stage** Inmates were transferred from solitary confinement to another prison, where they would labor with the inmates who were already housed there. Maconochie's mark system played a major role in Crofton's

Irish system during this second stage when prisoners worked to earn marks as they finished assigned tasks.

3. **Third Stage** After earning enough marks in the second stage, prisoners were sent to an open institution that looked more like a military barrack. Six staff members supervised the convicts as they worked and earned marks or credits for their productivity. The staff was also responsible for communicating to the public that once prisoners earn enough marks to pass through stage three, they would be capable of work in free society under a ticket of leave.

4. **Fourth Stage** The final stage meant that prisoners had earned the requisite number of marks needed to earn conditional release or their ticket of leave. It is in this stage where the foundations for modern day parole are most recognizable. Once prisoners earned their ticket of leave, they were released into the community and supervised by local police. The former prisoners had to submit reports on a monthly basis to police. Eventually, Crofton would appoint a special civilian inspector to supervise the former prisoners, which would then influence the progression to modern day parole officers.

The other concept that would evolve out of the development of parole is **indeterminate sentencing**. For Maconochie's or Crofton's approaches to conditional release to work, there had to be a way that the marks or good credits earned could encourage prisoners to work toward a shorter sentence and/or progress to the next stage. Under **determinate sentencing**, judges impose a fixed number of years convicted defendants are to serve under custody and they must be released when time has been served. Indeterminate sentencing models rely on judges sanctioning convicted offenders to a range of years to serve in custody. To illustrate, a determinate sentence would be a prison term of five years and an indeterminate sentence would be one that calls for a minimum of three years and a maximum of five years. It was recognized that demonstrating good behavior and working toward enough marks/credits and moving to the next stage would not be as much as an incentive if prisoners could not reduce their time imprisoned, as would be the case under determinate sentencing.

PAROLE IN THE UNITED STATES

In the United States, the term "parole" was first used in an 1846 letter to the Prison Association of New York to refer to type of conditional release. In that same year, Massachusetts was the first state to establish an official parole service, where an agent was appointed to assist released prisoners. The Civil War detracted attention from justice-related issues so little progress was made across the country that furthered the development of parole. By 1870, however, a renewed awareness in the harsh environment of the nation's penitentiaries came to be scrutinized. A more humanitarian approach to the practice of incarceration was advocated based more on the philosophy of rehabilitation rather than pure incapacitation or deterrence. The National Prison Association, which is known today as the American Correctional Association, was formed in 1870 to address the problems of the penitentiary system. Prison administrators, members of Congress, and prominent citizens from the States and abroad gathered in Cincinnati, Ohio, and issued a set of declarations by which the existing corrections system would be reformed.

These principles stressed the value of treatment for inmates based on their individual needs, an indeterminate sentencing scheme by which inmates can earn their way out of prison, vocational and educational training, labor that was purposeful instead of as punishment, and noncorporal methods of discipline that made use of rewards rather than punishment for conformity. The introduction of a system whereby released inmates could continue their treatment in the community was also introduced during this era. Crofton's Irish system was also part of the "Declaration of Principles" document where the above-noted concepts were emphasized. In 1876, these principles would be put into practice with the opening of the **Elmira Reformatory** in New York.

The Elmira Reformatory

The Elmira Reformatory, under the direction of its first general superintendent, **Zebulon R. Brockway**, presented on the reformatory at the American Prison Association meeting, was the prototype institution. Young males aged sixteen to thirty were the typical prisoners held at Elmira, and Brockway's approach was to work with each inmate on an individualized basis. Upon arrival, Brockway met with the inmates and assessed their potential for reform based on their behaviors and thought patterns. During these meetings, which could be considered predecessors to what occurs during intake in some secure residential facilities or community corrections programs, Brockway took detailed notes about each inmate (Johnson, Wolfe, and Jones 2003). Inmates would also learn what would be expected of them as they progressed through the institution's three-tiered ranking system.

Each tier, or grade, had various privileges or lack thereof, and inmates would be distinguished in ranking by their assigned uniforms (Warner 1885). Starting from the grade furthest away from release, grade-three inmates would be fairly isolated. They would eat meals in their rooms, did not have access to visitors, could not receive or send letters, or borrow books from the library. The uniform for the grade threes was dark red without any cap. At grade two, inmates were allowed visitors, communication via mail, and library borrowing privileges. However, eating meals in their rooms was mandatory. Their uniform was a dark colored suit with a scotch cap. The first grade included the privileges of those in grade two, but now the inmates could eat in the dining hall. Unlike the inmates in grades two and three who worked mostly tedious tasks, grade-one inmates were assigned jobs that were thought to improve their chances for obtaining employment post-release. Grade-one uniforms were blue and the inmates wore a navy cap.

After being classified based on their conduct and success in the interventions available at the facility, such as training for trade and education, inmates would start their stay at Elmira in the second grade of classification. If they exhibited good behavior and completed their work tasks and their studies, the inmates would earn additional privileges at grade one, the last grade of promotion before becoming eligible for parole or being released early from custody from Elmira. If, however, they were not behaving well, were not productive workers, and/or not completing their educational requirements, they could be sent to grade three, which would mean they would have to earn their way to grade two, one, and then finally release. The decision as to whether an inmate would be released was determined by Elmira Reformatory managers, which was legislated by what would in effect become a statute that allowed for indeterminate sentences in New York. On average, the maximum amount of time inmates would spend at Elmira was around three years. Time spent on parole was six months and the released men would receive assistance from Elmira officials in securing employment and housing.

By the 1950s, all states had adopted some form of discretionary parole and in 1977, over 70 percent of those incarcerated exited prison as parolees. A quarter-century later, however, the tide began to turn. See Figure 6.1 for a timeline of the first 100-year history of parole in the United States. Public disillusionment with

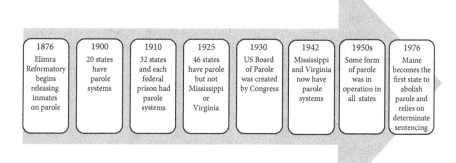

1876	1900	1910	1925	1930	1942	1950s	1976
Elmira Reformatory begins releasing inmates on parole	20 states have parole systems	32 states and each federal prison had parole systems	46 states have parole but not Mississippi or Virginia	US Board of Parole was created by Congress	Mississippi and Virginia now have parole systems	Some form of parole was in operation in all states	Maine becomes the first state to abolish parole and relies on determinate sentencing

Figure 6.1 US Parole Timeline: The First 100 Years.

the use of rehabilitation and indeterminate sentencing systems was becoming widespread across the country. Recidivism rates began to climb as well, prompting legislatures across the country to abolish parole.

Justifications for and against Parole

Critics of parole contend that (1) parole is too lenient; (2) it is an infringement on judicial sentencing authority; (3) it takes away the pardoning powers of the chief executive, which would be the governor at the state level and the president at the federal level; and (4) it allows unchecked discretion by the parole board. Advocates are quick to reply with numerous advantages of parole:

1. Parole is more humanitarian than long prison sentences.
2. Parole allows time between the criminal act and possible release from imprisonment for heated emotions to settle down and actions of the offenders to be viewed more calmly years later. This presents an opportunity to mitigate sentences where harshness appeared justified at the time they were handed down by the judge.
3. Parole offers offenders a chance to reduce their prison terms even though they are guilt of serious crimes. However, in prison many inmates have aged and matured and are no longer likely to recidivate.
4. Parole is accepted as a way to control inmate behavior by offering the possibility of early release for those willing to participate in prison programs and cooperate with officials.
5. Supervision in the community is less costly than secure custody.
6. While on parole, offenders can be gainfully employed, pay taxes, and support his or her family.
7. Supervised release into the community tends to be safer and more effective than simply discharging inmates from prison.

Dual Meaning of Parole

While some form of parole remains the typical method by which inmates are released from prison, the nature of parole has changed considerably from its origins. There are really two meanings of parole. First, parole is the conditional release of an offender from incarceration, usually by a parole board, after part of the prison sentence has been served. Offenders can be released directly to the community with supervision of a parole officer or they can be sent to a halfway house or community-based residential facility for a short stay, and then released into the community under supervision. Similar to being on probation, the parolee must comply with specific conditions while on parole. The second meaning of parole is when an offender spends a period of time under supervision in the community. Thus, parole is really the continuation of an offender's sentence outside the prison walls. Today, you might hear the term "post-release community supervision" used as the new term for parole, but it generally is the same practice. Some states where the new term is commonly communicated are California, New York, and Ohio.

It is important to note that traditional parole is considered a **discretionary release** from prison; there is no right to parole. In jurisdictions where parole has been "abolished," there are typically two other mechanisms for release: (1) **supervised mandatory release** and (2) **expiration** or **unconditional mandatory release**. Supervised mandatory release is the required discharge of an inmate to conditional supervision (similar to parole in this regard) at the expiration of a certain time served as determined by law or parole guidelines. Expiration or unconditional mandatory release involves releasing an offender from custody with no additional supervision; the offender may not be returned to prison for any part of the original sanction. This form of release usually applies in cases of commutation, pardon, or end of sentence.

Eligibility requirements for parole differ by jurisdiction. Some states set that a person can legally be released from prison at the end of the minimum term less good time. Others establish that a certain fraction (e.g., one-half or two-thirds of the original sentence) of the minimum or the maximum sentence must be served before an inmate is eligible for release. In some states, offenders appear before the parole board automatically when they are eligible. In other jurisdictions, offenders have to apply. In some states, parole boards hold an initial hearing with inmates shortly after they arrive at prison and set a **presumptive parole date**. This date is when the inmate will be released, assuming the inmate does not violate any laws or prison rules and continues to follow any treatment or other programs while incarcerated. As the date approaches, the parole board receives a report from prison staff as to the behavior and conduct of inmates whose parole dates are approaching. If all is going well, the inmate is released on the presumptive parole date. If there are concerns, a parole board hearing is held that follows the same considerations as those noted above for cases where no presumptive parole date is set. If there have been conduct problems, the parole board can reschedule a new presumptive release date.

Characteristics of Parole Boards

Depending on the state, a parole board is either consolidated or autonomous. **Consolidated boards** are comprised of individuals who are part of the department of corrections. **Autonomous boards** are those that operate as an independent agency of the government. Most members of state parole boards are hired on as full-time employees via appointment by the governor. A few states have boards that are composed of part-time members who have full-time careers in other occupations outside of the parole board. The size of parole boards differs as well in that some are as small as two members or as large as twelve or more. The US Parole Commission is charged with parole release decisions for individuals housed in federal institutions, but parole is not an option for offenders who committed crimes after November 1, 1987. Parole was eliminated with the passage of the Sentencing Reform Act of 1984. Federal inmates can still earn good time credit that can reduce their time spent in prison, however. Judges can also add on a period of supervised release in the community to the original incarceration sentence. Thus, while the

	Number per 100,000 US adult residents			US adult residents on—		
Year	Community supervision[a,b]	Probation	Parole	Community supervision[a,b]	Probation	Parole
2000	2,162	1,818	344	1 in 46	1 in 53	1 in 285
2000	2,215	1,864	351	1 in 45	1 in 54	1 in 285
2010	2,067	1,715	356	1 in 48	1 in 58	1 in 281
2011	2,017	1,663	358	1 in 50	1 in 60	1 in 279
2012	1,984	1,634	356	1 in 50	1 in 61	1 in 281
2013	1,946	1,603	348	1 in 51	1 in 62	1 in 287
2014	1,911	1,568	348	1 in 52	1 in 64	1 in 288
2015	1,872	1,526	350	1 in 53	1 in 66	1 in 285
2016	1,811	1,467	349	1 in 55	1 in 68	1 in 287

NOTE: Rates are based on most recent data available and may differ from previously published statistics. Rates are based on the total community supervision, probation, and parole population counts as of December 31 of the reporting year and were computed using the estimates of the U.S. resident population of persons age 18 or older from the U.S. Census Bureau for January 1 of the following year.

[a]Includes adults on probation and parole.

[b]For 2008 to 2016, detail may not sum to total because the community supervision rate was adjusted to exclude paroless who were also on probation.

Figure 6.2 Rates of US Adult Residents on Community Supervision, Probation, and Parole, 2000, 2005, and 2010-2016
SOURCE: Bureau of Justice Statistics, Annual Probation Survey and Annual Parole Survey, 2000, 2005, 2010–2016; and U.S. Census Bureau, National Intercensal Estimates, 2001, 2006, and 2011–2017

official practice of discretionary parole in the federal system has been prohibited legislatively, there is still resemblance of a functional early release process. A similar conclusion can also be drawn for states who have statutorily abolished discretionary parole such as Maine, Illinois, Virginia, Florida, and Washington. Yet, there are still inmates in prison who were sentenced prior to the implementation of these laws who have, and will, come up for consideration for early, discretionary release with the decision made by a parole board. Based on the most recent data available, 1 in every 287 US residents is under some form of parole supervision. Figure 6.2 displays the rates of individuals under community supervision, whether probation or parole from 2000 to 2016.

THE PAROLE RELEASE DECISION

Like most stages in the criminal justice system, parole follows its own process from consideration of parole, to decision, to carrying out the terms of the release. This process varies from state to state and the federal system. It is important to note that discretionary parole is not a right, but a privilege as set forth in a decision by the US Supreme Court decision in the case of *Greenholtz v. Inmates of the Nebraska Penal and Correctional Complex* (1979). Since parole is not a requirement whereby every inmate is eligible, the composition and practices of parole boards are not often reviewed by another government authority when release is denied. If you recall, this reason is one that has been offered as a criticism to parole.

Critical Thinking Exercise

Go to https://caselaw.findlaw.com or www.oyez.org and search for the *Greenholtz v. Inmates of the Nebraska Penal and Correctional Complex* (1979) case. Compare and contrast the concurring and dissenting opinions. Do you think the case was decided appropriately? Is the decision that parole is a privilege and not a right adequately justified? Explain.

Nonetheless, research confirms that persons released under conditional supervision tend to recidivate less than those who are released outright without any supervision (Vito, Higgins, and Tewksbury 2017; Ostermann 2015; Schlager and Robbins 2008; Ireland and Prause 2005). To kick off the parole release process, the first step is for inmates to apply for parole consideration, or, in some states, considering inmates for parole is automatic based on the date of eligibility, or the date by which an inmate could be evaluated for release based on their original sentence. To illustrate, if the judge hands out a sentence of thirty-two to fifty months with consideration for parole after thirty-two months in prison, consideration for release on parole can be made once thirty-two months and one day are served. The decision whether to release the inmate after the application is filed or if an automatic review is due lies with the parole board. The parole board can grant, deny, or defer inmates' requests for discretionary release. If state or federal parole guidelines are mandated for use, then the parole board follows those guidelines and reviews inmates' files and records.

Parole Guidelines

Parole guidelines were a result of charges of discrimination and disparity in parole board decisions whereby parole board members did not follow any uniform standards when it came to granting or denying parole. Even though inmates can appeal a parole decision, parole guidelines provide a basis to justify the outcome that is more transparent and understandable to the inmate and the public. The guidelines provide ranges of time that should be served prior to release based on the seriousness of the offense and prior criminal history. Some guidelines also include the probability of success while on parole, as such, parole boards often utilize instruments that are similar to risk assessments where a variety of factors are listed and inmates are scored based on where they fall on these items. Typical items on assessment instruments are

1. age when first admitted to a correctional facility;
2. history of revocations for felony offenses when under supervised release;
3. prior incarcerations;
4. employment history;
5. the offense that led the offender to the current prison sentence;
6. offender's age at time of parole consideration;
7. whether the offender is a confirmed security threat group (i.e., gang) member;
8. educational, vocational, and certified on-the-job training programs completed during the current prison sentence;
9. participation in substance use or mental health programs while serving current prison sanction;
10. prison infractions and other disciplinary issues while incarcerated;
11. current prison custody level.

Items 1–6 are considered static factors that do not change, no matter how much time passes or how many programs an inmate completes while incarcerated. Items seven to eleven are dynamic factors that can change over time. Each item is given a point value and then a total score is calculated by adding the values together. In some states, the lower the total score means the higher the probability of success on parole. In some states it is the higher score that corresponds to better outcomes; it all depends on the instrument being used. For example, one of the earliest and consistently validated instruments used to predict parole outcomes is the Salient Factor Score (SFS). The US Parole Commission (2010) uses the SFS as does the state of Connecticut. The SFS leans toward the dynamic items as indicators of likelihood of successful parole completion. The SFS score is then inserted into a table that categorizes offenses based on their seriousness with more-severe crimes being listed in higher categories. When considering the category of the offense and SFS score, the parole board can determine the length of time, typically in ranges of months, a person should serve in prison before being considered eligible for release on parole. To illustrate, look at Figure 6.3. If there is an inmate with an SFS score of seven who was convicted of involuntary manslaughter, a category four offense, this individual would have had to have served at least twenty months before being eligible for release on parole.

Once it is determined that inmates can be considered for parole, the next step in the parole decision process is for the board to hold a parole hearing where the eligible inmate appears before the parole board members or **hearing officers** to answer questions. Hearing officers are not parole board members, but they conduct the hearings and make recommendations to the parole board for consideration. Often, this hearing occurs in the prison, but in some places, the hearing may be conducted via video conferencing. In a few states, inmates can be represented by attorneys during the hearing even though the proceeding is not considered one

GUIDELINES FOR DECISION–MAKING

[Guidelines for Decision-Making, Customary Total Time
to be Served before Release (including jail time)]

OFFENSE CHARACTERISTICS:	OFFENDER CHARACTERISTICS: Parole Prognosis (Salient Factor Score 1998)			
Severtiy of Offense Behavior	Very Good (10–8)	Good (7–6)	Fair (5–4)	Poor (3–0)
Category One	Guideline Range			
	<=4 months	<=8 months	8–12 months	12–16 months
Category Two	Guideline Range			
	<=6 months	<=10 months	12–16 months	16–22 months
Category Three	Guideline Range			
	<=10 months	12–16 months	18–24 months	24–32 months
Category Four	Guideline Range			
	12–18 months	20–26 months	26–34 months	34–44 months
Category Five	Guideline Range			
	24–36 months	36–48 months	48–60 months	60–72 months
Category Six	Guideline Range			
	40–52 months	52–64 months	64–78 months	78–100 months
Category Seven	Guideline Range			
	52–80 months	64–92 months	78–110 months	100–148 months
Category Eight*	Guideline Range			
	100+ months	120+ months	150+ months	180+ months

Figure 6.3 Guidelines for Parole Decision-Making of the US Parole Commission.
SOURCE: U.S. Parole Commission Rules and Procedures Manual. Washington, DC: US Parole Commission, 2010. Accessed on September 2, 2018. https://www.justice.gov/sites/default/files/uspc/legacy/2010/08/27/uspc-manual111507.pdf.

in which the right to counsel is required. Some hearings are quite short with few questions asked of the inmate seeking release. In other hearings, they are more involved where witnesses, victims, and evidence for or against the inmate are presented much like an adversarial proceeding. In addition to the hearing, the parole board or the hearing officers consider a number of records, including the police file, the presentence investigation report, and correctional documents (e.g., infraction report, good time credits, program participation records, and the like). It is also an expectation that inmates have a plan for what they will do for housing, employment, and if needed, treatment in the community for drug use and/or mental health disorder or similar needs. Most prisons have case managers who assist inmates in preparing their post-release plans. There are varying criteria for the granting of parole that are taken into consideration by the parole board:

- risk of recidivism,
- the chances the inmate will conform to parole rules and regulations,
- whether release would be bad for overall prison morale,
- the realistic chances of suitable employment and living conditions presented in the inmate's plan,
- the community's willingness for the parolee to return,
- whether the release would promote disrespect for the law,
- whether the inmate has served about the average time for persons convicted for the same crime,
- whether the person could benefit from further involvement in prison training and educational or rehabilitative programs.

Web Activity

Go to https://www.nytimes.com/interactive/projects/documents/parole-hearing-transcripts-diana-ortiz-and-herbert-murray?ref=nyregion. It is the transcript for two convicted murderers at their parole hearing. Did anything strike you as concerning when reading this transcript? Are there other questions you would have liked to uncover the answers to during the hearing? Based on the reading of the transcript, would you have granted or denied parole to Ortiz? Murray?

Conditions of Release

Once the parole board decides to grant parole, or if there are inmates eligible for supervised mandatory release, the next step is for inmates to learn of, and agree in writing to, the conditions of their supervision. In many ways, it is at this stage where there is a lot of overlap between probation and parole, which may be why there is some confusion as to how the two community control approaches differ from one another. To recap, probation is a sentence handed down by the judge and it occurs in lieu of a jail or prison sentence; parole occurs after some time is served in prison. Common conditions of parole include the following as adapted from the American Probation and Parole Association's sample Rules for Probation and Parole (n.d.):

1. You may not possess firearms or any other deadly weapons.
2. You are subject to searches for prohibited items at the discretion of your parole officer.
3. Report to the parole officer as directed and permit the officer to visit you at your home or place of employment when necessary.

4. Respond promptly to any summons to appear in court.
5. Report any change of address to your parole officer within seventy-two hours and do not leave _____ without permission from your probation/parole officer.
6. Make every effort to seek and maintain employment and inform your parole officer of any change in your employment status.
7. Obey all federal, state, county criminal laws and city ordinances.
8. You may not unlawfully possess, use, sell or distribute controlled substances of any kind.
9. Notify your parole officer of any new arrest within seventy-two hours.

Special conditions may also be imposed, such as compliance with drug testing, participation in treatment programs, wearing a GPS device, or non-association with known offenders (e.g., gang members) or the victim(s) of the crime(s) for which the defendant was convicted. How do we know if the conditions are being met? This responsibility falls to the state or federal parole authority and its officers.

PAROLE OFFICERS AND PAROLEES

Parole officers are responsible for overseeing those individuals serving their time in the community after release from prison, regardless whether discretionary or mandatory supervised release. In some ways, parole officers carry out their duties by combining the supervisory and rehabilitative skills of a probation officer and the protection of public safety role typically associated with law enforcement officers. Even before an inmate is released to post-control community supervision, parole officers begin meeting with these individuals to assist them in making plans for where they will leave, what they will do for employment, and find treatment programs for mental health and/or substance use disorders after release. If there are other health issues or related, parole officers may also help locate care in the community when possible.

After release, parolees meet with their parole officer, who then uses the results of a risk assessment instrument, as discussed in Chapter 5, to determine the intensity of parole supervision, types of treatment programs, and how parolees will be monitored in the community. The frequency of contacts is positively correlated with parolees' risk levels in that those who are classified as higher risk receive more contacts by their parole officer with at least one being face-to-face contact in addition to contacts made via telephone, electronic communications, and collaterally. **Collateral contacts** are those the parole officer makes to verify information about the parolee. For example, a parole officer may call the parolee's employer or treatment program provider to ensure that the parolee is complying with the conditions of their supervision. Similarly, parolees who have a significant history of substance use in their past, will also take more drug tests while on supervision.

The assessment instruments also determine the nature of how parolees will be monitored in the community and this will drive the caseload sizes of parole officers. In general, there are three types of caseloads: regular, intensive, and special.

Within the regular type, offenders who are assessed as very low risk for recidivism and are nonviolent could be monitored by what is known as **administrative parole**, which requires no contacts with the parole officer over the length of time under supervision. Parolees may be required to submit to their parole officer a list of what they are doing to either secure or maintain employment, training, treatment, housing, and the like at specified intervals. If the parolee has a history of substance use, it is possible that the parole officer will require the parolee to get tested for drugs, even those there few contacts between offenders on an administrative caseload. The caseload size, or the number of parolees per parole officer, for administrative parole can be higher than other kinds of case types given the infrequency of contacts and minimal risk levels.

Moving up the levels of risk means increased contacts between parolees and parole officers. The higher the risk, the lower the caseload size since more interaction and supervision will be necessary to protect the public safety (that law enforcement role) and to ensure the parolees are following through with their post-release conditions and successfully reintegrating to the community (the probation office role). Intensive caseloads are composed of parolees who are high risk and require multiple contacts a month. Special caseloads are reserved for those offenders who have specific treatment needs, such as mental health, substance use disorders, co-occurring disorders, or committed certain crimes such as sex offenses. Parole officers will work with treatment providers and other agencies in the community to address parolees falling under a specialized caseload, which requires more involvement to ensure parolees are following their treatment plans and conditions of their supervision. Whether intensive or special caseload, there is a requirement for more contacts between parole officer and parolees, as well as concentrated supervision by the parole officer.

Web Activity

Finding effective ways to monitor parolees and assist parole officers in carrying out their jobs is something that automatic kiosks can help facilitate. Learn more about this practice by going to https://www.nij.gov/topics/corrections/community/Pages/auotated-kiosks-can-help-manage-caseloads-of-low-risk-clients.aspx#note1 and watching this video: https://www.youtube.com/watch?v=6lqp5vVBqb0. Do you think the kiosks are effective? Why or why not? What other technological innovations do you think could help in managing caseloads?

As noted in Chapter 5 with probation officers, there are recommended caseload minimums by the American Probation and Parole Association. Many jurisdictions' correctional budgets, however, are limited so hiring enough parole officers to reach the recommended caseload maximums is not often possible. The recommended caseload for clients that require intensive supervision should have a parolee to officer ratio of 20 to 1; for caseloads of moderate- to high-risk parolees that ratio should be 50 to 1; the parolee-to-officer ratio for low-risk offenders should be 200 to 1; and administrative caseloads 1,000 (or higher) to 1, due to the infrequency of required contacts. When parole officers' caseloads are too high, it can be challenging to ensure that supervision conditions are being met and that parolees are leading law-abiding lives. Similar to probationers, if parolees do violate the terms of their supervision, (i.e., a **technical violation**) and/or commit a new crime (i.e., a **new crime violation**) while on post-release control, they could have their parole revoked. Parole revocation is not automatic; it requires a formal process similar to probation's.

Web Activity

First, watch "Life on Parole" on *Frontline*: https://www.pbs.org/wgbh/frontline/film/life-on-parole/. Of the four persons followed, who seemed most likely to be successful? Who did you think was most likely to return to prison? Why? Second, go to https://www.pbs.org/wgbh/frontline/article/whats-happened-to-jessicavaughn-rob-and-erroll/ and find out how Jessica, Vaugh, Rob, and Erroll fared. Were you surprised? Why or why not? What indicators led you to conclude what you did?

PAROLE REVOCATION PROCESS

Once parole officers determine that a parole violation has occurred, a formal revocation process begins regardless if the violation falls under the technical or new crime category. For new crime violations, parolees can also be prosecuted through criminal justice system proceedings just like someone who is not on parole but has been arrested for committing an offense. The next step in the proceeding is for the parole officer to file a **notice of revocation of parole**. This notice states that a technical and/or new crime violation has been committed by the parolee and a hearing date is set to determine whether parole should be revoked and the parolee returned to prison to complete the remainder of their sentence minus any time spent under post-release community supervision in the community. Prior to and during the **revocation hearing**, some due process rights must be guaranteed because the outcome of the hearing could result in the loss of liberty in a secure facility. These rights, as held in *Morrissey v. Brewer* (1972), include

1. advance written notice of the alleged violation in a timely manner,
2. right to hear evidence against them,
3. right to present evidence, witnesses, and to speak their own behalf,
4. the opportunity to confront and cross-examine witnesses and refute testimony,
5. right to a neutral hearing body that must be detached from the parole officer making the allegation of the violation in seeking revocation,
6. explanation for the finding that parole will be revoked and rationale to support that decision in written form.

Critical Thinking Exercise

In the case of *Morrissey v. Brewer* (1972), the United States Supreme Court (USSC) determined that while parolees have limited due process rights, as noted under the "Parole Revocation Process" section of this chapter, they do not have a general right to an attorney to represent them. The USSC left it up to the hearing body to make the determination whether an attorney should be provided to the parolee for the hearing. Some states, however, do provide counsel in many cases. Do you think the USSC was correct in redirecting the decision for counsel to the states, or should they have made the right to appointed counsel mandatory for parole revocation hearings? Defend your response.

In many states, the parole board will be the detached and neutral body that decides whether parole will be revoked. For states that no longer have parole boards and/or for offenders released on mandatory supervised release, there are alternative hearing bodies. Some states have an entity similar to a parole board to hear cases related to technical and new crime violations. Other states return to the sentencing court to conduct revocation hearings.

OTHER MECHANISMS OF RELEASE FROM PRISON AND SENTENCE REDUCTIONS

Besides parole and expiration of sentence, some prisoners may be released from prison earlier than their stipulated sentence if granted **clemency**. Clemency is granted for several reasons. These can include correcting a sentence where a person was sentenced unjustly, to show mercy or forgiveness to individuals who were rightly convicted and sentenced to prison, or to remedy sentences that are disproportionate to the severity of the crime. Sometimes, you will see this called **executive clemency** because these officials are the head of their respective levels of government and have primary decision-making authority over many matters pertaining to the government, and in the case of corrections, this includes the prison system. The president has the power to grant clemency to inmates housed in federal prisons and the governor for those in state prisons. Typically, clemency begins with a petition submitted by the persons seeking it or an attorney on their behalf.

At the federal level, inmates apply for a certificate of pardon through the Office of the Pardon Attorney at the US Department of Justice (DOJ). The application is six pages in length and petitioners are asked what type of relief they are pursuing (e.g., reduction of prison sentence, remission of fine and/or restitution, or both). The person then completes the form by responding to a series of questions about their current confinement, whether they ever applied for clemency previously, whether their case is under appeal or was appealed, information about the offense(s) that led to the current prison sentences and past criminal history, and why they are seeking clemency. The petition is then reviewed by the DOJ and a recommendation is sent to the president who will then determine whether to grant or deny the petition.

At the state level, a similar petition process for clemency is followed, though there may be slight differences across states. In Ohio, for example, the petitioner submits an application to the Adult Parole Authority of the Ohio Department of Rehabilitation and Correction whose representative then submits it to the parole board. The parole board then makes a recommendation to the governor who renders the final decision. In other states, like Rhode Island or Mississippi, a formal application is not required as inmates just petition directly, in written form, to the governor.

Web Activity

Compare and contrast the clemency processes across the states by going to https://www.cjpf.org/clemency-al/. How many states use parole boards to review the initial petition and then make a recommendation to their respective governors? How many use official application forms? What other differences or similarities do you find?

There are two categories of clemency. The first is an **executive pardon** and the second a **commutation of sentence**. When offenders receive pardons, they are cleared of their crime(s), which results in restoration of most of their civil rights and clean criminal record. Pardons can be granted at any point prior to conviction and sentencing, while the offender is in prison, or years after a sentence has been served. A commutation of sentence grants the offender a reduction in prison time where the number of months or years remaining to be served are decreased. Another type of commutation is based on status such as a person sentenced to death is now sentenced to life in prison, or from life without parole to life with the possibility of parole sanction. Before President Barack Obama ended his final term in office, over 300 people convicted of nonviolent drug crimes convicted under the harsh drug laws of the 1970s and 1980s received clemency in the form of a sentence commutation with some offenders' sentences being reduced by several years to decades.

Web Activity

To learn more about the federal clemency process go to: https://www.justice.gov/pardon. This website also contains statistics of the process and outcomes of petitions made: https://www.justice.gov/pardon/clemency-statistics. Which president received the most petitions? The least? Who granted the most and least? Do you think any historical events or social context factors affected the outcomes? Detail.

REENTRY

Regardless of exit method, approximately 95 percent of state inmates will be released from incarceration at some point (Hughes and Wilson 2002). On average, there have been around 600,000 persons released from state and federal prisons annually since 1990 (Carson and Golinelli 2013). It was not until the early to mid-2000s that a focused concern on the success of these formerly incarcerated persons as they transitioned into free society gained national attention. This interest became known as the **reentry movement** with researchers, government officials, social service providers, and academics advocating and developing programs to respond to the adverse consequences of decades of sanctioning practices based on retributive and incapacitative philosophies whereby more and more persons were behind bars serving increasingly longer sentences. There was also recognition that the release of inmates will happen regardless of sentencing motivations. Thus, in order to reduce recidivism, save money, and ensure effective transitions for these former inmates, reentry had to be addressed in a more organized and collaborative approach than what was currently being done across many states and the federal government, which was minimal at best.

Reentry is the transition period of persons who are soon to be released or have recently been released from prison or jail back into the community. It involves providing services and assistance to these individuals and their families. After 9/11, states were in debt, the economy was souring, and unemployment was high compared to the booming years of the late 1990s. When the recession hit between 2007 and 2009, states had to devise ways to defray costs, and imprisoning offenders is very expensive. Couple the budget cuts with the fact that the "get-tough" policies in the 1980s led to overcrowded prisons, states had to come up with alternative models to save money while trying to maintain the relatively low crime rates the nation had been experiencing for several years.

In general, there are two mechanisms to reduce prison crowding and its cost. There are **front-door options** that involve community-based sanctions like probation instead of prison or jail, as were discussed in Chapter 5 of this text. **Back-door options** involve early-release mechanisms such as parole, transitional placement in a community-based correctional facility, or simply being released from prison without any assistance or supervision. The focus on reentry programs and services, most notably in the areas of employment, housing, and behavioral health, are critical when back-door options are implemented. Of specific concern are individuals with substance use and/or mental health disorders, who have an even greater risk of recidivism. It is estimated that over 70 percent of state prisoners have struggled with either one or both of these conditions (James and Glaze 2006; Peters, Wexler, and Lurigio 2015).

Barriers and Challenges to Reentry

Offenders face a multitude of barriers and challenges upon release that must be addressed in order to see reductions in recidivism and to improve adjustment outcomes for both formerly incarcerated persons and the people who live in the communities to which they return. The majority of these barriers and challenges fall under the categories of health services, employment and education, housing, transportation, and legal issues.

Critical Thinking Exercise

How likely would you be able to start over if you were given $200 and one small bag of personal items? Could you find a place to live, a job, and other necessities with so little to start with? What would help you in your transition from custody to free society?

Health Services

Physical health problems are more prevalent among the offender population, particularly those with mental illnesses with co-occurring substance use problems (La Vigne et al. 2008). Issues such as hypertension, diabetes, hepatitis A, B and C, communicable diseases, tuberculosis, HIV/AIDS, asthma, and heart disease are some of the potential physical health issues that need to be addressed, as physical healthcare is also important for recovery. Substance use disorders often accompany and can intensify these health problems. Drug use and intoxication are common in the months following release, and without sustained advocacy and follow-up, those with substance use problems are likely to relapse and engage in other negative behaviors. Similarly, mental health disorders alone or co-occurring with substance use disorders are also prevalent among the incarcerated population. It is important to identify the healthcare needs of persons returning to society and ensure that they are provided access to medication and treatment after release. Failure to address these health issues decreases the likelihood of successful reentry into communities. To overcome this barrier, proper treatments and interventions in the community should be accessible to individuals upon their return to the community and thereafter.

Employment and Education

Obtaining employment represents one of the greatest barriers to formerly incarcerated persons' successful reintegration into the community. At its most basic level, employment provides former prisoners with a consistent source of funding for necessary food, shelter, clothing, transportation, and other basic amenities. It also provides a new social network that supports positive behaviors and serves as a protective factor against future criminal activity. The lack of adequate education, sufficient career development, and educational and vocational training programs contribute to higher recidivism rates. Educational programs offered to inmates while incarcerated and then continued out in the community after release are important pathways to helping the formerly incarcerated secure employment, reducing recidivism and enhancing quality of life (West 2016). Being gainfully employed assists ex-offenders in obtaining and maintaining housing and decreases the likelihood of returning to crime.

Housing

Securing safe, decent, affordable housing is a major challenge for people exiting prison, During the early days and weeks after release from custody, many formerly incarcerated persons live with family members, friends, or a significant other. For those ex-inmates who find it difficult to reunite with those they left behind while they were incarcerated, there are few housing options available. Even with government assistance programs like Section 8 Housing under the US Department of Housing and Urban Development, some categories of felonies are disqualified from housing benefits. These include sex offenses, drug trafficking crimes, violent offenses, and some types of fraud offenses.

Without stable housing, not only is there stress involved, it is also a challenge to provide a reliable address to use while completing a job application and fulfilling the terms of post-release supervision if applicable. Without a job, it is problematic to complete the paperwork to rent or purchase an apartment or home. Unfortunately, for some, returning to crime may be viewed as a viable option to earning money legitimately and finding a place to live.

Transportation

Depending on where formerly incarcerated persons are returning, transportation may be more challenging. In rural areas, there are limited options to rely on public transportation and in more urban areas, the costs to take public transportation such as time, fares, and pickup locations may present their own barriers for some individuals. For ex-offenders under post-release supervision, many are required to make office visits and participate in treatment, holding a job and/or job seeking, or vocational programs as a condition of their release. If they are not able to access transportation, they could be found in violation and returned to prison.

Legal Issues

Many ex-offenders face substantial legal problems after release, which have often been left unsettled while incarcerated. Examples of these legal issues are

1. restoring lost voting rights,
2. taking care of past-due child support payments,
3. reinstating driving privileges,

4. overcoming barriers that mandate occupational licenses such as those required in certain health, education, and legal professions,
5. needing assistance obtaining acceptable documentation necessary to obtain employment and housing such as driver's license or other photo identification, social security card, and birth certificate.

Of all the legal issues above, obtaining personal identification is critical upon release, as it is a prerequisite for achieving the more long-term reentry goals of finding a job, opening a banking account, and securing housing. These legal problems often prevent formerly incarcerated persons from obtaining and maintaining stable housing and employment, which are two of the most significant predictive factors for whether they are likely to return to prison or face homelessness or other hardships.

Critical Thinking Exercise

Assume you are a volunteer at a newly formed local reentry assistance organization. You are being asked to put together a pamphlet on how to help recently released inmates obtain personal identification. What would you include in this document? What else do you think would be helpful?

Reentry Programming and Services

Fortunately, largely due in part to the reentry movement, numerous local, state, and federal agencies and nonprofit organizations across the country provide reentry programming and assistance. Reentry efforts that make connections even before inmates return to the community and that continue over the first year after release are essential. Some state departments of corrections and the federal government have reentry planning services or programs for inmates preparing for release from custody. During this planning, which can occur upon admission with updates made during their prison stay and just prior to release, inmates are asked to note:

1. where they will live immediately upon release and then longer term housing arrangements;
2. what their transportation plans are from the prison and thereafter;,
3. what agencies in the community can provide resources they need such as employment, education, mental and physical health services, and identification such as driver's license, social security card, and/or birth certificate;
4. what they will do during their leisure time;
5. who they can rely on for social support such as family, friends, or community members.

With the passage of the **Second Chance Act of 2008**, financial support through federal grant funding has increased the number of formalized reentry programs across the US, state, local, and tribal governments and nonprofit agencies, and organizations can apply for grant funding to develop and implement programs to assist individuals being released from prison, jails, and juvenile institutions. Recently funded projects have included programs that provide assistance for adults with co-occurring substance use and mental disorders, the creating and supporting reentry courts, and mentoring and transitional services for juveniles. A major key to success in reentry programming is to develop coordinated partnerships with state and local criminal justice and social services agencies, organizations, and health service providers to efficiently and appropriately deliver needed support and services to formerly incarcerated populations.

Critical Thinking Exercise

Researchers at the RAND Corporation have been analyzing and reporting on numerous issues from crime to workers in the workplace since 1948. They have devoted a considerable effort toward examining programs and practices to reentry. Pick one report available at https://www.rand.org/topics/prisoner-reentry.html and share with a classmate what you find promising and would recommend to your local or state policy makers or practitioners to implement to improve reentry outcomes.

Evidence-Based Practices to Reentry

Evidence-based practices (EBPs) have been recognized as a very effective and efficient model to work with across the medical, substance use, and mental health and social work fields—the major areas that are vital to reentry success for a large proportion of ex-offenders. It requires an integration of the best research evidence; patients' or clients' input regarding their values, beliefs and concerns; and the clinician's expertise on services and treatments available to the client (Sackett et al. 1996). By taking into account these combined elements, clients are then presented with viable options for choosing services most appropriate for them. Under EBPs, clients are also more likely to be invested in their reentry success since their perspectives are taken into consideration. As such, we are more likely to observe increases in the likelihood of clients achieving positive outcomes from participating in reentry programs and recovery support services in the community. Research continues to find support for the **eleven principles of effective intervention** when it comes to reentry (Matthews, Hubbard, and Latessa 2001, p.455-56; and as cited in Willison et al. 2017, p. 32):

1. Interventions are behavioral in nature and involve the use of reinforcement and modeling of prosocial behaviors and problem-solving skills.
2. Services should be matched to the risk levels of the program participants where, as discussed in Chapter 5, intensive services should be applied to those who are higher risk in order to see the most significant effects.

3. Service referrals should be related to individuals' assessed criminogenic needs (e.g., anti-social attitudes, anti-social friends, substance use, lack of empathy, and impulsive behavior).
4. Clients' personality and learning styles should be responsive to the treatment method, modality, and service provider.
5. Forty to 70% of time in treatment should consist of intensive services for higher risk individuals over three to nine months.
6. Programs and interventions are highly structured with deviations from the plan enforced firmly, consistently, and fairly by service providers.
7. Treatment staff are trained in behavioral interventions and interact with clients in constructive ways utilizing constructive and interpersonal supervision and communication strategies.
8. Clients are monitored over the course of the treatment noting any setbacks and reinforcing gains.
9. Services for relapse prevention and aftercare are accessible and clients are trained to practice prosocial behaviors.
10. Clients' family members and significant others learn how to help them when confronted with challenging situations that could lead to deviant behaviors.
11. High advocacy and brokering activities for clients occur frequently if services are appropriate and available in the community.

Web Activity

For a snapshot of some promising programs and the populations served, go to https://csgjusticecenter.org/wp-content/uploads/2013/11/ReentryMatters.pdf. You just might find your state is doing something noteworthy for offender reintegration.

Programs and services that apply the eleven principles can expect to reduce recidivism by at least 30 percent. A common theme across these principles is matching treatment programs and services to the needs of clients and helping facilitate that the right approaches are targeted to the right clients in the right setting under the guidance of professionals who are trained in behavioral interventions.

To increase the probability of success in applying these principles, case management is promising. Case management is an approach to service delivery that requires knowledge and understanding of community resources along with assessment, intervention, and negotiation skills. Primary functions of the case manager include (1) assessment of client's strengths, weaknesses, and needs; (2) planning for unique services for each individual based on their needs and preferences; (3) locating needed services and resources and linking clients to them; (4) coordinating and monitoring services provided; (5) case advocacy for unavailable resources and (5) identification and outreach (Phillips, Kemper, and Applebaum 1988; Levine and Fleming 1987).

A major advantage to case management approaches are that they can assist clients in overcoming the challenges and barriers to service they face when attempting to avail them. This assistance can increase the probability of treatment attendance, program, completion, and client goal attainment. Increased length of time in treatment has been significantly associated with positive outcomes in terms of decreased drug use and criminal behavior and increased employment (Hubbard et al. 1989). In addition, case management techniques that link mental health services and other resources to offenders returning to the community can play a vital role in reducing symptoms of these disorders (Scott 2008). Research studies have also consistently documented that case management approaches to service delivery reduce recidivism among offender populations (Broner et al. 2003; Yamatani and Spjeldnes 2011; Cullen et al. 2012; Bahr, Masters, and Taylor 2012).

One example of a type of case management is **strengths-based case management** (SBCM) and recent calls for its use in reentry practices have been made (Hunter et al. 2016). SBCM empowers clients as it provides them with an opportunity to identify their own strengths and to use these strengths as a mechanism to lead them toward their success in recovery and increases the probability of reentry success. Six core principles of strengths-based practice are: (1) People can recover, reclaim, and transform their lives; (2) The focus is on an individual's strengths rather than deficits; (3) The community is viewed as having an abundance of resources; (4) The client is the director of the helping process; (5) The relationship between case manager and client is primary and essential; and (6) The primary setting for treatment is in the community.

The five functions of SBCM case manager are assessment, planning, linkage, monitoring, and advocacy. During assessment, case managers, working along with clients, identify clients' skills and abilities, support clients in setting their treatment and reentry success goals, and determine how these goals would be met. Case managers also assist clients in accessing their identified services and resources and also work to resolve any challenges or barriers their clientsight face. They also engage in case advocacy for their clients for needed resources or accommodation. In general, research suggests that SBCM increases the likelihood of positive outcomes such as client employability and reduced drug use (Pantalone, Iwamasa, and Martell 2010; Bahr, Masters, and Taylor 2012; Hunter et al. 2016). Comparing the eleven principles of effective intervention with the core principles of SCBM, we can see that there is significant overlap. Reentry programs would benefit from applying these standards to increase the probability that larger percentages of formerly incarcerated persons will transition into their respective communities successfully upon release and in the years to follow.

SUMMARY

This chapter presented the various mechanisms by which individuals are released from incarceration and the challenges and barriers individuals face as they transition from time spent in secure facility to adjusting to live in the community.

The meaning and history of parole practices were discussed followed by the factors that go into release decisions and the characteristics of the parole boards that make those decisions. The role of parole or post-control community supervision officers and their relationships with parolees were explored along with the conditions of release and revocation processes should those conditions be violated.

The latter part of the chapter covered the reentry movement and the importance of connecting ex-offenders with services and programs to increase their chances for success as they reenter the community. Approaches that follow the eleven principles of effective intervention and utilize evidence-based practices like strengths-based case management were also detailed as well as the Second Chance Act of 2008. Over the past fifteen-plus years, more attention has been paid and grant funding made available to programs and services aimed at guiding and supporting the post-release success of the thousands of individuals who are released from secure custody annually.

KEY WORDS

administrative parole
autonomous boards
back-door options
banishment
Zebulon R. Brockway
clemency
collateral contacts
commutation of sentence
consolidated boards
Sir Walter Crofton
determinate sentencing
discretionary release
eleven principles of effective intervention
Elmira Reformatory
evidence-based practices

executive clemency
executive pardon
expiration or unconditional mandatory release
front-door options
hearing officers
indentured servants
indeterminate sentencing
intermediate system
Irish system
Alexander Maconochie
mark system
new crime violation
notice of revocation of parole

parole d'honneur
parole officers
presumptive parole date
parole guidelines
reentry
reentry movement
revocation hearing
Second Chance Act of 2008
strengths-based case management (SBCM)
supervised mandatory release
technical violation
ticket of leave
transportation

DISCUSSION QUESTIONS

1. The governor of a newly formed state in the mid-1800s wants to begin a system of parole and is debating between the Maconochie and the Crofton models. Which would you recommend? Why?

2. It is now present day and the governor is being asked to consider an autonomous parole board to replace the consolidated board currently in place. You are part of a team asked to list the pros and cons of each type of board or come up with an alternative method that can reduce the probability that the state is biased in its decisions to release individuals from prison, but also ensure that

public safety is not at risk. Comparing your list, which one would be more likely to meet these ends? Defend.

3. Assessment instruments are frequently being used by parole boards to determine a person's probably of success while on parole. Some of the items are dynamic factors that can change over time, and research demonstrates that these are strong predictors of success. Of these, which factors should be addressed, both during, and immediately upon release from incarceration? Whereshould funding and programming be directed? Why did you choose these over other factors?

4. Given the barriers to reentry for formerly incarcerated persons, which ones do you think can be more easily addressed compared to others? Why? What would an ideal reentry process look like in your state? Be sure to address the majority of the issues for maximum success.

5. Should it be mandatory for state prison systems to have reentry programming that connects to the services and programs in the communities where persons return? Why or why not?

SUGGESTED READINGS

Hunter, B. A., A. S. Lanza, M. Lawlor, W. Dyson, and D. M. Gordon. (2016). "A Strengths-Based Approach to Prisoner Reentry: The Fresh Start Prisoner Reentry Program." *International Journal of Offender Therapy and Comparative Criminology* 60(11), 1298–1314.

Latessa, E. J., S. L. Listwan, and D. Koetzle. D. (2014). *What Works (and Doesn't) in Reducing Recidivism.* Waltham, MA: Anderson.

Ogletree, C. J., and A. Sarat, eds. (2012). *Life without Parole: America's New Death Penalty?* New York, NY: NYU Press.

Petersilia, J. (2003). *When Prisoners Come Home: Parole and Prisoner Reentry.* New York, NY: Oxford University Press.

Reamer, F. G. (2016). *On the Parole Board: Reflections on Crime, Punishment, Redemption, and Justice.* New York, NY: Columbia University Press.

Ricciardelli, R., and Adrienne M. F. Peters, eds. (2017). *After Prison: Navigating Employment and Reintegration.* Waterloo, ON: Wilfrid Laurier University Press.

Council of State Governments. (2017). *Reducing Recidivism: States Deliver Results.* Retrieved from https://csgjusticecenter.org/wp-content/uploads/2017/06/6.12.17_Reducing-Recidivism_States-Deliver-Results.pdf.

US Department of Justice (2016). *Roadmap to Reentry: Reducing Recidivism through Reentry Reforms at the Federal Bureau of Prisons.* Accessed October 4, 2018. https://www.justice.gov/archives/reentry/file/844356/download.

West, R. J. (2016). *Reexamining Reentry: The Policies, People, and Programs of the United States Prisoner Reintegration Systems.* Lanham, MD: Rowman and Littlefield.

Willison, J. B., S. B. Rossman, C. Lindquist, J. H. Walters, and P. K. Lattimore. (2017). *Second Chance Act Adult Offender Reentry Demonstration Projects Evidence-Based Practices: Prosocial Behavior Change Techniques.* Accessed September 15, 2018 from https://www.ncjrs.gov/pdffiles1/nij/grants/251444.pdf.

REFERENCES

American Probation and Parole Association. n.d. "Rules of Probation and Parole" (sample). Accessed September 2, 2018. http://www.appa-net.org/psn/docs/Rules_of_Probation_ Parole.pdf.

Bahr, S. J., A. L. Masters, and B. M. Taylor. (2012). "What Works in Substance Abuse Treatment Programs for Offenders?" *The Prison Journal 92*(2), 155–174.

Broner, N., H. Nguyen, A. Swern, and S. Goldfinger. (2003). "Adapting a Substance Abuse Court Diversion Model for Felony Offenders with Co-occurring Disorders: Initial Implementation." *Psychiatric Quarterly 74*(4), 361.

Carson, A., and D. Golinelli. (2013, December 19). *Prisoners in 2012: Trends in Admissions and Releases 1991–2012.* p. 4. (NCJ 243920). Washington, DC: Bureau of Justice Statistics.

Cullen, A. E., A. Y. Clarke, E. Kuipers, S. Hodgins, K. Dean, and T. Fahy. (2012). "A Multisite Randomized Controlled Trial of a Cognitive Skills Programme for Male Mentally Disordered Offenders: Social–Cognitive Outcomes." *Psychological Medicine 42*(3), 557.

Hubbard, R. L., M. E. Marsden, J. V. Rachal, H. J. Harwood, E. R. Cavanaugh, and H. M. Ginzburg. (1989). *Drug Abuse Treatment. A National Study of Effectiveness.* Chapel Hill: University of North Carolina Press.

Hughes, T., Wilson, D.J. (2002). *Reentry Trends in the United States.* Washington, DC: Bureau of Justice Statistics.

Hunter, B. A., A. S. Lanza, M. Lawlor, W. Dyson, and D. M. Gordon. (2016). A Strengths-Based Approach to Prisoner Reentry: The Fresh Start Prisoner Reentry Program. *International Journal of Offender Therapy and Comparative Criminology 60*(11), 1298–1314.

Ireland, C. S., and J. Prause. (2005). Discretionary Parole Release: Length of Imprisonment, Percent of Sentence Served, and Recidivism. *Journal of Crime and Justice 28*(2), 27–49.

James, D. J., and L. E. Glaze. (2006). *Mental Health Problems of Prison and Jail Inmates.* Washington, DC: US Dept of Justice, Office of Justice Programs, Bureau of Justice Statistics

Johnson, H. A., N. T. Wolfe, and M. Jones. (2003). *History of Criminal Justice.* 33rd ed. Cincinnati: Anderson.

La Vigne, N., E. Davies, T. Palmer, and R. Halberstadt. (2008). *Release Planning for Successful Reentry.* Washington DC: Urban Institute Justice Policy Center.

Levine, I. S., and M. Fleming. (1987). *Human Resource Development: Issues in Case Management.* Rockville, MD: National Institute of Mental Health.

Matthews, B., D. J. Hubbard, and E. Latessa. (2001). "Making the Next Step: Using Evaluability Assessment to Improve Correctional Programming." *Prison Journal* 81, no. 4: 454–472.

Ostermann, M. (2015). "How Do Former Inmates Perform in the Community? A Survival Analysis of Rearrests, Reconvictions, and Technical Parole Violations." *Crime & Delinquency 61*(2), 163–187.

Pantalone, D. W., G. Y. Iwamasa, and C. R. Martell. (2010). "Cognitive-Behavioral Therapy with Diverse Populations." In *Handbook of Cognitive-Behavioral Therapies,* edited by K. Dobson, 445–462. New York: Guilford Press.

Peters, R. H., H. K. Wexler, and A. J. Lurigio. (2015). Co-occurring Substance Use and Mental Disorders in the Criminal Justice System: A New Frontier of Clinical Practice and Research. Accessed October 4, 2018. https://www.apa.org/pubs/journals/features/prj-0000135.pdf.

Phillips, B., P. Kemper, and R. Applebaum. (1988). The Evaluation of the National Long Term Card Demonstration. 4: Case Management under Channeling. *Health Services Research 23*(1), 67–81.

Sackett, D., W. Rosenberg, G. J. Muir, R. Haynes and W. Richardson. (1996). Evidence-Based Medicine: What It Is and What It Isn't. *British Medical Journal* 312: 71–72.

Schlager, M. D., and K. Robbins. (2008). Does Parole Work? Revisited: Reframing the Discussion of the Impact of Postprison Supervision on Offender Outcome. *Prison Journal 88*(2), 234–251.

Scott, R. (2008). "Interventions to address violence associated with mental illness." *Australasian Psychiatry, 16*(6), 405–411.

U.S. Parole Commission Rules and Procedures Manual. (2010). Washington, DC: US Parole Commission. Accessed September 2, 2018. https://www.justice.gov/sites/default/files/uspc/legacy/2010/08/27/uspc-manual111507.pdf.

Warner, C. D. (1885). "A Study of Prison Management." *North American Review 140*(341), 291–308.

Vito, G. F., G. E. Higgins, and R. Tewksbury. (2017). "The Effectiveness of Parole Supervision: Use of Propensity Score Matching to Analyze Reincarceration Rates in Kentucky." *Criminal Justice Policy Review 28*(7), 627–640.

West, R. J. (2016). *Reexamining Reentry: The Policies, People, and Programs of the United States Prisoner Reintegration Systems.* Lanham, MD: Rowman and Littlefield.

Willison, J. B., S. B. Rossman, C. Lindquist, J. H. Walters, and P. K. Lattimore. (2017). *Second Chance Act Adult Offender Reentry Demonstration Projects Evidence-Based Practices: Prosocial Behavior Change Techniques.* Accessed September 15, 2018 from https://www.ncjrs.gov/pdffiles1/nij/grants/251444.pdf.

Yamatani, H., and Spjeldnes, S. (2011). "Saving Our Criminal Justice System: The Efficacy of a Collaborative Social Service." *Social Work, 56*(1), 53–61.

CASES

Greenholtz v. Inmates of the Nebraska Penal and Correctional Complex, 442 U.S. 1. (1979).
Morrissey v. Brewer, 408 U.S. 471 (1972).

CHAPTER 7

Juvenile Corrections

CHAPTER OUTLINE

AFTER READING THIS CHAPTER,
YOU SHOULD BE ABLE TO:

- Discuss the early institutions established to handle problem youths
- Identify two common residential facilities for youths and discuss each
- Distinguish between preventive detention and therapeutic detention
- Discuss state training schools
- Identify the expectations and goals of probation, as well as issues in its operation
- List and define different probation-plus programs
- Discuss home confinement and the use of EMS
- Define restorative justice and discuss its use in juvenile corrections
- Define aftercare and compare it to probation

INTRODUCTION

While most of this book covers adult corrections, it is important to consider juvenile corrections in our discussion. Juveniles were once held in the same facilities as adults prior to the reform movement for juveniles that began in the 1800s and culminated with the establishment of the first separate juvenile court system in 1899. Institutions for juveniles became commonplace in the 1820s as society recognized that children were different from adults. One major driver for a separate juvenile system was the belief that youths could be rehabilitated and deserved second chances, unlike adult offenders who were often seen as deserving of their punishment and not as amenable to treatment efforts.

EARLY HISTORY

Throughout most of history the young were considered either property or people. The very young, from birth to age five or six, held much the same status as any other property in society. They were subject to being bought, sold, and disposed of just as any other property. Once the individual reached the age of five or six, he or she became a full-fledged member of society and was expected to act according to the same mandates placed on all "adult" members of society (Aries 1962).

The general view that children were the same as adults extended to the realm of legal sanctioning. Prior to reaching the status of "adult," children who committed a crime were dealt with by the father, and the father, as "owner," was responsible to the victim. Once children became "adults," they were subject to the same rules and regulations as all adults (Empey 1982). There did not exist a separate system for dealing with youthful offenders. Society could sanction youths in the same way as it could adults. The law made no distinction based on the age of the offender. In fact, youths could be (and were) sentenced to death for various deviant actions. While many youths could be sentenced to death, few received such a sentence, and most of those who did were never put to death (Platt 1977). Faust and Brantingham (1979) claimed that a process of **nullification**, or refusal to enforce the law against children, took place because of the lack of penalties geared specifically for juvenile offenders.

Changes in the methods of dealing with problem youths corresponded to the changes occurring in American society of the early 1800s. Responses to problem youths grew out of the establishment of ways to handle poor people in the cities (see Rothman 1971, 1980). A key aspect of addressing poverty was to train the poor for employment, beginning early in life. Removing a child from bad societal influences and the substandard training they received from their poor parents was seen as an important step in creating productive citizens. Early evidence of this was in 1555 when the English established the **Bridewell Institution** in London to handle youthful beggars. While the primary emphasis of the institution was dealing with poor and destitute youths, in practice the institution handled all problem youths, including delinquents. The establishment of institutions in the early 1800s in the United States closely followed the ideas of the Bridewell Institution.

Houses of Refuge

The first official and separate institutions for juveniles were known as the **houses of refuge** and were developed by prominent Quakers along with the political backing of local and state policy makers. These institutions were established to separate youths from the detrimental environment of the city. The first house of refuge was established in New York City in 1825 and was followed by institutions in Boston (1826) and Philadelphia (1828). The New York City House of Refuge was funded by the state government but privately managed. The state generated the money for operating the house of refuge by placing a head tax on passengers arriving from overseas and with the proceeds from the license fees on taverns, circuses, and theaters. These taxes were seen as appropriate sources by the reformers of the time (known as the **child savers**) who blamed alcohol consumption, immigration, and commercial entertainment for crime committed by juveniles.

Central aspects of the house of refuge were education, skills training, hard work, religious training, parental discipline, apprenticeships, and indeterminate sentences (Pisciotta 1983). The goal was to produce productive members of society. Indeterminate sentences reflected the idea that each youth may need individual attention. Where one youth may benefit from a short period of intervention, another child may require extended assistance. The belief that the best methods of training lay in the realm of the family and the church was a cornerstone of intervention. The houses of refuge were envisioned as shelters and sanctuaries that would protect and nurture children while avoiding the corrupting influences of the city and the poor family (Rothman 1971).

Houses of refuge also served to separate children from the criminogenic influences of adult workhouses and jails (Krisberg and Austin 1978). Placing poor and problem juveniles in adult institutions meant enhanced contact with adult criminal offenders. Adult institutions would be "schools for crime" that produced more problems than they solved. The houses of refuge supposedly differed by offering education and training in useful skills within a setting that allowed for control and discipline of the children.

The first placements by the courts into the houses of refuge were youths who would be considered status offenders who really did not commit crimes. They were more likely to be vagrants or neglected children. Sometimes, juveniles were placed in the facilities despite parental objections. The length of the commitment was contingent upon a youth's need, age, and labor skills. The house of refuge was not as rosy as it might appear at first glance—there were some who criticized the strict discipline used against the children and the separation of the sexes. Apparently, some of the admitted children were also not fans of the operations of the house of refuge as many ran away from the facilities.

Once children entered the house of refuge, most of their day was spent working under supervision. Labor was believed to be important to education and discipline, but it also helped financially support the facility. Boys' tasks involved the manufacturing of brushes, chairs, brass nails, and shoes. Girls' jobs revolved around typical domestic chores such as sewing uniforms and doing laundry. Education typically meant religious instruction, mostly centered on the evangelical tradition. The youths in the house of refuge also received very basic educational skills.

The daily operations and the impact of these institutions was questionable. Many of the activities were far removed from the real world. Daily operations followed a military behavior model which included enforced silence, marching to and from different activities, the wearing of uniforms, and swift and habitual corporal punishment (Rothman 1971). Apprenticeships often failed to be more than simple slave labor. Many of the apprenticeships were on farms in the country and some youths were apprenticed to ship captains. Exploitation of the youths by the institutions was common. Children were bribed, beaten, and even subjected to extended incarceration if the monetary interests of the administrators were at stake (Pisciotta 1982).

The houses of refuge also failed in other respects. In many ways they were nothing but new prisons. They were tremendously overcrowded. In the mid-1800s, the construction of larger institutions for children was needed as more and more youths were being incarcerated. The overcrowding was partly due to the admission of the poor and destitute, delinquent youths, and poverty-stricken adults and adult offenders. The overcrowding altered the goals of education and training to simple custody and discipline. The establishment of institutions like the **Lyman School for Boys** in 1848 by the state of Massachusetts eliminated the housing of adult and juvenile offenders in the same facility but carried on the tradition of overcrowding and related problems. In general, the early houses of refuge failed to provide their stated goals and settled into a process very reminiscent of that of the adult prisons and jails that had previously been the norm for handling youths.

Reformatories

The child savers did not give up on rescuing children from lives of crime and poverty when the houses of refuge failed to live up to their promise. These reformers continued to encourage state and local governments to create other institutions that became known as **reformatories**. Proponents of the house of refuge approach argued that the principles underlying their intervention were correct—just poorly executed. The emphasis on education, training, and parental discipline led to the establishment of "cottage" reformatories.

A **cottage** setup was intended to closely parallel a family. Each cottage had surrogate parents who would oversee the training and education of a small number of problem youths. Care and concern typical of family life would be the norm in the cottages. Youths were separated from the criminogenic features of the urban environment by establishing cottages in the country and on farms. Youths would learn hard, honest work. The idea of indeterminate sentencing also carried over to the cottage approach.

Another method of dealing with youths, in accordance with the cottage idea, entailed placing juveniles in foster homes. These placements were primarily apprenticeships and were seen as an alternative to institutionalization. Youths were to be trained to enter a worthwhile occupation.

Unfortunately, like the earlier houses of refuge, these new reformatories faced many of the same problems. The cottages became terribly overcrowded to the point that custody became the primary concern. Apprenticeships proved to be little more than slave labor, and youths often fled at the first opportunity. One analysis of 210 apprenticed individuals found that 72 percent of the youths either ran away or returned to the institution (Pisciotta 1979). The harsh treatment of the youths in the institutions led to running away, the setting of fires, and the emergence of various sexual problems (Pisciotta 1982). The inability to handle some youths prompted the establishment of special facilities such as the **Elmira Reformatory** in 1876. Unfortunately, Elmira accepted both juveniles and young adults and negated the premise of separating youths from criminogenic older offenders. A final problem with the institutions was the continued mixing of both deviant and destitute youths in the same facilities. The institutions considered that being poor was closely tied to deviant activity and, as a result, intervened in the lives of lower-class individuals regardless of the existence (or lack) of a delinquent or criminal act.

Institutions for Females

As with adult corrections, the early focus of juvenile corrections was on males. Little attention was paid to females, due to the relatively small number of females sent to institutions. Female offenders were typically dealt with in the same institutions as males. Separate institutions for girls began to appear in the mid-1800s. One of the most well-known facilities for females was the **Lancaster State Industrial School for Girls** in Massachusetts. Most of the girls sent here came from poor, immigrant families (Brenzel 1983). Institutions for female youths were set up as family cottages.

Institutions for girls aimed to produce women capable of being good house-wives and mothers (Brenzel 1983). Marriage and parenthood was the vision for the future of the girls. Unfortunately, the institutions for females suffered from the same problems as those for males. Lancaster and similar institutions tended to be little more than prisons for youths. They were characterized by overcrowding, lack of treatment, and strict discipline.

The New Juvenile System

The establishment of the juvenile court in Cook County (Chicago), Illinois, in 1899 meant a truly separate system for handling problem youths. This included a separate correctional system for youths. No longer were adult institutions or shared adult/juvenile institutions the default for youthful offenders. New facilities were needed to handle youths processed by the new juvenile courts. One of the first of the new institutions was the Illinois State School at St. Charles, Illinois, which opened in 1905 (Platt 1977). Most of the new institutions were based on the cottage reformatory model.

JUVENILE INSTITUTIONAL CORRECTIONS TODAY

Two common types of facilities for juveniles found in nearly every state are deten-tion centers and **state training schools**. Detention centers are often administered at the county level and are akin to jails for adults. Their primary purpose is to hold ju-veniles awaiting the next stage in the juvenile process. In addition to these facilities, nearly every state will have at least one state-controlled training school, which is the juvenile equivalent to adult prisons. They are secure residential facilities designed to care for juveniles for longer durations than a detention center. Many training schools are large institutions, with significant numbers dating back to before 1900.

States have a range of other residential facilities for handling youths beyond detention centers and state training schools. The Office of Juvenile Justice and De-linquency Prevention (OJJDP) lists five other types. These are shelters, group homes, boot camps, ranch/wilderness camps, and residential treatment centers. A brief description of each is found in Box 7.1.

A correctional census of juvenile residential facilities is conducted every two years by OJJDP. The count is based on a one-day census. The most recent one-day count, taken October 28, 2015, indicates that there is over 48,000 youths residing in almost 1,900 juvenile residential facilities (Sickmund et al. 2017). Fifty-four per-cent of the facilities are public facilities, handling 69 percent of the youths. Resi-dential treatment centers are the most common type of facility (39%), followed by detention centers at 36 percent. State training schools account for only 10 percent of facilities (Hockenberry et al. 2016). The size of the facilities varies a great deal. State training schools and other long-term secure institutions typically house over 200 youths (Sickmund et al. 2017). Conversely, most group homes hold fewer than 50 residents, while detention centers and residential treatment centers generally house from 21 to 150 youths.

BOX 7.1

Types of Residential Centers

- Detention center A short-term facility that provides temporary care in a physically restricting environment for juveniles in custody pending court disposition and, often, for juveniles who are adjudicated delinquent and awaiting disposition or placement elsewhere or are awaiting transfer to another jurisdiction.

- Shelter A short-term facility that provides temporary care similar to that of a detention center, but in a physically unrestricting environment. Includes runaway/homeless shelters and other types of shelters.

- Reception/diagnostic center A short-term facility that screens persons committed by the courts and assigns them to appropriate correctional facilities.

- Group home A long-term facility in which residents are allowed extensive contact with the community, such as attending school or holding a job. Includes halfway houses.

- Boot camp A secure facility that operates like military basic training. There is emphasis on physical activity, drills, and manual labor. Strict rules and drill instructor tactics are designed to break down youth's resistance. Length of stay is generally longer than detention but shorter than most long-term commitments.

- Ranch/wilderness camp A long-term residential facility for persons whose behavior does not necessitate the strict confinement of a long-term secure facility, often allowing them greater contact with the community. Includes ranches, forestry camps, wilderness or marine programs, or farms.

- Residential treatment center A facility that focuses on providing some type of individually planned treatment program for youth (substance use, sex offender, mental health, etc.) in conjunction with residential care. Such facilities generally require specific licensing by the state that may require that treatment provided is Medicaid-reimbursable.

- Long-term secure facility A specialized type of facility that provides strict confinement for its residents. Includes training schools, reformatories, and juvenile correctional facilities.

- Other Includes facilities such as alternative schools and independent living, etc.

SOURCE: Sickmund, M., T. J. Sladky, W. Kang, and C. Puzzanchera. 2017. "Easy Access to the Census of Juveniles in Residential Placement." Accessed on February 26, 2018. http://www.ojjdp.gov/ojstatbb/ezacjrp/.

Two-thirds of the youths are being held after being adjudicated. The remainder are being held while awaiting some form of adjudication or placement (Sickmund et al. 2017). Just 5 percent of youths in custody are status offenders. The number of youths in residential placement has dropped from over 105,000 in 1977 to just over 48,000 in 2015. This translates into a 54 percent decrease and is the lowest number since 1975. The mean length of stay in facilities is 129 days (roughly four months), with the median stay being 69 days (Sickmund et al. 2017). Many of the facilities were built in the 1970s and earlier (Roush and McMillen 2000).

Information on the demographic background of those held is also gathered in the biannual census. The most recent data show that most residents are male (85%) (Sickmund et al. 2017). Looking at racial breakdown, blacks make up 42 percent of those in residential facilities, followed by whites at 31 percent and Hispanics at 22 percent. The racial data show that blacks are confined at a disproportionate rate compared to their population representation. In terms of age, 28 percent of the residents are age seventeen. Just over one-quarter are age 16 and 18 percent are age fifteen (Sickmund et al. 2017).

The number of youths held in adult prisons has fallen to 993 in 2015 from roughly 4,000 in 2000 (Sickmund et al. 2017). In addition, 4,200 youths were held in adult jails (with 80% being held as adults) in 2015. This number is also down from its high of almost 9,500 in 1999 (Sickmund et al. 2017).

Web Activity

For the latest available statistics on juveniles in custody in state prisons, go to the website of the Office of Juvenile Justice and Delinquency Prevention Statistical Briefing Book and click on Juveniles in Corrections. Available at: https://www.ojjdp.gov/ojstatbb/ezacjrp/.

The cost of confining youths is substantial. The Justice Policy Institute (2014) noted that the average yearly cost of confining a youthful offender is just under $149,000, with a daily average cost of $966. The costs also vary a great deal from state to state. The lowest cost is in Louisiana (roughly $47,000 per year) and the highest cost is in New York (almost $353,000 per year).

Web Activity

The Justice Policy Institute offers insight into the costs of confining youths and relates these costs to things like recidivism, educational attainment, and other factors. You can read more about this at http://www.justicepolicy.org/uploads/justicepolicy/documents/sticker_shock_final_v2.pdf.

Critical Thinking Exercise

Investigate the number of youths held in facilities in your state. What types of facilities are there? What is the demographic characteristics of the youths held in the facilities? How does this compare to the general population of the state?

Detention Centers

Every state has **detention centers**, often administered at the county level. Detention centers are akin to jails for adults. Their primary purpose is to hold juveniles awaiting the next stage in the juvenile process. Youths who are arrested or otherwise detained by the police are typically taken to a detention center. This will include youths who have committed a delinquent act or status offense. Juveniles who violate court orders or probation may also find themselves spending time in detention centers.

The first role of these centers is akin to the bail decision in the adult criminal justice system. The decision has to be made (often in consultation with the local prosecutor's office) whether to hold or release the youth, pending further processing. Holding juveniles in detention should be reserved for the most serious of offenders or those youth likely to abscond. In 2014, almost 213,000 delinquency cases (roughly 22%) involved detention. Youths are detained for an array of cases. One-third of youths in detention are there for personal offenses. Thirty percent are there for public order offense. Another 28 percent are there for property crime cases and 9 percent for drug crimes (Hockenberry and Puzzanchera 2017). Status offenders add another 4,200 youths to the detention roles. This represents 7 percent of all status offense cases.

Web Activity

A great deal of information is available on youths processed through the juvenile system. Hockenberry and Puzzanchera (2017) offer a compilation of data and explanation on a range of issues, including detention. You can investigate this material at https://www.ojjdp.gov/ojstatbb/njcda/pdf/jcs2014.pdf.

Detention centers are designed for short periods of confinement and were not meant to be used as sanctions. Despite this fact, detention centers often hold children for extensive periods of time, sometimes longer then they are held in state training schools. Based on the 2015 census, almost 40 percent of youths in detention centers have been there from 14 to 60 days. An additional 26 percent have been held for over 60 days (with roughly 1% held over 545 days) (Sickmund et al. 2017). Just over 35 percent are held and released within two weeks.

Black youths predominate in detention centers. Blacks comprise 42 percent of those detained, far exceeding their proportion of the youthful US population (Sickmund et al. 2017). Whites make up 36 percent. Interestingly, these detention figures more closely mirror the numbers of youths who are brought forth for possible detention. Roughly one-quarter of each nonwhite category are detained, while 18 percent of whites are detained. In terms of sex of the youth, males make up 79 percent of detainees. At the same time, less than one of every four males is detained (24%), while less than one in five females is detained (17%).

The initial decision to detain a youth is usually made by a detention worker or probation officer. The requirements for decisions vary across jurisdictions, but generally follow guidelines outlined by the National Council of Juvenile and Family Court Judges (NCJFCJ). The timing of a detention hearing should be within one business day but no longer than forty-eight hours of a youth being detained (National Council of Juvenile and Family Court Judges [NCJFCJ] 2005). These hearings should include the youths, legal representation, the prosecutor and court personnel, and the youth's parent/guardian. The basis for detaining the youth should be on the following:

- The juvenile might present a danger to society.
- The juvenile may have contact with his/her victim.
- The juvenile may fail to appear for future proceedings.
- The juvenile may be a danger to him/herself.
- There is no adequate home/alternative placement for the child upon release (NCJFCJ 2005).

Courts and jurisdictions may use a variety of assessment instruments in determining who to detain. Of the different factors that may prompt a detention decision, the risk of additional offending and being a danger to the community is the most important. One assessment instrument that specifically addresses this type of risk is the Ohio Youth Assessment System. This system is largely based on the risk of future offending and can be applied to different stages of system processing. For the detention decision, six factors are significant predictors of future arrest. These factors are

- any prior offense;
- current charge for a status, misdemeanor or felony offense;
- first contact with the system at age fifteen or younger,
- family members have been arrested;
- difficulty controlling anger;
- having a negative attitude toward the system (Latessa, Lovins, and Ostrowski 2009).

The authors have demonstrated that this instrument can distinguish between low-, medium-, and high-risk individuals.

Web Activity

More information of detention risk assessment can be found in "Juvenile Detention Risk Assessment: A Practice Guide to Juvenile Detention Reform," which can be accessed from http://www.aecf.org/m/resourcedoc/aecf-juveniledetentionrisk assessment1-2006.pdf

There are two types of detention that are somewhat at odds with one another. These are preventive detention and therapeutic detention. **Preventive detention** restricts youths by placing them in secure institutions, generally for the safety of the community or the youth. Legally, the use of preventive detention was settled in the case *Schall v. Martin* in 1984. In that case, the US Supreme Court ruled that preventive detention was permissible in keeping with the *parens patriae* (or state as parent) philosophy of the juvenile court. Despite its legality, there is still debate over the use of preventive detention.

Therapeutic detention strives to be more treatment oriented by providing diagnosis, remediation, and rehabilitation programs. In practice, however, detention centers have become catch-all institutions that attempts to serve all kinds of youth—those who need to be restrained, assisted, treated, and those whom no one knows quite what to do with. This is evident in the data on length of time spent in detention presented earlier. Detention is not just a temporary placement until a more definitive placement is made. For many youths it serves as a primary placement.

Detention can be either secure or nonsecure. **Secure detention** involves placing youths in a locked facility until future court appearances or the youth is transferred to a state correctional facility. **Nonsecure detention** is used more often for less serious offenders who are not a threat to the community or themselves and for youths who have been victims of abuse or neglect and need assistance. Rather than placement in a jail setting, youths are sent to small group homes that are not securely locked. Nonsecure detention may allow youths to attend regular school during the day before returning to the center at night. These centers may also be referred to as **day-night centers**.

The ideal detention situation is to hold youths for as short a time as possible. As noted earlier, detention is supposed to be used while youths are awaiting either further system processing (such as juvenile court proceedings) or movement to another type of facility or intervention. Programming, therefore, should address short-term needs of youths. The reality is that many youths spend considerable time in detention, which prompts the need for various types of programming.

One immediate need is programming to help maintain simple order in the facility. Behavior modification is an often-used approach and many detention centers use **token economy programs**. These programs use points to reward detained youths for appropriate behavior (such as good behavior, cleaning one's room, and participating in facility programs) and subtract points for inappropriate behavior (such as lying, being disrespectful, fighting, or failing to participate in required activities). Over time, youths can use accumulated points to "purchase" items from the center's store (such as food, drinks, or games) or to get extra privileges, such as free time or television time. The underlying idea is that of **operant conditioning**, which holds that behavior is learned through reinforcements.

The other typical form of programming in detention is education. Detention centers are required to make certain that school-aged youths continue to receive their education while in the facility. This is particularly important when youths spend lengthy periods of time in custody. Stephens and Arnette (2000, 4) note that "academic educational services should be the focus of detained and incarcerated youth's institutional experience." The goal is to provide youths the tools needed to be successful in life outside the facility. This means that the educational programs should include basic academic skills, high school completion, GED preparation, special education, social skills training, life skills training, and pre-employment preparation (Stephens and Arnette 2000). Youths also need preparation and support to transition back to regular school settings upon release from detention or other residential facilities.

Web Activity

Read more about educational needs of youths in detention, as well as the hurdles for youths returning to school in the community in "From the Courthouse to the Schoolhouse: Making Successful Transitions," at https://www.ncjrs.gov/pdffiles1/ojjdp/178900.pdf

---

In addition to educational services, detention is required to provide essential healthcare to the youths. This includes medical treatment, dental care, and mental health services, among others. Unfortunately, detention falls short in addressing these concerns. Gallagher and Dobrin (2007) note that few detention centers meet standards for healthcare as set by the National Commission on Correctional Health Care. Similarly, Barton (2012) points out that at least two-thirds of detained youths require some form of mental healthcare, but most of those needs go unaddressed. Many detained youths have some form of developmental disability, such as a learning disability, that is not addressed.

Training Schools

Training schools are often juvenile or youth correctional facilities and are the counterpart to adult prisons. Whatever the name, these institutions house adjudicated juveniles in secure, locked environments for extended periods of time (months to years). They house youths whom the juvenile court deems beyond the abilities of other lesser punishments to handle. Training schools can take a variety of physical forms. Some look like adult prisons with secure perimeters (high walls and/or fences), locked cells, their own medical and maintenance facilities, and isolation rooms for problem residents. Most of the institutions are much smaller than adult prisons, many of them housing fewer than fifty youths (Krisberg 2012).

Many training schools follow the cottage system in terms of their structure. This is based on the nineteenth-century reformatories that attempted to create a homelike environment that reformers felt was missing from youths' lives. Under the cottage system, juveniles are placed in small cottages with twenty to forty other youths. Unfortunately, cottages are often much different from a homelike atmosphere with loving parents. Cottage facilities are often little more than deteriorating, overcrowded dormitories.

Prior to placement in a particular institution, juveniles are sent to diagnostic and reception centers where they are assessed to determine which facility would best suit their needs. For example, some training schools specialize in treatment programs for sex offenders or offer specific academic, vocational, and therapy instruction. The diagnostic process can take anywhere from thirty to ninety days.

Several arguments have been advanced both supporting and opposing placement of youths in training schools. Proponents assert that training schools

- are just as effective as community alternatives and are necessary to protect the public,
- notify juveniles of the serious consequences of violating the law and deter future negative behaviors,
- remove the small number of habitual juvenile offenders from the community.

Opponents argue that training schools

- disrupt the family unit, particularly the families of male delinquents, as males often provide economic assistance to their families. Detaining a delinquent places every family member under even more stress and increases the chances that siblings will become involved in delinquency as well.
- increase the likelihood that confined youths will form a negative identity and see themselves as "bad" kids. They view their life chances in a less positive light compared to youth remaining in the community.
- separate youths from their families, which can lead to physical and emotional detachment problems. In turn, these juveniles often experience depression and isolation and are somewhat inept socially.
- solidify membership into the criminal subculture as delinquents housed with one another communicate the skills and values needed to succeed in this subculture to each other.

It is no surprise that opponents push for less reliance on training schools and more on development of community alternatives.

Roughly 12,000 youths were held in long-term secure confinement on any given day in 2015. The vast majority (87.3%) were males (Sickmund et al. 2017). In terms of race, close to half (43.2%) were black, far exceeding their proportion of the US population. Both whites and Hispanics accounted for roughly one-quarter of those in secure confinement (27.4% and 24.5%, respectively). As would be expected, the youths tend to be older, with most being age sixteen and older. Almost half (48.4%) are held due to a personal offense. Another one-quarter have committed a property offense and 12 percent are held for public order offenses (Sickmund et al. 2017).

Programming in state training schools is more extensive than in shorter-term residential facilities, such as detention. As in detention, behavior modification, typically through a token economy, is the primary means of controlling the youths. Besides earning extra privileges, points may be used to advance through steps of treatment programs or for shortening the time to release.

Educational programming, either academic or vocational, represent the primary daily activity of residents, particularly during the regular school year. The programming, however, is not the same as what youths receive in regular school classrooms. This is because the "students" in the institution typically have greater deficiencies and needs compared to students outside the institutions. Youths in custody are more likely to need remedial coursework, special education classes and assistance, and greater attention to in-class behavior (Council of State Governments Justice Center 2015). These facts mean that educational programming in long-term secure facilities faces obstacles to delivering basic education or vocational training.

Beyond academic programming, long-term secure institutions also offer other interventions. Life skills training and learning skills are common topics. Anger management, conflict resolution, and substance use resistance are also offered on a regular basis. Unfortunately, perhaps one of the most common forms of intervention in facilities is **boob tube therapy**. In essence, youths are parked in front of televisions for an inordinate amount of time. Sedlak and McPherson (2010a) report that youths in confinement watch roughly three hours of television every weekday, and this is more than youths in the general population.

Web Activity

Go to https://www.pbs.org/video/how-juvenile-corrections-can-help-reduce-mass-incarceration-1552011890/ and listen to Johnnie McDaniels, former executive director of the Henley-Young Juvenile Justice Center as he shares his insight how to shut the revolving door of justice starting with how youthful offenders are dealt with in our system. Do you think the way we treat youth has affected mass incarceration, which was discussed in Chapter 4? What meaningful ideas resonated with you and what the research supports in Mr. McDaniels's statement? Why?

Other Placements

Two other residential forms of corrections for youths are boot camps and wilderness experience programs. These programs have received a great deal of popular and professional attention since the 1980s. Both of these types of programs take youths out of their home environment and place them into an environment aimed at teaching them personal responsibility and success, often with a strong group component.

Boot camps for youths emerged in the late 1980s and grew quickly in popularity. By 2000 there were seventy boot camps in operation (Mackenzie and Freeland 2012). **Boot camps** (also called **shock incarceration**) are short-term programs incorporating a basic military model that relies on strict discipline, physical train-ing, and drilling. Each day follows a rigorous schedule including early rising, marching, calisthenics, classroom study, work details, and counseling (Clark, Aziz, and MacKenzie 1994). The amount of time spent on counseling and other treat-ment can vary a great deal from one camp to another. Boot camps emerged at a time of calls to "get tough" on crime. The assumption was that more punishment would deter crime and delinquency. Boot camps, with the heavy regimentation, fits into the get tough movement.

Boot camps have been subjected to evaluations on their effectiveness and re-ducing recidivism since the 1990s. Multiple studies report that boot camps do not reduce recidivism (Cronin, 1994; Peters, Thomas, and Zamberlan 1997; Parent 2003). Two meta-analyses (Lipsey 2009; Wilson, MacKenzie, and Mitchell 2005) found that boot camps were no more effective at reducing future offending by camp participants than reoffending by those not in boot camps. Camps utilizing a strong treatment component were more likely to have an impact (Wilson, MacKenzie, and Mitchell 2005).

Wilderness programs involve placing youths in physically challenging out-door settings, including ocean ships or wagon trains. The goal is to teach youths survival skills, limits, and self-esteem. The youths learn basic skills, including how to cook, obtain shelter from the elements, read a compass, and start fires. They do not do this alone. A key aspect of the program is learning to work with and depend on others. The assumption is that success in the program will give youths a sense of accomplishment and a belief that hard work and their own abilities can help them be successful in the normal environment outside the program.

Evaluations of the impact of wilderness programs have found mixed results. Lipsey and Wilson (1998) reported finding no effect on recidivism. In a meta-analysis of twenty-eight wilderness program evaluations, Wilson and Lipsey (2000) found positive results. Those participating in the programs exhibited lower delinquency. He also reported that more intensive physical challenges bring about the best results. The inclusion of individual, family, and group counseling also added to the programs' impact (Wilson and Lipsey 2000).

While boot camps and wilderness programs are still in operation, their popu-larity has diminished. This is due in large part to several deaths in the programs that received a great deal of media attention. These events raised concerns over the safety of the programs and led some jurisdictions to abandon such physically chal-lenging interventions for youths.

Critical Thinking Exercise

Despite the lack of evidence on the effectiveness of boot camps, wilderness expe-rience, and similar programs, they continue to receive public support. Why do you think this is the case? Would you support these programs? Why or why not?

INSTITUTIONAL LIFE

Life in an institution can be problematic. Rather than provide the care and reha-bilitation promised under parens patriae, institutional life brings with it a variety of problems and issues that may have a negative impact on the youths. Among these issues are victimization in the institution, misconduct, racial/ethnic tension, and mental health and substance disorders.

Victimization

Over half of the youths in custody experience at least one type of victimization. The 2003 Survey of Youths in Residential Placement found that 46 percent of youths were victims of theft, 29 percent were assaulted, 10 percent were robbed, and 4 percent were victims of some type of sexual assault (Sedlak, McPherson, and Basena 2013). Those who were victimized once are more likely to be victim-ized again. A recent study in Canada uncovered that roughly one-third of institu-tionalized youths were bullied (either physically of verbally), roughly 10 percent were assaulted, 10 percent were robbed, and 1 percent were sexually bullied (Connell et al. 2016).

The issue of rape in institutions receives a great deal of attention due to the Prison Rape Elimination Act of 2003, which mandates, among other things, mea-suring the extent of the problem. Beck and Rantala (2016) report that there were about 1,500 reports of sexual violence in juvenile institutions in 2012. Interest-ingly, 45 percent of the perpetrators were institutional staff.

In addition to actual victimization, youth also report significant levels of fear in institutions. The Survey of Youths in Residential Placement found that over one-third of youths fear being attacked. This fear is not restricted to fear of the other residents. One quarter fear attacks from institutional staff (Sedlak and McPherson 2010a). Even higher levels of fear (almost 50%) have been reported in a study of victimization in English institutions (Chan and Ireland 2009).

Inmate Misconduct

Victimization of youths by other youths in institutions is only one form of miscon-duct occurring in facilities. Among the various forms of misconduct are the pres-ence of weapons or drugs/illegal substances, refusing to participate in required activities, refusing to follow instructions, being in prohibited areas, and other dis-ruptive behaviors. In general, these are technical, and not criminal/delinquent, violations.

In a study of over 2,500 serious and violent male delinquents held in residen-tial facilities, Trulson et al. (2010) found that the youths committed an average of almost eight major violations (including assaults, thefts, and other delinquent acts) and seventy-nine minor misconduct violations in the institution. The major-ity of youths (57%) had fewer than five violations. Similar results emerge in a second study of over 4,600 youths released from a large Southern juvenile correc-tional system. Trulson (2007) reports that each youth committed approximately fifty-three misconduct incidents. This includes both serious victimizations (such as assault) and technical violations of institutional rules. Male residents committed more-serious violations than did females.

Racial/Ethnic Tension

Conflict between groups in the larger community do not stop at the door to correctional institutions. In many respects, the conflict is exacerbated when different individuals and groups are housed closely together in residential settings. Racial/ethnic tension is evident in juvenile institutions. This should not be surprising when more than two-thirds of those in residential placement are members of minority groups, particularly blacks and Hispanics. In essence, those who are "minorities" in the community are in the "majority in correctional settings. This results in what Bartollas and Sieverdes (1981) refer to as role reversal in the institution. White youths are in a foreign setting that makes them fearful and uncertain of their position vis a vis the traditional "minority" youths. The shift in position can make some youths feel threatened and others to feel more empowered (Bartollas and Sieverdes 1981). This tension in the institution may manifest itself in aggressive behavior, most often against members of other racial/ethnic groups. This is evident in staff reports of youths' behavior (Bartollas and Sieverdes 1981) and in how the staff interact with and refer to youths of different racial/ethnic groups (Bortner and Williams 1997).

Mental Health and Co-occurring Disorders

Youths in the juvenile justice system, particularly in residential settings, typically suffer from some type of mental health disorder, and these are often coupled with other co-occurring disorders, such as substance use. Cocozza, Skowyra, and Shufelt (2010) note that between 65 and 70 percent of young people with juvenile justice system contact have a mental health disorder. In a study of over 1,400 youths, 47 percent had a conduct disorder, 46 percent had a substance use disorder, one-third suffered from an anxiety disorder, and one out of five has a mood disorder (such as depression) (Shufelt and Cocozza 2006).

These levels of mental health problems are higher than those found among youths outside residential settings, indicating that the need for treatment is great in correctional facilities. Unfortunately, treatment for mental health and co-occurring disorders is severely lacking in institutions. A survey of almost 700 secure detention facilities found that 27 percent had no or poor mental health services for the youths. In addition, more than half of the staff had little or no mental health training (US House of Representatives 2004). Further, Sedlak and McPherson (2010b) note that most facilities do not evaluate youths for any mental health needs.

Mental health and co-occurring disorders are common and serious problems for incarcerated youths. These youths need specialized treatment but typically do not receive the appropriate, or any, assistance. Incarcerated youths have expressed a desire for more rehabilitation and feel that proper programming would have a greater impact on them than simple incarceration (Pealer, Terry, and Adams 2017).

Critical Thinking Exercise

In 2012, the United States Supreme Court ruled in *Miller v. Alabama* that juveniles could no longer be held in prison without the chance of parole. Watch "Second Chance Kids" on *Frontline*: https://www.pbs.org/wgbh/frontline/film/second-chance-kids/. What are the implications of the Court's ruling? Would you extend the ruling to adults who are convicted and sentenced to mandatory life in prison without the possibility of parole? Why or why not?

COMMUNITY CORRECTIONS

There is a wide variety of options besides confinement/detention available for juveniles when it comes to their disposition. These are generally subsumed under the heading of community corrections. On its surface, community corrections is distinct from institutional efforts in terms of its focus on rehabilitation and treatment. **Community treatment** is defined as the care, protection, and assistance to juveniles outside of a secure correctional environment. Examples include probation, individual and group counseling programs, vocational training, restitution, and community service. The placement of youths into foster homes, small group homes, and boarding schools in the community also fall under the umbrella of community treatment.

Community corrections is considered nonpunitive. Community corrections supporters argue that:

- community options allow youths to remain in the community but juveniles must also be under strict supervision thereby vindicating the law and protecting the public;
- community alternatives encourage rehabilitation by maintaining normal contacts with family members, schools, and other community organizations;
- by remaining in the community, youths can avoid the negative effects of confinemen;
- community treatments are cheaper than institutional options.

This is accomplished through a wide array of interventions that take place in the community.

Probation

Probation is the most common form of community treatment for juveniles. Probation was a cornerstone in the creation of the juvenile court. In many states, supporters of a separate system for juveniles saw probation as the primary step toward achieving the goals of the juvenile court. As the juvenile court movement spread, so did probation. Together, the development of the juvenile court and probation were justified as appropriate under the belief that juveniles could be rehabilitated and the public had a responsibility in protecting wayward youth.

The use of probation has increased markedly since the late 1980s. In 2014, almost 359,000 youths were placed on probation for delinquent offenses (see Figure 7.1). This represents almost two-thirds of the more than 291,000 youths who were adjudicated delinquent. Over 175,000 youths who were not adjudicated delinquent agreed to some form of probation. This figure includes almost 103,000 youths who were not formally adjudicated (not petitioned to court) but voluntarily agreed to probation supervision and almost 73,000 who were petitioned but not adjudicated as a delinquent (Sickmund et al. 2017). Probation also handles significant numbers of status offenders. Hockenberry and Puzzanchera (2017) report that 24,000 youths were placed on probation for a status offense violation in 2014. This represents more than half of all status offense cases adjudicated in juvenile court. Truancy is the most frequent status offense resulting in probation (45% of the cases), followed by liquor law violations (21%) and ungovernability charges (15%) (Hockenberry and Puzzanchera 2017).

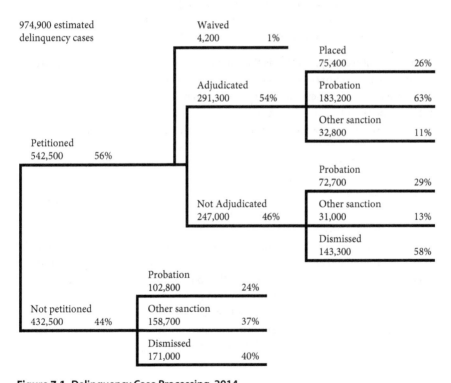

Figure 7.1 Delinquency Case Processing, 2014.
SOURCE: Hockenberry, S. and Puzzanchera, C. (2017). Juvenile court statistics, 2014. Pittsburgh: National Center for Juvenile Justice.

Web Activity

You can find a great deal of information on juveniles and probation in both the Hockenberry and Puzzanchera (2017) report: https://www.ojjdp.gov/ojstatbb/njcda/pdf/jcs2014.pdf, and on the Easy Access to Juvenile Court Statistics website: https://www.ojjdp.gov/ojstatbb/ezajcs/

There are several arguments in favor of probation:

- First, youths who are not a danger to themselves or others can be adequately supervised in the community.
- Second, probation provides the court the opportunity to put together a disposition that is individualized to the needs of the offender and the offense(s) committed.
- Third, the goals of community safety, accountability, and treatment can be accommodated by probation dispositions, even when the cases coming before the juvenile court are more serious than in the past.
- Finally, probation has become the sanction of choice, especially when it comes to status offenders.

One important role of probation is the completion of a **social history investigation (pre-disposition report)** prior to the court determining the actual disposition of a youth (see Box 7.2). A social history investigation includes information on the youth and his or her family. This report covers both legal information on the delinquent or status offense (including past offenses) and information on prior system contact/intervention. The social history information includes the child's age, family situation, education, development, and alcohol or other drug abuse, among other things.

Data for the social history investigation is gathered from a range of sources. Interviews with the youth, the youth's family, the victim, and the police provide information on the immediate event and past offending/problems. Police and court records also provide insight. Interviews with teachers and school personnel, along with copies of the child's cumulative school records give insight to the child's grades, discipline, and educational needs. Other information may come from social service agencies and community sources that have information on the youth. Probation officer conducting the investigation may ask for a psychologist/psychiatrist to examine the child for emotional problems or other issues that may be helpful in determining the appropriate programming for the youth. A summary of this information, along with a recommendation for disposition, is given to the judge.

Web Activity

You can see a social history form and format on the textbook website.

BOX 7.2

Social History Information

NAME

OFFENSE DATA

    Prior Offenses

    Current Offense

    Prior Court Involvement?

FAMILY DATA

    Father

        Present? Absent? Stepfather?

        Employment information (type of job, income, work hours)

        Problems—mental, emotional, drug/alcohol

    Mother

        Present? Absent? Stepmother?

        Employment information (type of job, income, work hours)

        Problems—mental, emotional, drug/alcohol

    Other Significant Adults

        Age, sex

        Relationship to child

    Siblings

        Positive resources to the child?

        Involvement in court

    Home Life

        Describe home and neighborhood

        Any traumatic experiences?

        Attitude of family members toward one another (caring, hostile, indifferent?)

        Prior involvement in counseling

    Child's Perception of Current Situation

        Remorseful? Hostile? Willing to work with the court?

        Family resistant or cooperative?

CHILD'S PERSONAL HISTORY

    Physical Health

        Medical History

        Drug/alcohol Involvement

School

    Academic/vocational aptitude

    Attendance

    Extracurricular activity

Leisure Time

    Interests, talents, activities

Treatment Efforts

    Medical or psychological evaluations

    Previous placement in residential or nonresidential programs

    Names of agencies currently or previously involved with child

RECOMMENDATIONS

Probation can be either informal or formal. **Informal probation** is typically used in cases involving youths committing minor transgressions and those who have limited (or no) offense histories. This probation often does not involve direct supervision by a probation officer. Instead, the youth is typically released on the promise/expectation that he/she will refrain from all future offending. Under **formal probation**, youths are closely monitored by a probation officer and, if they wish to remain in the community, they must carefully follow a set of strict conditions. These conditions may include reporting regularly to the probation officer, obeying the law, and attending school. A wide range of other specific conditions can be imposed by the judge or the probation officer. Restitution may be a requirement. The fact that most youths are not employed and have no funds to make payment to the victim means that restitution often takes the form of community service (more information on restitution appears later in this chapter). Counseling is another condition ordered for many probationers, as well as for the probationer's families. Other forms of treatment or intervention can also be ordered as a condition of probation.

Probation officers will utilize a range of approaches in working with youths. Often the officer will build a personal relationship with the youth and attempt to be a role model for the child. Probation caseloads, however, make it unrealistic for many officers to undertake this role. An alternative would be to find other adults to mentor youths on probation. One possible source of mentors is Big Brothers/Big Sisters. Mentors and mentoring program have been found to be effective at reducing antisocial behavior and increasing educational attainment and prosocial activity (Tolan et al. 2014).

A major expectation of probation is to supervise youths in the community. This entails contact with the youths, the families, schools, the police, social service agencies, and others in the community who may have useful insight to the youth. Interaction with these individuals and groups opens opportunities to address the needs of the probationers and establishing programs and interventions that utilize the strengths of the different participants. The probation officer assumes a role similar to that of a social worker, which can entail referral to other sources of help or providing counseling services him/herself. counseling often involves family therapy, reality therapy, rational emotive therapy, or client-centered therapy. These may be in individual or in group settings.

Traditionally, community corrections has focused on rehabilitation as its primary goal. With the advent on the conservative revolution in the 1980s, community corrections began to take on more of a social control model and less of the assisting role. While the rehabilitative aspects of community corrections, probation in particular, have not been overlooked, today's dispositions in the community have a heavier control dimension.

These programs are known as **probation plus** because they combine restrictive sanctions to community service orders. Probation-plus options seem to fit the conservative desire for punishment and the liberal desire for alternatives to secure confinement. Some examples of probation-plus programs are intensive probation supervision, home confinement, balanced probation, restitution, and restorative justice. Each of these is discussed below.

Intensive Probation Supervision

Intensive probation supervision means a juvenile is assigned to a probation officer who has a small caseload. These juveniles are contacted regularly and have more restrictions placed on their movements than a typical probationer. The primary goal of intensive probation supervision is keeping youths from being sent to a secure facility. The second goal is to control high-risk offenders in the community, putting them under stricter security than traditional probation provides. Maintaining community ties and reintegration is the third goal, as intensive probation supervision permits juveniles the opportunity to remain in school and with their families.

Intensive probation programs have received mixed reviews in the empirical literature with some showing positive results and others showing either negative results or no improvement over traditional sanctions. One thing is for certain, intensive probation supervision programs are cheaper than incarceration. Some studies have also demonstrated that intensive probation is more successful than traditional probation for some offenders. Offenders most likely to fail under an intensive probation supervision disposition are those who have committed petty crimes. Because intensive probation supervision clients are supervised more regularly and more closely, they are subject to more technical violations of their probation conditions. The failure rates under intensive probation supervision are higher than traditional probationers, which can negate the cost savings if these failed probationers are then sent to secure facilities.

Home Confinement

Home confinement entails releasing a youth to his/her parents/guardian with the requirement that he/she stay at home during certain time periods, such as after school and/or work, in the evenings, and on weekends. Home confinement has been commonly used for adults, but today we see that these alternatives are making their way into the juvenile justice system. Home confinement is also used in place of detention for those awaiting court hearings or other proceedings. Those on home confinement are monitored through visits and phone calls, typically by a probation officer.

An additional component of home confinement may be electronic monitoring. **Electronic monitoring** uses technology to monitor the location of an individual. Electronic monitoring can entail one of two primary systems or types—active and passive. *Active, or continuous signaling, systems* keep track of the offender on a continuous basis. A signaling device is typically strapped to the offender's ankle and a constant signal is transmitted to a receiver which logs the offender's presence or absence. A *passive, or programmed contact, system* requires periodic activation of the system to certify the presence of the individual. Electronic monitoring may also use **global positioning system (GPS) technology** employs satellites to locate a person or monitor his or her movements. GPS technology does not require a home monitoring device or the use of any telephone lines and makes it more difficult for offenders to abscond.

A probation officer or other individual typically checks on any recorded violation to confirm the information and take appropriate action. The computer system can be programmed to allow the offender to go to work, attend school, or participate in other activities. The system simply logs the times the offender leaves and returns home. A continuous computer printout of the offender's activity can be evaluated at any time.

Proponents of home confinement, with or without electronic monitoring, point to a variety of advantages. First, it can possibly alleviate the overcrowding of correctional institutions. Second, home confinement, particularly with electronic monitoring, enhances the ability to supervise offenders in the community and can incapacitate offenders better than simple probation. Third, home confinement reduces the costs of monitoring youths in the community compared to regular probation supervision. Finally, home confinement aides in reintegrating youths by maintaining family and friendship ties, as well as allowing them to stay in their home school.

Critical Thinking Exercise

The great changes in technology over the past three decades have led to various means of surveillance of youths in the community. What issues would wearing an electronic monitor have for youths in school and the community? Does the use of GPS infringe on a youth's right to privacy? Should limits be placed on this technology when used with juveniles? If so, what would those limits be?

Balanced Probation

In attempts to improve the success of probation programs, some jurisdictions have implemented balanced probation programs. These efforts aim to protect the community, hold the juvenile offender accountable, and individualize dispositions.

The idea behind **balanced probation** is the belief that youths are responsible for their behaviors and have an obligation to society to right their wrongs. Probation officers structure programs based on the individual offender with the focus on the juvenile accepting responsibility for his/her transgressions. Some scholars and practitioners have offered that balanced probation programs allow the juvenile probation system to have a more distinctive role than they currently serve in many jurisdictions.

Examples of balanced probation programs include having juveniles perform home repair and gardening for elderly community members, assisting in voter registration, painting homes and public buildings, and creating shelters for needy populations. Essentially, balanced probation youths agree to repair the damage they did to the victim and/or community such that they become reintegrated into society. Citizens often work together with juvenile probation offices to facilitate these types of activities. The jury is still out on the effectiveness of balanced probation programs, but they are certainly cheaper and avoid the stigmatization of secure confinement.

Restitution

A popularly utilized form of community treatment is victim **restitution**. Typically, restitution is tied to a probation disposition and is administered by the probation staff. In many respects, restitution is similar to balanced probation. One big difference is the fact that restitution is often mandated by the court as part of the official disposition. Restitution may be administered by probation or it can be an independent restitution program developed by local governments or private nonprofit organizations.

There are four general forms of restitution:

1. **Monetary restitution to the victim** A juvenile reimburses the victim for a crime or donates money to a charity or public cause.
2. **Monetary restitution to the community** In this form, the victim may not wish to have contact with the youthful offender. Instead, the restitution payment is made to a community fund.
3. **Service restitution to the victim** In this type of restitution, the youth provides a service to the victim directly, such as painting a fence that the youth damaged.
4. **Service restitution to the community** Under this approach juveniles provide service to the community, such as by working to clean up a playground or helping a community organization. This form is commonly used when victims do not wish to have contact with the offender.

The most widely used form of restitution in the United States is direct monetary restitution to the victim. In Europe, restitution to a charity is the most commonly used.

Regardless of type, restitution programs are quite flexible in that they can be required at any stage of the juvenile justice process. For example, intake officers can require them as part of a diversion program or judges can require them as a condition of probation. Most studies have shown that restitution programs are relatively effective and have recommended that their use be expanded.

Restitution programs have been criticized because, by their very nature, they would follow a philosophy of retribution rather than an orientation toward rehabilitation. This stance is due to its reliance on justice for the victim and on offender responsibility for acts committed rather than on inclusion of a treatment component. Those who take this position do not see the possibility that restitution itself can be rehabilitative for the offender. Restitution programs are also accused of widening the net because they give judges another option for a disposition in cases where juveniles may not face any sanction. Nonetheless, restitution programs have increased greatly in number since the late 1970s when few programs existed. Today, all fifty states and the District of Columbia have restitution programs codified by legislation.

Despite the growth in restitution programs, the actual use of restitution is limited. One impediment to restitution with youths is their inability to make payments. Most youths have limited or no funds and many are not employed or are not employable. A second concern is the fact that when imposed on youthful offenders, restitution is rarely paid in full. Lane et al. (2005) report that youths only pay about 10 percent of the total restitution ordered in California. Griffin and Thomas (2004) find that youths in Pennsylvania pay just under half of the amount ordered. While payments may not always meet the order, there is evidence that youths who are ordered to make restitution tend to recidivate at lower levels than those not participating (Latimer, Dowden, and Muise 2005).

Restorative Justice

A final probation-plus approach to be discussed here is restorative justice. These programs have become quite popular in recent years. The idea underlying **restorative justice** is to rely on nonpunitive methods to control crime and delinquency by turning the justice system into a healer rather than a distributor of retribution. The key to restorative justice is to restore all parties to the transgression (the victim, the offender, and the community) to their pre-offense state. Reconciliation between the victim and the offender is central to restorative justice programs, which is seen as vital since many victims and offenders know one another. Less formal processes in a cohesive social group (e.g., families or neighborhoods) are believed to facilitate the healing process as the relationship between victim and offender was damaged by the delinquent act. The ultimate objective is to return to the community a law-abiding member where he/she can play a productive, rather than destructive, role.

Restorative justice generally takes a variety of forms. These include victim–offender mediation, family group conferencing, neighborhood reparative boards, and sentencing circles. Of these, family group conferencing is most commonly used with youths. **Family group conferencings** brings together a facilitator, the youth, the victim, and their families and support groups. There is also the possibility of including criminal justice personnel, social workers, attorneys, and others.

The goal is to engender discussion on what took place, why it occurred, how to address the harm that was done, and how to keep it from happening again. The solution must be agreed upon by all parties. These conferences can be held either pre- or post-adjudication.

The success of restorative justice programs depends on how much stake the youth has in a particular group. If he or she does not care about his or her membership in that group, it is unlikely that he or she will accept responsibility for the transgressions. In addition, it is probable that the youth will show no remorse for his or her actions or take the time and energy to repair any harms caused by these actions. Since community involvement is vital to the success of restorative justice programs, lacking this element will certainly be problematic.

Critical Thinking Exercise

What forms of probation plus exist in your state? Which to you believe would be the most welcome in your community? Why? Which should be started in your community?

Aftercare

Beyond probation and different variations on probation, community corrections also includes interventions aimed at those youths who have been held in residential settings and are being released back into the community. Most youths held in residential facilities will be released prior to reaching the age of majority and aging out of the juvenile system. Many states have **aftercare** programs (the parallel to adult parole) to assist in transitioning back into the community and addressing issues the youths may still have.

Aftercare, just as with probation, is a mix of supervision and treatment. Youths have specific guidelines they must follow, typically including routine reporting to an aftercare officer. Aftercare will require youths to attend school (assuming they have not graduated from high school), abide by curfews, avoid drugs and alcohol, participate in counseling (individual or group), participate in other treatment/rehabilitation programs addressing their individual needs, or abide by a host of other requirements outlined by the aftercare officer. If youths do not follow the rules, their aftercare can be revoked, and they can be sent back to a secure residential facility.

The impact of aftercare on subsequent delinquency is not entirely clear. In one of the only national evaluations, Wiebush and colleagues (2005) report that youths in aftercare reoffend at roughly the same level as control youths released without aftercare services. Their data reveal that approximately 50 percent of the youths on aftercare are rearrested for new felonies, and four out of five (80%) are rearrested if technical violations are included in the analysis. Nellis (2009) claims that programs emphasizing mental health interventions and mentoring show some promise in reducing recidivism.

ISSUES IN COMMUNITY CORRECTIONS

Community supervision pits a number of competing goals against one another. Perhaps the two ends of the continuum of goals are retribution/punishment and treatment. Those working with youths under correctional supervision in the community are asked to address the entire continuum. This leads to **goal confusion**. The system does not know whether to view delinquents as hostile predators who must be controlled for the sake of others, or as wayward youths who need direction and help to overcome the forces leading them to misbehave (Morse 1999). This competition in approaches is nowhere more evident than in the "get-tough" movement since the 1980s and the "parens patriae philosophy" underlying the juvenile justice system.

On one hand, probation officers and other community correctional workers are asked to provide simple supervision of youths and to sanction them for transgressions. On the other hand, they are to provide an array of treatments and interventions to assist the youth. This conflict, if not resolved, can cause stress for the workers and lead to job burnout and a great deal of personnel turnover in the agencies.

What is needed in community corrections is expanding the ideas of balanced probation to a more generalized **balanced approach** to intervention. This is a philosophy that "requires the system to provide balanced attention to the need for competency development, accountability, and community safety and requires efforts to restore, to the greatest extent possible, the victim and community to their precrime status" (Kurlychek, Torbet, and Boynski 1999, 3). The offender is held accountable for his behavior, while at the same time receiving assistance and rehabilitative programming. This approach combines traditional rehabilitation, restorative justice, and classical retributive criminology.

The balanced approach is evident in several programs. One prime example from the 1990s is the Gang Violence Reduction Program in Chicago. This program combined the efforts of the police and probation to increase supervision of violent and potentially violent gang members, while providing counseling, employment training, and job placement (Howell and Hawkins 1998). Boston also combined police and probation services in Operation Night Light to provide surveillance and compliance with services mandated under probation (Urban, Cyr, and Decker 2003). Pennsylvania has taken the balance approach a step further by amending it general purpose clause for the juvenile system to explicitly incorporate balanced and restorative justice principles.

The balanced approach should help to reduce any goal confusion. This is especially likely as community corrections turns to **evidence-based practices**. These are interventions that research has shown to be successful in reducing recidivism and achieving positive outcomes, such as reduced substance use, increased educational attainment, and successful completion of treatment programs. The movement toward evidence-based intervention has grown greatly in recent years.

SUMMARY

Juvenile corrections faces a number of issues that need attention. Both institutional and community corrections struggle with serving a massive number of youths with inadequate resources. This forces the system to rely on more punitive approaches to control youthful behavior. Correctional institutions do little more than warehouse youths to protect society, and community corrections tends to emphasize surveillance for the same purpose. Youths do not receive the treatment and programs needed to address the causes of their behavior and mitigate future transgressions. Mental health, substance use, and other issues often receive little or no attention in institutions or from community interventions. This situation is counter to the basic premise behind the development of a separate juvenile system that works for the care, education, and treatment of youthful offenders, rather than a system oriented toward simple punishment and control.

KEY WORDS

aftercare
balanced approach
balanced probation
boob tube therapy
boot camps
Bridewell Institution
child savers
community treatment
cottage
day-night centers
detention centers
electronic monitoring
Elmira Reformatory
evidence-based practices
family group
    conferencing
formal probation

global positioning
    system (GPS)
goal confusion
home confinement
house of refuge
informal probation
intensive probation
    supervision
Lancaster State Industrial
    School for Girls
Lyman School for Boys
nonsecure detention
nullification
operant conditioning
parens patriae
pre-disposition report
preventive detention

probation
probation plus
reformatories
restitution
restorative justice
Schall v Martin
secure detention
shock incarceration
social history investiga-
    tion (pre-disposition
    report)
state training schools
therapeutic detention
token economy
    programs
wilderness programs

DISCUSSION QUESTIONS

1. You are a state legislator and are working in a committee discussing proposed legislation to require juvenile court judges to use formal criteria to determine whether a youth should be detained in detention. Where do you stand? Why?

2. You are invited to a debate on the placement of youth in training schools. A coin is tossed with heads representing for training schools and tails against training schools. What side do you want the coin to land on? Why? Is one side more persuasive than the other? Defend.

3. Your local school district is calling on you to assist with having more family involvement for at-risk and delinquent youth. Based on the content in this chapter, what are the top five points you would share to decrease contact with juvenile corrections?

4. The juvenile prosecutor is seeking ideas for a diversionary program for youths who vandalize schools. You are a new expert in these types of programs and are being asked for a short report detailing a promising approach, its advantages, and limitations. What are you going to offer to the juvenile prosecutor and why?

5. Should parents or guardians of juveniles found responsible for their criminal or delinquent behavior be required to participate in their child's disposition in some way? Defend your response.

SUGGESTED READINGS

Barton, W. H. "Detention." *The Oxford Handbook of Juvenile Crime and Juvenile Justice,* edited by B. C. Feld and D. M. Bishop. New York: Oxford University Press. DOI:10.1093 /oxfordhb/9780195385106.013.0026.

Krisberg, B. "Juvenile Corrections: An Overview." In *The Oxford Handbook of Juvenile Crime and Juvenile Justice,* edited by B. C. Feld and D. M. Bishop. New York: Oxford University Press. DOI:10.1093/oxfordhb/9780195385106.013.0026.

Lipsey, M. W., and D. B. Wilson. (1998). "Effective Intervention for Serious Juvenile Offenders: A Synthesis of Research." In *Serious and Violent Juvenile Offenders: Risk Factors and Successful Intervention,* edited by R. Loeber and D. P. Farrington, 313–345. Thousand Oaks, CA: SAGE.

MacKenzie, D. L., and R. Freeland. (2012). "Examining the Effectiveness of Juvenile Residential Programs." In *The Oxford handbook of Juvenile Justice,* edited by B. C. Feld and D. M. Bishop, 771–798. New York: Oxford University Press.

Trulson, C. R., M. DeLisi, J. W. Caudill, S. Belshaw, and J. W. Marquart. (2010). "Delinquent Careers behind Bars." *Criminal Justice Review* 35, 200–219. http://doi.org/10.1177/0734016809360326.

REFERENCES

Aries, P. (1962). *Centuries of Childhood.* New York: Knopf.

Bartollas, C., and C. M. Sieverdes. 1981. "The Victimized White in a Juvenile Correctional System." *Crime & Delinquency* 27: 534–543.

Barton, W. H. (2012). "Detention." In *The Oxford Handbook of Juvenile Crime and Juvenile Justice,* edited by B. C. Feld and D. M. Bishop. New York: Oxford. DOI:10.1093/ oxfordhb/9780195385106.013.0026

Beck, A. J., and R. R. Rantala. (2016). *Sexual Victimization Reported by Juvenile Correctional Authorities, 2007–12.* Washington, DC: Bureau of Justice Statistics.

Bortner, M. A., and L. M. Williams. (1997). *Youth in Prison: We the People of Unit Four*. New York: Routledge.

Brenzel, B. M. (1983). *Daughters of the State: A Social Portrait of the First Reform School for Girls in North America, 1856–1903*. Cambridge, MA: MIT Press.

Chan, J. P. K., and J. L. Ireland. (2009). "Fear of Bullying among Adult, Young, and Juvenile Prisoners: Its Association with Perpetration, Victimisation, and Behavioural Predictors." *International Journal of Prisoner Health* 5: 223–232.

Clark, C. L., D. W. Aziz, and D. L. MacKenzie. (1994). *Shock Incarceration in New York: Focus on Treatment*. Washington, DC: US Department of Justice.

Cocozza, J. J, K. R. Skowyra, and J. L. Shufelt. (2010). *Addressing the Mental Health Needs of Youth in Contact with the Juvenile Justice System in System of Care Communities: An Overview and Summary of Key Issues*. Washington, DC: Substance Abuse and Mental Health Services Administration.

Connell, a., Farrington, D.P., & Ireland, J.L. (2016). Characteristics of bullies and victims among incarcerated male young offenders. *Journal of Aggression, Conflict, and Peace Research, 8*, 114–123.

Council of State Governments Justice Center. (2015). *Locked Out: Improving Educational and Vocational Outcomes for Incarcerated Youths*. New York: Council of State Governments Justice Center.

Cronin, R. C. (1994). *Boot Camps for Adult and Juvenile Offenders: Overview and Update*. Washington, DC: National Institute of Justice.

Empey, L. T. (1982). *American Delinquency: Its Meaning and Construction*. Homewood, IL: Dorsey Press.

Faust, F. L., and P. J. Brantingham. (1979). *Juvenile Justice Philosophy: Readings, Cases and Comments*. St. Paul, MN: West Group.

Gallagher, C. A., and A. Dobrin. (2007). "Can Juvenile Justice Detention Facilities Meet the Call of the American Academy of Pediatrics and National Commission on Correctional Health Care? A National Analysis of Current Practices." *Pediatrics* 119: 815–816.

Griffin, P., and D. Thomas. (2004). "The Good News: Measuring Juvenile Outcomes at Case Closing." *Pennsylvania Progress* 10, no. 2: 1–6.

Hockenberry, S., and C. Puzzanchera. (2017). *Juvenile Court Statistics, 2014*. Pittsburgh, PA: National Center for Juvenile Justice.

Hockenberry, S., A. Wachter, and A. Sladky. (2016). *Juvenile Residential Facility Census, 2014: Selected Findings*. Washington, DC: Office of Juvenile Justice and Delinquency Prevention.

Howell, J. C., and J. D. Hawkins. (1998). "Prevention of Youth Violence." In *Youth Violence*, edited by M. Tonry and M. H. Moore, 189–261. Chicago: University of Chicago Press.

Justice Policy Institute. (2014). *Sticker Shock: Calculating the Full Price Tag for Youth Incarceration*. Washington, DC: Justice Policy Institute.

Krisberg, B. (2012). "Juvenile Corrections: An Overview." In *The Oxford Handbook of Juvenile Crime and Juvenile Justice*, edited by B. C. Feld and D. M. Bishop. New York: Oxford. DOI:10.1093/oxfordhb/9780195385106.013.0030.

Krisberg, B., and J. Austin. (1978). *The Children of Ishmael*. Palo Alto, CA: Mayfield.

Kurlychek, M., P. M. Torbet, and M. Bozynski. (1999). *Focus on Accountability: Best Practices for Juvenile Court and Probation*. Washington, DC: US Department of Justice and Delinquency Prevention.

Lane, J., S., Turner, T. Fain, and A. Sehgal. (2005). "Evaluating an Experimental Intensive Probation Program: Supervision and Official Outcomes." *Crime & Delinquency* 51: 26–52.

Latessa, E., B. Lovins, and K. Ostrowski. (2009). *The Ohio Youth Assessment System: Final Report*. Cincinnati, OH: University of Cincinnati.

Latimer, J., C. Dowden, and D. Muise. (2005). *The Effectiveness of Restorative Justice Practices: A Meta-Analysis*. Ottawa, Canada: Canada Department of Justice. Cited in N. Rodriguez. (2007). Restorative Justice at Work: Examining the Impact of Restorative Justice Resolutions on Juvenile Recidivism. *Crime & Delinquency* 53, 355–379.

Lipsey, M. W. (2009). "The Primary Factors That Characterize Effective Interventions with Juvenile Offenders: A Meta-Analytic Overview." *Victims and Offenders* 4:124–147.

Lipsey, M. W., and D. B. Wilson. (1998). "Effective Intervention for Serious Juvenile Offenders: A Synthesis of Research." In *Serious and Violent Juvenile Offenders: Risk Factors and Successful Intervention*, edited by R. Loeber and D. P. Farrington, 313–345. Thousand Oaks, CA: SAGE.

MacKenzie, D. L., and R. Freeland. (2012). "Examining the Effectiveness of Juvenile Residential Programs." In *The Oxford Handbook of Juvenile Justice*, edited by B. C. Feld and D. M. Bishop, 771–798. New York: Oxford University Press.

Morse, S. (1999). "Delinquency and Desert." *Annals of the American Academy of Political and Social Science* 564:56–80.

National Council of Juvenile and Family Court Judges (2005). *Juvenile Delinquency Guidelines: Improving Court Practice in Juvenile Delinquency Cases*. Reno, NV: National Council of Juvenile and Family Court Judges.

Nellis, A. (2009). *Back on Track: Supporting Youth Reentry from Out-of-Home Placement to the Community*. Washington, DC: Juvenile Justice and Delinquency Prevention Coalition—The Sentencing Project.

Parent, D. G. (2003). *Correctional Boot Camps: Lessons from a Decade of Research*. Washington, DC: National Institute of Justice.

Pealer, J., A. N. Terry, and K. R. Adams. (2017). Voices from Inside the Walls: Views of the Juvenile Justice System from the Youthful offenders. *Corrections: Policy, Practice, and Research*, 2:130–147.

Peters, M., D. Thomas, and C. Zamberlan. (1997). *Boot Camps for Juvenile Offenders: Program Summary*. Washington, DC: US Department of Justice.

Pisciotta, A. W. (1979). "The Theory and Practice of the New York House of Refuge, 1857–1935." Unpublished PhD diss., Florida State University.

Pisciotta, A. W. (1982). "Saving the Children: The Promise and Practice of *Parens Patriae*, 1838–98." *Crime & Delinquency* 28:410–425.

Pisciotta, A. W. (1983). Race, Sex and Rehabilitation: A Study of Differential Treatment in the Juvenile Reformatory, 1825–1900. *Crime & Delinquency* 29: 254–269.

Platt, A. M. (1977). *The Child Savers: The Invention of Delinquency*. Chicago: University of Chicago Press.

Rothman, D. J. (1971). *The Discovery of the Asylum: Social Order and Disorder in the New Republic*. Boston: Little, Brown.

Rothman, D. J. (1980). *Conscience and Convenience: The Asylum and Its Alternatives in Progressive America*. Boston: Little, Brown.

Roush, D., and M. McMillen. (2000). *Construction, Operations, and Staff Training for Juvenile Confinement Facilities*. Washington, DC: Office of Juvenile Justice and Delinquency Prevention.

Sedlak, A. J., and K. S. McPherson. (2010a). *Conditions of Confinement: Findings from the Survey of Youth in Residential Placement.* Washington, DC: US Department of Justice.

Sedlak, A. J., and K. S. McPherson. (2010b). *Youth's Needs and Services: Findings from the Survey of Youth in Residential Placement.* Washington, DC: US Department of Justice.

Sedlak, A. J., K. S. McPherson, and M. Basena. (2013). *Nature and Risk of Victimization: Findings from the Survey of Youth in Residential Placement.* Washington, DC: Office of Juvenile Justice and Delinquency Prevention.

Shufelt, J. S., and J. C. Cocozza. (2006). *Youth with Mental Health Disorders in the Juvenile Justice System: Results from a Multi-state Prevalence Study.* Delmar, NY: National Center for Mental Health and Juvenile Justice.

Sickmund, M., T. J. Sladky, W. Kang, and C. Puzzanchera. (2017). "Easy Access to the Census of Juveniles in Residential Placement." Available http://www.ojjdp.gov/ojstatbb/ezacjrp/

Stephens, R. D., and J. L. Arnette. (2000). *From the Courthouse to the Schoolhouse: Making Successful Transitions.* Washington, DC: Office of Juvenile Justice and Delinquency Prevention.

Tolan, P. H., D. B Henry, M. S. Schoeny, P. Lovegrove, and E. Nichols. (2014). "Mentoring Programs to Affect Delinquency and Associated Outcomes of Youth at Risk: A Comprehensive Meta-analytic Review." *Journal Experimental Criminology* 10:179–206.

Trulson, C. R. (2007). "Determinants of Disruption: Institutional Misconduct among State-Committed Delinquents." *Youth Violence and Juvenile Justice* 5: 7–34. https://doi.org/10.1177/1541204006295162.

Trulson, C. R., M. DeLisi, J. W. Caudill, S. Belshaw, and J. W. Marquart. (2010). "Delinquent Careers behind Bars." *Criminal Justice Review* 35: 200–219. https://doi.org/10.1177/0734016809360326

US House of Representatives. (2004). Incarceration of Youth Who Are Waiting for Community Mental Health Services in the United States. US House of Representatives. https://www.hsgac.senate.gov/imo/media/doc/040707juvenilereport.pdf

Urban, L. S., J. L. St. Cyr, and S. H. Decker (2003). "Goal Conflict in the Juvenile Court: The Evolution of Sentencing Practices in the United States." *Journal of Contemporary Criminal Justice* 19: 454–479.

Wiebush, R. G., D. Wagner, B. McNulty, Y. Wang, and T. N. Le. (2005). *Implementation and Outcome Evaluation of the Intensive Aftercare Program: Final Report.* Washington, DC: Office of Juvenile Justice and Delinquency Prevention.

Wilson, S., and M. Lipsey. (2000). "Wilderness Challenge Programs for Delinquent Youths: A Meta-Analysis of Outcome Evaluations." *Evaluation and Program Planning* 23: 1–12.

Wilson, D. B., D. L. MacKenzie, and F. N. Mitchell. (2005). *Effects of Correctional Boot Camps on Offending.* Campbell Collaboration. https://www.campbellcollaboration.org/better-evidence/effects-of-correctional-boot-camps-on-offending.html.

CHAPTER 8

Correctional Effectiveness

AFTER READING THIS CHAPTER, YOU SHOULD BE ABLE TO:

- Discuss the deterrent impact on offending, both general and collective
- Distinguish between collective and selective incapacitation
- Discuss the evidence on the incapacitative effect of imprisonment
- Talk about the "what works" argument and the different positions on whether rehabilitation works
- Define and discuss the principles of risk, need, and responsivity
- Relate the importance of treatment fidelity for rehabilitation
- Identify and discuss various cognitive-behavioral therapies

PUNISHMENT RATIONALES

The ultimate goal of correctional intervention is to address the level of crime in society. How the level of crime is affected will differ if one considers the philosophical rationale underlying corrections. Three primary mechanisms through which corrections may have an impact are deterrence, incapacitation, and rehabilitation. This chapter addresses each of these possibilities and the evidence on the impact of each.

DETERRENCE

Deterrence can affect crime in two general ways. In the first, the hope is that the threat of punishment will deter potential offenders from committing crime. Correctional intervention with past offenders should serve as an example to other potential law violators and deter those individuals from committing crime. This form of deterrence is called general deterrence. **General deterrence** looks at the effect of punishing one individual on the future behavior of other persons.

The second way corrections can have a deterrent impact falls into the category of **specific deterrence**. A specific deterrent effect is evident if an individual offender who has been incarcerated/punished refrains from violating the law again after release or post punishment. The assumption is that the experience of punishment deters the individual from engaging in future illegal activity. The incarceration/punishment is not expected to affect anyone other than the targeted individual. The focus in this chapter is on a specific deterrent effect of correctional intervention.

Many evaluations of specific deterrence look to the effect of imprisonment on subsequent offending. These evaluations typically consider the recidivism rate of individuals who have been released after a period of incarceration. These evaluations present a bleak picture for specific deterrence. In one early analysis, Glaser (1964) reported that roughly one-third of prison releases were eventually reincarcerated. These individuals were not deterred from further offending by their initial punishment. This result reflects only reincarceration, which is an extreme measure of recidivism in light of the fact that many offenses do not result in a prison sentence. Other measures, such as simple rearrest, could reveal even greater levels of recidivism. Langan and Levin (2002) noted that two-thirds of offenders released from prison were rearrested within three years, almost half were reconvicted, and 25 percent were reincarcerated. Alper, Durose, and Markman (2018) reported that 44 percent of state prison releasees are rearrested within one year of release, 68 percent are rearrested within three years of release, and 83 percent are rearrested with nine years. Excluding arrest for technical violations of probation or parole has little impact on these figures (82% are arrested within nine years for *new* offenses).

Web Activity

The National Institute of Justice produced a good summary about deterrence and its impact. This can be accessed at https://www.ncjrs.gov/pdffiles1/nij/247350.pdf.

An alternative method for analyzing specific deterrence considers success on parole. The releasee has experienced a period of confinement and is being given supervised/conditional release. Any violation that could result in being returned to the institution or indicate noncompliance could be considered a form of recidivistic behavior. Based on data for parole releasees in 2016, Kaeble (2018) notes that 30 percent of all those released fail to comply with the terms of release. For imprisonment to have a deterrent effect on crime, it should be influenced by the length of time offenders spend in prison prior to release on parole, but some studies point to either minimal influence, or to an opposite effect in that the longer the prison term, the higher the probability of reoffending.

Comparing the recidivism rate for parolees who serve differing amounts of time in an institution reveals the impact of incarceration on subsequent offending. Babst, Koval, and Neithercutt (1972) looked at almost 15,000 burglars paroled in 1968 and 1969 and examined the recidivism rate for twenty-two groups of burglars categorized by drug use, alcohol use, prior record, and age at release. The study results revealed no consistent relationship between the time served and parole outcome after one year when comparing similar groups of subjects (Babst, Koval, and Neithercutt 1972).

Beck and Hoffman (1976) and Gottfredson, Gottfredson, and Garofalo (1977) also examined the impact of sentence length on parole outcome. In the first study, the authors divided subjects into five groups based on their risk of recidivating while on parole. Using a two-year follow-up, the authors reported that, in general, there is more recidivism as the length of time served in prison increased (Beck and Hoffman 1976). Significantly, individuals who were given better odds for a good prognosis for success on parole tended to do worse as the amount of time spent in prison increases. Gottfredson, Gottfredson, and Garofalo (1977) divided their subjects into nine separate categories based on various discriminating factors. Results revealed that the time served in prison was related to higher recidivism as the time served increased to forty-nine months for three groups of subjects and there was no impact on recidivism for four categories of parolees. Time served had a positive impact for those who spend fifty months or more in prison (Gottfredson, Gottfredson, and Garofalo 1977). The results of these studies strongly suggest that the length of imprisonment has a differential effect for different risk subjects.

One major problem with these parole evaluations is the inability to randomly assign parolees to varying lengths of time served and then compare the parole outcome figures. In one study, Berecochea and Jaman (1981) randomly varied the time served, with one group serving six additional months in prison. Looking at twelve- and twenty-four-month follow-up figures, the authors found no statistically significant differences in the likelihood of return or returns for new complaints. They concluded that the severity of punishment is unrelated to recidivism (Berecochea and Jaman 1981). The major problem with this study was that the six-month difference in length of imprisonment may not have been sufficient for a specific deterrent effect to become viable.

Critical Thinking Exercise

Public support for capital punishment, lengthy prison terms, and other sanctions is very strong. Given the evidence on the deterrent impact of sanctions, how do you explain the public support? What would you suggest should be done to improve the deterrent impact of sanctions? Is it possible to make them more effective?

It is important to remember that these recidivism figures underrepresent the number of ex-inmates who reoffend. This is true for both the general ex-inmate population and for those released on parole. Measuring recidivism as return to incarceration is a high bar to meet. Many individuals reoffend, are arrested, and processed without being sent to prison confinement. This means that simple imprisonment fails to deter a large proportion of those who are incarcerated.

Death Penalty

The ultimate form of punishment is the death penalty. Recall that early punishments often involved both **capital** and **corporal sanctions** whereby even those actions falling under the *corporal* category (i.e., physical imposition of harm to the body) would result in the death of the convicted person. The end goal of *capital* sanctions (i.e., punishment by death) is the legally authorized execution of the convicted. Currently, there are forty-one federal crimes punishable by death, with the majority involving murder or engaging in behaviors that result in death. Treason, espionage, bank robbery involving a kidnapping, or the intent to kill by mailing harmful items are the only nonmurder-involving offenses whereby a person can be sentenced to death. There are twenty-nine states that have capital punishment whereby lethal injection is the primary method of execution.

In early history, and often proceeding into current times, is the belief that executions for certain offenses would deter their future occurrences in two ways: through general deterrence and/or specific deterrence. Ideally, both would prove to have utility by carrying out the punishment, so that fewer of these death eligible offenses would occur in society. Specific deterrence is achieved as those who are punished by death cannot commit another crime, let alone, murder, after they are executed. Research studies, however, do not find strong evidence in favor of the general deterrent effect.

Sorenson et al. (1999) examined the impact of executions over a fourteen-year period in Texas and reported that monthly homicide rates are unrelated to the number of executions. Katz, Levitt, and Shustorovich (2003) analyzed annual state-level data from 1950 to 1990 and observed that the death penalty has little, if any, impact on homicide rates. One strong explanation for the lack of a deterrent effect is the small number of executions that take place relative to the number of people convicted and those sentenced to death. There is also a great deal of variation over time in homicide rates, making it difficult to inform any changes in homicide to the rare executions (Donohue and Wolfers, 2006; Katz, Levitt, and Shustorovich 2003). Donohue and Wolfers (2006) noted that the uncertainty of executions makes it difficult to assume that the death penalty would have much of an impact on homicide rates.

An alternative possible impact of executions is an increase in subsequent offending. Bowers and Pierce (1980) claimed that there are two more homicides in the month immediately following an execution and one more in the second month after an execution than would be normally expected. It appears that the use of the death penalty causes an absolute increase of three homicides after the execution. They refer to this as the **brutalization effect** of the death penalty (Bowers and Pierce 1980). Other researchers (Bailey 1998; Cochran, Chamlin, and Seth 1994; Cochran and Chamlin 2000) also report a brutalization effect as a result of executions.

Web Activity

Go to http://www.ncsl.org/research/civil-and-criminal-justice/death-penalty.aspx to learn more about state laws and procedures related to the death penalty. What United States Supreme Court case rulings in the past decade or so surprised you? Next, go to https://deathpenaltyinfo.org/state-and-federal-info/state-by-state to learn more about your state and its practices regarding capital punishment. If your state no longer has the death penalty as a form of punishment, in what year was it abolished? Why do you think it was abolished when it was? If your state still has the death penalty as an option, how many people are on death row to date? How many were executed in the last two years? Do these numbers surprise you?

INCAPACITATION

Corrections can have an impact independent of changing an offender's future behavior by simply imprisoning the individual and keeping him from offending while incarcerated or by otherwise controlling him. Incapacitating an individual keeps the subject from committing crimes against society while in an institution. **Incapacitation** provides control over the individual, thus precluding behavior that is harmful to society.

An incapacitation effect rests on several assumptions concerning criminal activity. Since incapacitation addresses the time period in which the offender is under system control, it is necessary to assess the individual's base rate of offenses every year. Using this figure, it is possible to estimate the number of offenses that are averted through the incapacitation of an individual. For example, if it is assumed that an individual commits ten crimes per year, the incapacitative effect of a one-year prison sentence is a reduction of crime by ten offenses for every person so incarcerated. This also assumes that there is a constant rate of offending over time and an individual's criminal career is not simply put on hold while incapacitated. That is, the inability to commit ten crimes (for example) while incarcerated are not just committed the year after release from incarceration. The inability to make this assumption would result in no incapacitative effect because the time served would simply postpone and not eliminate the level of offending.

Incapacitation can take two different forms—collective and selective. **Collective incapacitation** refers to the imposition of sentences upon everyone committing the same crime with no consideration of individual circumstances. For example, all burglars receive the same sentence. The basis of collective incapacitation is the legal finding of a specific past offense. **Selective incapacitation** emphasizes identifying high-risk offenders and subjecting only those individuals to greater or harsher intervention, while lower risk offenders receive minimal time in prison or receive an alternate punishment. The intent is to maximize the incapacitation effect without subjecting all offenders to long prison terms or control. A good example of selective incapacitation is *three-strikes laws* that mandate lengthy imprisonment for those convicted of a third offense.

The Collective Incapacitation of Imprisonment

The impact of collective incapacitation from imprisonment on the level of crime is not large. Clarke (1974) estimated that incarcerating boys prior to age eighteen would only result in a modest 1 to 4 percent decrease in the overall index crime rate. Greenberg (1975), using official records of adult offenders, claimed that doubling the amount of time spent in prison would only decrease crime by 0.6 percent to 4.0 percent. Peterson and Braiker (1980), examining the incapacitative effects on different groups of offenders found that incarceration reduced the level of burglary by only 6 percent, auto theft by 7 percent, armed robbery by 22 percent.

Other analyses suggest greater reductions from incapacitation. Changes in criminal justice system policies may result in varying incapacitation effects.

Petersilia and Greenwood (1978) estimated that a five-year mandatory sentence imposed on felony offenders would result in a 31 percent decrease in violent crimes and a 42 percent decrease in burglaries. Van Dine, Conrad, and Dinitz (1979), looking at data for Columbus, Ohio, claimed that a five-year mandatory sentence for a first felony offense would result in a 17.4 percent decrease in violent index crimes. Finally, Cohen (1983) reported that five-year mandatory sentences for repeat offenders would reduce index crimes by Washington, DC, arrestees by almost 14 percent.

Collective incapacitation can also be examined in terms of the number of people who need to be incarcerated to bring about varying reductions in crime. Cohen (1978) estimated the level of increased incarceration necessary to achieve a 10 percent reduction in index crime, a reduction of 100 index crimes, and a 10 percent reduction in violent crimes for different states (see Table 8.1). The table shows that small reductions in crime require large increases in the percent of people sentenced to prison. For example, a 10 percent reduction in the California index crime rate requires a corresponding 157.2 percent increase in the prison population. The smallest change related to a decrease in index crimes appears in Mississippi, where it is still necessary to increase the incarcerated population by 33.7 percent. Wermink et al. (2013), using data from the Netherlands, claimed that it is necessary to incarcerate an additional 5,707 offenders to avert 400 convictions. It is clear that collective incapacitation requires incarcerating a large number of offenders to bring about even small reductions in crime.

Bringing about an incapacitative effect is not cheap. Walker (1985) estimated that, nationally, a 25 percent incapacitation effect requires the incarceration of 1,200,000 new prisoners. Each of these new prisoners requires bed space and

Table 8.1 Level of Change Needed in Imprisonment Necessary for Incapacitation

	Percent Increase in Prison Population Needed to Achieve:		
State	10% Decrease in Index Crimes	Reduction of 100 Index Crimes	10% Decrease in Violent Crime
California	157.2	36.1	22.8
New York	263.5	67.2	57.0
Massachusetts	310.5	103.4	26.6
Ohio	82.5	34.7	12.0
Kentucky	86.1	44.8	16.0
New Hampshire	118.0	98.9	8.4
Mississippi	33.7	39.1	13.0
North Dakota	122.0	144.2	19.6

SOURCE: Adapted from Cohen, J. 1978. "The Incapacitative Effect of Imprisonment: A Critical Review of the Literature." In Deterrence and Incapacitation: Estimating the Effects of Criminal Sanctions on Crime Rates, edited by A. Blumstein et al., 187–243. Washington, DC: National Academy Press.

upkeep. Henrichson and Delaney (2012) computed the yearly costs of imprison-ment at \$31,286 per inmate for states. Based on Walker's projected increase in needed beds, the increased costs to the states would exceed \$375 billion! This does not include the costs of constructing the space.

It would appear that the costs of collective incapacitation, both in terms of numbers of incarcerated persons and the related dollars, outweigh the benefits ac-crued from the effort. A possible solution to this would be the incapacitation of only the individuals who are a clear threat to society. Such selective incapacitation may eliminate the need to increase the prison population in order to bring about lower levels of crime.

The Selective Incapacitation of Imprisonment

Under selective incapacitation, the emphasis is on the identification of offenders who pose a high risk to society. These individuals are subjected to longer periods of incarceration than are lower risk offenders. Advocates of selective incapacita-tion point to the lower cost of incarcerating only a portion of all offenders as well as to a presumed savings in the number of future offenses.

The key to selective incapacitation is identifying the high-risk individuals who should be incarcerated to have the greatest impact on crime. Greenwood (1982) surveyed almost 2,200 prison inmates in California, Texas, and Michigan who were serving time for burglary or robbery and combined their behavior with official documents concerning past behavior, arrests, convictions, and incarcera-tions. Based on that information, Greenwood (1982) composed a seven-item scale that purportedly distinguishes between high-, medium-, and low-rate offenders. The scale included:

- prior conviction for the same offense,
- incarcerated for more than 50 percent of the preceding two years,
- conviction before the age of sixteen,
- served time in a juvenile facility,
- drug use in the preceding two years,
- drug use as a juvenile,
- employed less than 50 percent of the preceding two years.

Greenwood (1982) applied this scale to California and Texas prisoners to test its incapacitative effect. He suggested that by reducing the time served by low- and medium-risk inmates and increasing the terms for high-risk offenders, it would be possible to reduce robbery by 15 percent while lowering the California prison population by 5 percent. The same 15 percent reduction under a collective inca-pacitation approach that would require a 25 percent increase in the prison popula-tion. While the California robbery results support a selective incapacitation argument and approach, the results for burglary in California and both burglary and robbery in Texas are not supportive. A 15 percent decrease in California bur-glary requires a 7 percent increase in the number of prisoners in California (Greenwood, 1982). In Texas, a 10 percent decrease in robbery and a 10 percent decrease in burglary requires a 30 percent increase and a 5 percent increase in the prison population, respectively. Despite the contradictory results, advocates of selective incapacitation often point to the 15 percent robbery reduction accompanied with the 5 percent decrease in the prison population in California in support of the approach (Greenwood, 1982).

Web Activity

Greenwood's (1982) report on selective incapacitation is available at https://www.rand.org/pubs/reports/R2815.html. There are also other related materials imprisonment at this site.

Selective incapacitation has been criticized on methodological grounds. Visher (1986) points out that there are serious problems with the data used in Greenwood's (1982) analysis, including the inability of some inmates to accurately recall past events and time periods, problems with estimating the level of offending prior to incarceration, and large differences between California, Texas, and Michigan offense rates. Reanalyzing the data, Visher (1986) found a selective incapacitative effect of only 5 to 10 percent in California and increased crime in both Texas and Michigan. An additional problem is the difficulty in predicting future behavior, which is a cornerstone of selective incapacitation. Any error in predicting who is high risk will impact any incapacitative effect.

Several problems impact any selective incapacitative effect. First, incapacitation assumes that the rate of offending remains constant over time and any offender whose career would end during the time served in prison would limit the value of incarceration. Second, most analyses rest on the prison population, however, prison inmates are not representative of the entire criminal population and any results based on studies of inmates have questionable generalizability. Finally, selective incapacitation rests on punishing high risk offenders more than low risk offenders. This means punishing an individual for potential dangerousness and not just actual behavior. Selective incapacitation imposes longer sentences in order to avoid what might happen if an individual is released. Given the poor ability to accurately predict future behavior, this approach subjects many individuals to unnecessary punishment. This raises concerns over whether society should punish a person for what "might" happen and not just what has happened. In summary, although selective incapacitation holds much intuitive appeal, there does not seem to be a solid empirical basis for invoking the process.

Incapacitation: Concluding Thoughts

Incarcerating offenders holds a great deal of appeal to the general public. One argument for doings so is to keep offenders from committing more crime against society, and locking up an offender means he cannot commit an offense while incapacitated. Three-strikes laws that require life sentences are a prime example of an incapacitative approach to eliminating crime. Unfortunately, the effect of incapacitation on levels of crime is not promising. Simply locking people up for specific time periods (collective incapacitation) has minimal impact on crime levels. Attempts to lock up subgroups of offenders based on their high-risk of offending (selective incapacitation) have not fared much better. The results suggest that any significant incapacitative effect requires the incarceration of significantly more offenders, with the concomitant costs to society of housing those offenders.

REHABILITATION

Rehabilitation has been the dominant orientation in corrections for most of the past 200 years. This is evident in the growth of prisons in the early 1800s that focused on repentance and reformation. The hope was that confinement and reflection would lead inmates to overcome the forces that led them to offend.

The emphasis on rehabilitation received a great boost in the 1900s with the rise of psychological and sociological theories that espoused positivistic views of behavior. The primary issue in corrections was that social and environmental factors caused individuals to offend. The solution to crime was to rehabilitate offenders. A wide range of treatment programs were used throughout the twentieth century. Unfortunately, crime persisted and the evidence on effective correctional rehabilitation was not realized.

Web Activity

The move toward rehabilitation has gained momentum over the past decade due to a number of factors. Petersilia offers insight to the move in "Beyond the Prison Bubble" (available at https://www.nij.gov/journals/268/pages/prison-bubble.aspx). Read this document and make a list of the arguments/rationales for the shift in correctional programming.

The "What Works" Argument

Rehabilitation came under serious question in 1974 (p. 25) when Martinson said "with few and isolated exceptions, the rehabilitative efforts that have been reported so far have had no appreciable effect on recidivism." The basis for this assessment was an examination of 231 studies of rehabilitation published between 1945 and 1967 undertaken by Lipton, Martinson, and Wilks (1975). This review considered evaluations in which there was a control group, an outcome measure attributable to the treatment, sufficient information about the intervention and evaluation for making a judgment, a sufficient sample size to make inferences, and a sound research methodology. Among the intervention techniques examined were counseling, educational and vocational training, medical treatment, psychological therapy, probation, parole, and community programs. While the effect of these various programs on recidivism was negligible, they did reveal positive impact on other factors, such as improved attitudes and educational attainment.

This assessment of little or no effect of rehabilitation on recidivism appears in a variety of other reports both prior to and since the work of Martinson (1974) and Lipton, Martinson, and Wilks (1975) (see, for example, Fishman 1977; Gensheimer et al. 1986; Whitehead and Lab 1989; Wright and Dixon 1977). The Lipton, Martinson, and Wilks (1975) findings were examined by the National Academy of Sciences. That report concluded that the original authors "were reasonably accurate and fair in their appraisal of the rehabilitation literature" (Sechrest, White, and Brown 1979). The major point of departure in the reanalysis involved the feeling that the earlier analysis *overstated the effectiveness* of the reviewed programs. Sechrest, White, and Brown (1979) claim that the earlier report fell short in its criticism of the studies and overlooked a variety of critical problems within the research reports.

Not all researchers, however, were ready to sound the death knell for rehabilitation. One leading proponent of rehabilitation (Palmer, 1975) noted that certain programs have positive effects on certain individuals under certain conditions. Palmer (1975) argued that the emphasis should not be on finding a single intervention that would be effective for all offenders. Martinson (1979) agreed that there are instances in which rehabilitation has a positive impact on behavior. Support for the belief that some programs work with some select individuals also can be found in reviews by Graziano and Mooney (1984), Garrett (1985), and Mayer et al. (1986). The greatest impact appears in other outcome measures (e.g., psychological adjustment, academic improvement, institutional adjustment) besides recidivism, and more-rigorous studies find less of an impact on recidivism.

The basic view that rehabilitation is not effective in reducing recidivism held sway from the Martinson (1974) proclamation largely until the turn of the century. Cullen (2013) notes, however, that the "nothing works" claims sowed the seeds of a resurgence of interest in rehabilitative efforts. Rehabilitation proponents shifted their emphasis from blind faith in rehabilitation to identifying those efforts that were effective at reducing recidivism and the keys to effective interventions.

Andrews et al. (1990) jump started the rehabilitation approach in an analysis that showed treatment has a definite positive impact on recidivism. The authors conducted a meta-analysis of program effects on recidivism and reported significant effect sizes of treatment. This positive outcome, however, emerges only for certain types of interventions. Andrews et al. (1990) specifically note that "appropriate" services have a mean effect size of 0.30 (meaning reduced recidivism), while "inappropriate" of "deterrence" based interventions have mean effect sizes of roughly -0.06 (higher recidivism). The key to effective interventions, according to Andrews et al. (1990), is implementing programs that pay attention to the principles of risk, need, and responsivity. We will return to these principles later.

The positive findings for rehabilitation programming finds support in a number of studies. Lipsey (1990, 1999, 2009; and Lipsey and Wilson 1993, 1998) offer extensive evaluations of the rehabilitation literature. Throughout the analyses, the author finds positive effects from rehabilitative treatment. For example, Lipsey and Wilson (1998) report a mean effect size of 0.12. This can be translated as a *12 percent reduction in recidivism.* The practical implication of the finding needs to consider the assumed base level of recidivism independent on the intervention (Cullen 2013). Lipsey and Wilson (1998) assumed a base recidivism rate of 50 percent, thus the 0.12 mean effect size would translate into a 6 percent reduction in the base recidivism rate (base rate of 50% multiplied by the 0.12 effect size equals 6%). This finding reflects the results of 200 evaluation studies.

Lipsey (1990, 2009) notes that there is a great deal of heterogeneity across the studies included in the meta-analyses, with different types of treatment having different effects. Treatments that focus on interpersonal skills, cognitive-behavioral interventions, multimodal approaches, and community-based programs typically have a greater impact than other interventions (Lipsey and Wilson, 1998; Lösel 1995). Lipsey (1990) argues that research on the impact of rehabilitation needs to consider the type of treatment, the setting in which it is delivered, the method of evaluation, and other factors when assessing the evidence. Lowenkamp, Latessa, and Smith (2006) note that interventions with stronger program integrity (that is, strong program implementation, good offender assessment, etc.) are more effective at reducing recidivism than those that have weak integrity. To a great extent these arguments point to the principles of risk, need, and responsivity, to which we now turn.

Risk, Need, and Responsivity

The key in effective correctional rehabilitation is paying attention to three basic principles—**risk, need, and responsivity** (Andrews et al., 1990). In essence, these principles go to identifying and matching the correct individuals to the correct interventions. It also requires that the interventions are implemented properly.

Risk. The risk principle states that treatment should be targeted at higher risk offenders. For those who are at a higher risk for reoffending, there is a greater margin for improvement than for those who are low risk. For example, an intervention has a greater chance to impact an individual who has a higher likelihood to reoffend and offends often, while the same intervention has a lower chance to change rare behavior. Smith, Gendreau, and Swartz (2009) state that those at a higher risk "have more room for change in comparison with their lower risk counterparts" (154). A focus on risk factors is common at many points in the criminal justice system, especially in corrections. Examples of using risk as a deciding factor are in bail decisions, sentencing, probation and parole decisions, and correctional housing.

Risk factors for reoffending fall into several categories, including family, peers, antisocial attitudes, past criminal behavior, and substance use. Family factors related to offending include poor parental supervision, abuse and maltreatment, harsh and inconsistent discipline, low familial affection, and poor family bonding. Peer risk factors typically consider antisocial and pro-criminal friends, family members, and associations. An individual's attitudes and beliefs are also related to future offending, particularly antisocial attitudes, anger, and negative feelings toward rules and societal values. Perhaps the greatest risk factor for future offending is past criminal behavior. Those with a history of alcohol and other substance use are also at a greater risk for antisocial behavior.

Need. The need principle simply refers to making certain the treatment addresses the needs of the individual. Too often rehabilitation programming is viewed as "one size fits all" and little consideration is paid to individual offenders and circumstances. Existing and new treatment programs are simply offered to all inmates or offenders. This may be done for a variety of reasons—it is the only program available, there is a blind belief in the value of the program for all offenders, it is the pet project of an agency or individual, or some other reason. Ideally, interventions will be targeted at the needs of the offenders.

The need principle is closely related and tied to the risk principle. High risk factors are those that need to be targeted in interventions and programming. For example, individuals who have substance use problems need substance use treatment and those with antisocial attitudes and anger issues require treatments that address those issues. Unfortunately, that is not what happens in many cases. It is not unusual that inmates will voluntarily participate in alcohol and substance use treatment when they do not have those problems, solely because participation earns points toward release or makes them appear cooperative, which gains them more privileges. The assessment of risk and needs should go hand in hand when considering what would be the appropriate and most effective treatment. Treatment needs to focus on risk factors related to recidivistic behavior (Cullen 2013).

Responsivity. The responsivity principle addresses how interventions are initiated and carried out. Not all offenders will respond to treatment or to different treatment protocols in the same say, thus the intervention has to fit the individual. Responsivity can be subdivided into two parts. These are general responsivity and specific responsivity. General responsivity involves teaching prosocial behavior. Gendreau (1996) notes that general responsivity rests on cognitive-behavioral interventions, social learning techniques, and interventions that focus on behavioral change. Specific responsivity is the recognition of differences between individuals and the circumstances and needs. The intervention, therefore, has to consider those differences and mold treatment to address each individual. This basically means matching the rehabilitation and the offender. Specific responsivity does not necessarily mean that the interventions are totally different from one person to another. Instead, it recognizes that how an intervention is implemented needs to be adapted for the characteristics of the individual. For example, teaching and modeling prosocial behaviors may need to be done in different ways for individuals based on their learning styles, maturity, and other factors.

Another aspect of responsivity is **treatment fidelity**. Fidelity (also referred to as therapeutic integrity) addresses how well the treatment was implemented. Was the intervention offered in accordance with how it was meant to be offered? Did the individual receive all components of the program and at the appropriate level? Were those offering the treatment qualified and experienced enough to meet program guidelines and expectations? Essentially, fidelity asks whether the intervention as truly "responsive" to the needs of the individuals in the program. This use of fidelity/therapeutic integrity is a common concern in corrections practices (Lowenkamp, Latessa, and Smith 2006; Smith et al. 2009).

The three principles of effective intervention have been found to be valid through a number of analyses. One project in particular (Smith et al. 2009) used meta-analysis to assess each of the principles. In regard to general responsivity, a meta-analysis of twenty-one studies reveals overwhelming positive mean effect sizes (i.e., reductions in recidivism), with cognitive-behavioral interventions having a better impact than other interventions. Looking at differences for higher and lower risk offenders, Smith et al. (2009) report that four of the six analyses included in their research show support for the risk principle. Five studies were included in the meta-analysis of the need principle. Adherence to the need principle in the studies resulted in uniformly positive outcomes (Smith et al., 2009). These results illustrate that correctional rehabilitation, particularly when in is conducted in light of the risk, need, and responsivity principles, can be effective at lowering recidivism.

Cognitive-Behavioral Interventions

Contemporary advocates of rehabilitation generally agree that interventions should be behavioral and address the cognitive processes that lead to antisocial activity. Such interventions would seek to alter the decision-making processes of individuals, help offenders to identify prosocial responses to challenges, and develop skills and techniques for avoiding problem behavior. These programs utilize structured social learning approaches that model appropriate behavior and skills. These programs generally fall under the heading of **cognitive-behavioral therapy** (CBT).

Web Activity

A great deal of information on cognitive-behavioral therapy is available on the web. One good starting point to explore this topic is at https://www.psychologytoday.com/us/basics/cognitive-behavioral-therapy. This site provides a good, succinct introduction to CBT and has links to a variety of other papers and materials on the topic.

Various programs appear under the CBT heading. multisystemic therapy, the Cognitive Thinking Skills Program, and functional family therapy are three examples. The idea that behavior is affected by a wide array of social and environmental factors underlies **multisystemic therapy** (MST) (Cullen and Gendreau, 2000). MST is a community-based intervention that attempts to address family, peer, school, community, and other influences that may prompt or lead to deviant behavior. The actual intervention will vary based on the needs of the individual, and it is dynamic and changes according to the needs and progress of the client. Each client receives intensive services, in the community, from a team of therapists who are held accountable for the successes or failures of the program (Cullen and Gendreau, 2000). Evaluations of MST reveal reduced delinquency and improvements in risk-related behaviors (Borduin et al. 1995; Brown et al. 1999).

The **Cognitive Thinking Skills Program** (CTSP) is also a multimodal intervention that utilizes a range of techniques targeting cognitive-behavioral problems (Gaes et al. 1999). The CTSP focuses on identifying cognitive deficits and inappropriate decision-making by individuals. Typical problems are impulsive behavior, egocentric activity, selfishness, and an inability to express oneself (Gaes et al. 1999). Highly trained program staff offer seventy hours of skills training to clients. CTSP has been adopted across Canada, as well as in several US states and the United Kingdom. Gaes et al. (1999), reviewing evidence on CTSP, report that fewer treatment subjects recidivate than nontreatment control clients. While the differences tend to be statistically significant, many of the differences are small. The most promising findings emerge from CTSP implementation in community settings (Gaes et al. 1999).

The final CBT program to be reviewed here, **functional family therapy** (FFT), has many of the same elements of those presented above, with a focus on the family unit and high-risk youths. FFT takes place over three months and incorporates up to 30 one-hour sessions (fewer for less serious cases) and involves three phases addressing engagement and motivation, behavior change, and generalization (Sexton and Alexander 2000). The program addresses a number of risk factors, including negativity, lack of motivation, poor parenting skills, poor communication, and lack of social support. A major focus is on the relationship between the parents/family and the youth (CrimeSolutions.gov 2011; Sexton and Alexander 2000). Evaluations of FFT reveal lower recidivism, particularly when the therapists adhere strongly to the program guidelines (i.e., there is high program fidelity) (CrimeSolutions.gov 2011).

These three programs are indicative of the positive outcomes post- CBT interventions. The increased use of cognitive-behavioral interventions has prompted several meta-analytic reviews. Smith and colleague's (2009) meta-analytic review of correctional programming that incorporates risk, need, and responsivity includes a number of CBT interventions. Without exception, the CBT studies report positive mean effect sizes (although some are small and not significant). Lipsey, Chaptman, and Landenberger (2001) considered fourteen evaluations that included experimental or quasi-experimental designs with a focus on recidivism. Lipton et al. (2002) examined forty-four studies of programs from around the globe. Overall, CBT significantly reduced recidivism, although there is a great deal of variability in impact among the studies. In a final analysis of fourteen studies from the United States and Canada, Lipsey and Landenburger (2006) report the combined result was statistically significant and in favor of CBT. Unfortunately, while all fourteen studies reported positive results, only four were statistically significant from zero, indicating the overall results were driven by only a few projects.

Rehabilitation: Concluding Thoughts

The end of the twentieth century saw rehabilitation come under fire for not having a positive impact on recidivism. This assessment is largely attributable to the pronouncement of Martinson (1974). While some saw this as a death knell for correctional treatment, it actually spurred on initiatives to identify effective rehabilitation and scientifically demonstrate the positive impact of rehabilitation on reduced recidivism. Led by Andrews and associates (1990), rehabilitation advocates have demonstrated that interventions focusing on the principles of risk, need, and responsivity are effective at reducing recidivism and that those results are statistically significant. This positive impact has been shown in a wide range of analyses, including major meta-analyses of treatment (see, for example, Lipsey 1992, 1995; Lipsey and Wilson 1998).

It is important to note, however, that rehabilitative interventions are not a cure-all. A mean effect size of 0.20 (typically a larger effect size in analyses) translates in a change in recidivism from 50 percent to 40 percent. This 10 percent reduction is noteworthy and signals that rehabilitation is effective. At the same time, 40 percent still recidivate. This means that the intervention is only effective for a portion of the offenders. The focus needs to be on what needs to change to make the intervention more effective. Was the assessment of risk and/or need flawed? Was the program fidelity weak? What needs to be done to improve the intervention? These questions (and others) do not mean that rehabilitation failed. They simply mean that there is still work to be done.

Critical Thinking Exercise

In light of the growing support for rehabilitation, society continues to incarcerate massive numbers of individuals every year. Why is this the case? Should this continue? Why or why not? What should the future direction be for the correctional system?

SUMMARY

Corrections seeks to impact crime and offenders in a variety of ways. The primary expectation is that correctional interventions will reduce the recidivistic behavior of those sent to the correctional system. Deterrence, incapacitation, and rehabilitation are the primary mechanisms used to bring about reductions in recidivism. None of these approaches, either alone or together, have eliminated crime or recidivistic behavior. Arguments can be, and have been, made for each correctional intervention. Even if recidivism remains a major concern, the use of corrections will not cease. For many people, corrections is not about recidivism from deterrence, incapacitation or rehabilitation. Instead, corrections is simply a form of punishment for what the offender did. Punishment as a form of retribution or "just desserts" is enough for many people. It makes people feel better just to strike back at the offender. Correctional interventions are not going to cease, regardless of the rationale underlying the choice. What is evident is the fact that rehabilitation appears to have the greatest impact, and increased attention needs to be paid to interventions that comply with the principles of risk, need, and responsivity.

KEY TERMS

brutalization effect
capital sanctions
cognitive-behavioral
   therapy
Cognitive Thinking Skills
   Program (CTSP)

collective incapacitation
corporal sanctions
functional family therapy
general deterrence
incapacitation
multisystemic therapy

risk, need, and
   responsivity
selective incapacitation
specific deterrence
treatment fidelity

DISCUSSION QUESTIONS

1. A news report claims that crime has been going up and your friends start to argue that the state should just "lock them all up" so that they cannot hurt anyone else. What are the pros and cons of such an incapacitative argument? Is there a way to choose who to lock up to cut the crime rate?

2. You make a pitch for more rehabilitation programming and are accused of being too soft on crime. Justify your position. How much of an impact can rehabilitation have on crime?

3. One of the candidates for governor calls for increased sanctions to deter crime. He claims that the system has been too soft on crime and says that changes can reduce the level of crime by deterring individuals. How would you respond to this argument? What evidence can you offer to back up your position?

4. You overhear an argument about the effectiveness of correctional rehabilitation. A friend knows you have studied rehabilitation and asks you what can be done to improve the effectiveness of rehabilitation programming. How would you answer him? What factors would you discuss?

5. Cognitive-behavioral therapy (CBT) has been identified as a cornerstone of effective rehabilitation treatment. Explain what this is and identify and discuss various interventions that include CBT.

SUGGESTED READINGS

Cullen, F. T. (2013). "Rehabilitation: Beyond Nothing Works." In *Crime and Justice in America, 1975–2025*, edited by M. Tonry, 299-376. Chicago: University of Chicago Press.
Lipsey, M. W. (2009). The Primary Factors that Characterize Effective Interventions with Juvenile Offenders: A Meta-Analytic Overview. *Victims and Offenders* 4: 124–147.

Nagin, D. S., F. T. Cullen, and C. L. Jonson. (2009). "Imprisonment and Reoffending." In *Crime and Justice: A Review of Research*, vol. 38, edited by M. Tonry, 115–200. Chicago: University of Chicago Press.

Tonry. M. (2008). "Learning from the Limitations of Deterrence Research." In *Crime and Justice: A Review of Research*, vol. 37, edited by M. Tonry, 279–311. Chicago: University of Chicago Press.

Wermink, H., R. Apel, R. Nieuwbeerta, and A. A. J. Blokland. (2013). "The Incapacitation Effect of First-Time Imprisonment: A Matched Samples Comparison." *Journal of Quantitative Criminology* 29: 579–600.

REFERENCES

Alper, M., M. R. Durose, and J. Markman. (2018). *2018 Update on Prisoner Recidivism: A 9-Year Follow-Up Period (2005–2014)*. Washington, DC: Bureau of Justice Statistics.

Andrews, D. A., I. Zinger, R. D. Hoge, J. Bonta, P. Gendreau, and F. T. Cullen. (1990). "Does Correctional Treatment Work?: A Clinically Relevant and Psychologically Informed Meta-Analysis." *Criminology* 28: 369–404.

Babst, D. V., M. Koval, and M. G. Neithercutt. (1972). "Relationship of Time Served to Parole Outcome for Different Classifications of Burglars Based on Males Paroled in Fifty Jurisdictions in 1968 and 1969." *Journal of Research in Crime and Delinquency* 9: 99–116.

Bailey, W. C. (1998). "Deterrence, Brutalization, and the Death Penalty: Another Examination of Oklahoma's Return to Capital Punishment." *Criminology* 36, no. 4: 711–734.

Beck, J. L., and P. B. Hoffman. (1976). "Time Served and Release Performance: A Research Note." *Journal of Research in Crime and Delinquency* 13: 127–132.

Berecochea, J. E., and D. R. Jaman. (1981). *Time Served in Prison and Parole Outcome: An Experimental Study. Report No. 2*. Sacramento: California Department of Corrections.

Borduin, C. M., B. J. Mann, L. T. Cone, S. W. Henggeler, B. R. Fucci, D. M. Blaske, and R. A. Williams. (1995). "Multi-Systemic Treatment of Serious Juvenile Offenders: Long-Term Prevention of Criminality and Violence." *Journal of Consulting and Clinical Psychology* 63: 569–578.

Brown, T. L., S. W. Henggeler, S. K. Schoenwald, M. J. Brondino, and S. G. Pickerel. (1999). "Multisystemic Treatment of Substance Abusing and Dependent Juvenile Delinquents: Effects on School Attendance at Posttreatment and 6-Month Follow-Up." *Children's Services: Social Policy, Research and Practice* 2: 81–93.

Bowers, W. J., and G. L. Pierce. (1980). "Arbitrariness and Discrimination under Post-Furman Capital Statutes." *Crime & Delinquency* 26, no. 4: 563–632.

Clarke, S. (1974). "Getting 'em Out of Circulation: Does Incarceration of Juvenile Offenders Reduce Crime?" *Journal of Criminal Law and Criminology* 65: 528–535.

Cohen, J. (1983). "Incapacitation as a Strategy for Crime Control: Possibilities and Pitfalls." *Crime and Justice*, 5: 1–84.

Cochran, J. K., and M. B. Chamlin. (2000). "Deterrence and Brutalization: The Dual Effects of Executions." *Justice Quarterly* 17, no. 4: 685–706.

Cochran, J. K., M. B. Chamlin, and M. Seth. (1994). "Deterrence or Brutalization? An Impact Assessment of Oklahoma's Return to Capital Punishment." *Criminology* 32, no. 1: 107–134.

Cohen, J. (1978). "The Incapacitative Effect of Imprisonment: A Critical Review of the Literature." In *Deterrence and Incapacitation: Estimating the Effects of Criminal Sanctions on Crime Rates*, edited by A. Blumstein, J. Cohen, and D. Nagin. Washington, D.C.: National Research Council, National Academy of Sciences.

CrimeSolutions.gov. (2011). "Program Profile: Functional Family Therapy (FFT)." Retrieved from https://crimesolutions.gov/ProgramDetails.aspx?ID=122.

Cullen, F. T. (2013). "Rehabilitation: Beyond Nothing Works." In *Crime and Justice in America, 1975–2025*, edited by M. Tonry, 299–376. Chicago: University of Chicago Press.

Cullen, F. T., & Gendreau, P. (2000). Assessing correctional rehabilitation: Policy, practice, and prospects. Criminal justice, 3(1), 299–370.

Horney, J., Peterson, R., MacKenzie, D., Martin, J., & Rosenbaum, D. (2000). Policies, processes, and decisions of the criminal justice system. *Criminal Justice 2000*, 3: 1–6.

Donohue, J., and J. Wolfers. (2006). "Uses and Abuses of Empirical Evidence in the Death Penalty Debate." *Stanford Law Review* 58: 791–846.

Fishman, R. (1977). "An Evaluation of Criminal Recidivism in Projects Providing Rehabilitation and Diversion Services in New York City." *Journal of Criminal Law and Criminology* 68: 283–305.

Gaes, G. G., T. J. Flanagan, L. L. Motiuk, and L. Stewart. (1999). Adult Correctional Treatment. Crime and Justice, 26: 361–426.

Garrett, C. J. (1985). "Effects of Residential Treatment on Adjudicated Delinquents: A Meta-Analysis." *Journal of Research in Crime and Delinquency* 22: 287–308.

Gendreau, P. (1996). "The Principles of Effective Intervention with Offenders." In *Choosing Correctional Interventions That Work: Defining the Demand and Evaluating the Supply*, edited by A. T. Harland, 117–130. Thousand Oaks, CA: SAGE.

Gensheimer, L. K., J. P. Mayer, R. Gottschalk, and W. S. Davidson. (1986). "Diverting Youth from the Juvenile Justice System: A Meta-Analysis of Intervention Efficacy." In *Youth Violence: Programs and Prospects*, edited by S. J. Apter and A. P. Goldstein, 39–56. New York: Pergamon.

Glaser, D. (1964). *The Effectiveness of a Prison and Parole System*. Indianapolis, IN: Bobbs-Merrill.

Gottfredson, D. M., M. R. Gottfredson, and J. Garofalo. (1977). "Time Served in Prison and Parole Outcomes among Parolee Risk Categories." *Journal of Criminal Justice* 5: 1–12.

Graziano, A. M., and K. Mooney. (1984). *Children and Behavior Therapy*. New York: Aldine.

Greenberg, D. (1975). "The Incapacitative Effect of Imprisonment: Some Estimates." *Law and Society Review* 9: 541–580.

Greenwood, P. W. (1982). *Selective Incapacitation*. Santa Monica, CA: RAND.

Henrichson, C., and R. Delaney. (2012). *The Price of Prisons: What Incarceration Costs Taxpayers*. New York: Vera Institute of Justice. Retrieved from https://www.vera.org/publications/price-of-prisons-what-incarceration-costs-taxpayers.

Kaeble, D. (2018). *Probation and Parole in the United States, 2016*. Washington, DC: Bureau of Justice Statistics.

Katz, L., S. Levitt, and E. Shustorovich. (2003). "Prison Conditions, Capital Punishment, and Deterrence." *American Law and Economics Review* 5: 318–343.

Langan, P. A., and D. J. Levin. (2002). *Recidivism of Prisoners Released in 1994*. Washington, DC: Bureau of Justice Statistics.

Lipsey, M. W. (1990). "Juvenile Delinquency Treatment: A Meta-Analytic Inquiry into the Variability of Effects." In *Meta-analysis for Explanation*, edited by T. D. Cook, H. Cooper, L. V. Hedges, R. J. Light, T. A. Lewis, and F. Mosteller, 83–127. New York: Russell Sage Foundation.

Lipsey, M. W. (1992). "Juvenile Delinquent Treatment: A Meta-Analytics Treatment Inquiry into the Variability of Effects." In *Meta-Analysis for Explanation: A Casebook*, edited by T. D. Cook, H. Cooper, D. S. Cordray, H. Hartmann, L. V. Hedges, R. J. Light, T. A. Lewis, and F. Mosteller. New York: Russell Sage Foundation.

Lipsey, M. W. (1995). "What Do We Learn from 400 Research Studies on the Effectiveness of Treatment with Juvenile Delinquency?" In *What Works: Reducing Reoffending*, edited by J. McGuire, 63–78. West Sussex, UK: Wiley.

Lipsey, M. W. (1999). "Can Rehabilitative Programs Reduce the Recidivism of Juvenile Offenders? An Inquiry into the Effectiveness of Practical Programs." *Virginia Journal of Social Policy and Law* 6: 611–641.

Lipsey, M. W. (2009). "The Primary Factors that Characterize Effective Interventions with Juvenile Offenders: A Meta-Analytic Overview." *Victims and Offenders* 4: 124–147.

Lipsey, M. W., G. L. Chapman, and N. A. Landenberger. (2001). "Cognitive-Behavioral Programs for Offenders." *Annals of the American Academy of Political and Social Sciences* 578: 144–157.

Lipsey, M. W., and N. A. Landenberger. (2006). "Cognitive-Behavioral Interventions." In *Preventing Crime: What Works for Children, Offenders, Victims, and Places*, edited by B. C. Welsh and D. P, Farrington, 57–71. New York: Springer.

Lipsey, M. W., and D. B. Wilson. (1993). "The Efficacy of Psychological, Educational, and Behavioral Treatment." *American Psychologist* 48: 1181–1209.

Lipsey, M. W., and D. B. Wilson. (1998). "Effective Interventions for Serious Juvenile Offenders: A Synthesis of Research." In *Serious and Violent Juvenile Offenders: Risk Factors and Successful Interventions*, edited by R. Loeber and D. P. Farrington, 313–345. Thousand Oaks, CA: SAGE.

Lipton, D., R. Martinson, and J. Wilks. (1975). *The Effectiveness of Correctional Treatment: A Survey of Treatment Evaluation Studies*. New York: Praeger.

Lipton, D. S., F. S. Pearson, C. M. Cleland, and D. Yee. (2002). The effectiveness of cognitive behavioural treatment methods on offender recidivism. In *Offender Rehabilitation and Treatment: Effective Programmes and Policies to Reduce Re-offending*, by J. McGuire, 79–112. Hoboken, NJ: John Wiley & Sons.

Lösel, F. (1995). "The Efficacy of Correctional Treatment: A Review and Synthesis of Meta-Evaluations." In *What Works: Reducing Reoffending*, edited by J. McGuire, 79–114. West Sussex, UK: Wiley.

Lowenkamp, C. T., E. J. Latessa, and P. Smith. (2006). "Does Correctional Program Quality Really Matter? The Impact of Adhering to the Principles of Effective Intervention." *Criminology and Public Policy* 5: 575–594.

Martinson, R. (1974). "What Works? Questions and Answers about Prison Reform." *Public Interest* 35: 22–54.

Mayer, J. P., L. K. Gensheimer, W. S. Davidson, and R. Gottschalk. (1986). "Social Learning Treatment within Juvenile Justice: A Meta-Analysis of Impact in the Natural Environment." In *Youth and Violence: Problems and Prospects*, edited by S. J. Apter and A. P. Goldstein, 24–38. New York: Pergamon.

Palmer, T. (1975). "Martinson Revisited." *Journal of Research in Crime and Delinquency* 12:133–152.

Petersilia, J., and P. W. Greenwood. (1978). "Mandatory Prison Sentences: Their Projected Effects on Crime and Prison Populations." *Journal of Criminal Law and Criminology* 69: 604–615.

Peterson, M. A., and H. B. Braiker. (1980). *Doing Crime: A Survey of California Prison Inmates.* Santa Monica, CA: RAND.

Sechrest, L., S. O. White, and E. D. Brown. (1979). *The Rehabilitation of Criminal Offenders: Problems and Prospects.* Washington, DC: National Academy Press.

Sexton, T. L., and J. F. Alexander. (2000). *Functional Family Therapy.* Washington, DC: Office of Juvenile Justice and Delinquency Prevention.

Smith, P., P. Gendreau, and K. Swartz. (2009). "Validating the Principles of Effective Intervention: A Systematic Review or the Contributions of Meta-Analysis in the Field of Corrections." *Victims and Offenders* 4: 148–169.

Sorensen, J., R. Wrinkle, V. Brewer, and J. Marquart. (1999). "Capital Punishment and Deterrence: Examining the Effect of Executions on Murder in Texas." *Crime & Delinquency* 45(4): 481–493.

Van Dine, S., J. P. Conrad, and S. Dinitz. (1979). *Restraining the Wicked: The Incapacitation of the Dangerous Criminal.* Lexington, MA: Lexington Books.

Visher, C. A. (1986). "Incapacitation and Crime Control: Does a 'Lock 'em Up' Strategy Reduce Crime?" *Justice Quarterly* 4: 513–544.

Walker, S. (1985). *Sense and Nonsense about Crime: A Policy Guide.* Monterey, CA: Brooks/Cole.

Wermink, H., R. Apel, R. Nieuwbeerta, and A. A. J. Blokland. (2013). "The Incapacitation Effect of First-Time Imprisonment: A Matched Samples Comparison." *Journal of Quantitative Criminology* 29: 579–600.

Whitehead, J. T., and S. P. Lab. (1989). "A Meta-Analysis of Juvenile Correctional Treatment." *Journal of Research in Crime and Delinquency* 26: 276–295.

Wright, W. E., and M. C. Dixon. (1977). "Community Prevention and Treatment of Juvenile Delinquency." *Journal of Research in Crime and Delinquency* 14: 35–67.

INDEX

Page numbers followed by *f* indicate figures; *t* indicates tables.